A Story of Her Own

A Story of Her Own

The Female Oedipus Complex Reexamined and Renamed

Nancy Kulish and Deanna Holtzman

JASON ARONSON
Lanham • Boulder • New York • Toronto • Plymouth, UK

Published in the United States of America
by Jason Aronson
An imprint of Rowman & Littlefield Publishers, Inc.

A wholly owned subsidary of
The Rowman & Littlefield Publishing Group, Inc.
4501 Forbes Boulevard, Suite 200, Lanham, Maryland 20706
www.rowmanlittlefield.com

Estover Road
Plymouth PL6 7PY
United Kingdom

British Library Cataloguing in Publication Information Available

Library of Congress Cataloging-in-Publication Data

Kulish, Nancy.
  A story of her own : the female Oedipus complex reexamined and renamed / Nancy
Kulish and Deanna Holtzman.
      p. cm.
  Includes bibliographical references and index.
  ISBN-13: 978-0-7657-0564-8 (alk. paper)
  ISBN-10: 0-7657-0564-8 (alk. paper)
  ISBN-13: 978-0-7657-0565-5 (alk. paper)
  ISBN-10: 0-7657-0565-6 (alk. paper)
  1. Oedipus complex. 2. Psychoanalysis. 3. Women—Psychology. I. Holtzman,
Deanna. II. Title.

  BF175.5.O33K85 2008
  155.3'33—dc22   2007037577

Printed in the United States of America

⊚™ The paper used in this publication meets the minimum requirements of
American National Standard for Information Sciences—Permanence of Paper
for Printed Library Materials, ANSI/NISO Z39.48-1992.

We dedicate this book to our mothers,
Marian and Letty.

~

Contents

~

Acknowledgments

We would like to give special thanks to three women who have helped us immensely in getting this book together. Our thanks to Eve Golden, M.D., for her always intelligent and cogent reading and editing; to Karen Holtzman, who, like a genie, could instantly find and obtain any obscure references or sources we needed; and to Mrs. Joanne Piatek, for her cheery diligence in assembling our bibliography. We also are grateful to innumerable colleagues for their encouragement and whose ideas have become incorporated into the development of our thinking and writing.

Our special thanks go to Bonnie Litowitz, Ph.D, for giving us permission to draw heavily on her unpublished presentation, "A Case Study in the Relationship of Theory to Language," given at the meetings of the American Psychoanalytic Association in Boston, June 21, 2003.

Special thanks to Krista Sprecher, Associate Production Editor at the Rowman & Littlefield Publishing Group, who appreciates and understands what we have been trying to say, and who has guided us so skillfully through all the final details of editing our manuscript.

The authors and publisher gratefully acknowledge permission for the following excerpts:

Excerpt from "Persephone Speaks" from MY MOTHER'S DAUGHTER: Four Greek Goddesses Speak by Doris Orgel. Copyright 2003 by Doris Orgel. Reprinted by permission of Henry Holt and Company.

"Tribute to the Angels [38]" (excerpt) by HD (Hilda Doolittle), from TRIL-OGY, copyright 1945 by Oxford University Press; Copyright renewed by Norman Holmes Pearson. Reprinted by permission of New Directions Publishing Corp.

From THE DIARY OF A YOUNG GIRL:THE DEFINITIVE EDITION by Anne Frank, edited by Otto Frank and Mirjam Pressler, translated by Susan Massotty, copyright 1995 by Doubleday, a division of Random House, Inc. Used by permission of Doubleday, a division of Random House, Inc.

"Pomegranate" in the House on Marshland from the FIRST FOUR BOOKS OF POEMS by Louise Gluck. Copyright 1968, 1971, 1972, 1973, 1974, 1975, 1976, 1977, 1978, 1979, 1980, 1985, 1995 by Louise Gluck. Reprinted by permission of Harper Collins Publishers.

"Persephone" originally published in the Summer 2000 issue of The Literary Review. Reprinted with permission from B.A. St. Andrews' estate.

Excerpt from NINETEEN EIGHTY-FOUR by George Orwell, copyright 1949 by Harcourt, Inc. and renewed 1977 by Sonia Brownell Orwell, reprinted with permission of the publisher.

87w from p.239, 241 from "Metamorphoses" by Ovid edited by Melville, A. D. (trans) (1988). By permission of Oxford University Press.

CHAPTER ONE

~

Introduction

What's in a name?

(Shakespeare, *Romeo and Juliet*, 2:2.1)

We begin this book with a dilemma—what to name it? As two female psychoanalysts who have tried over the years to understand and to help many women, naturally we are interested in the psychology of women. This interest, and our clinical experience, have led us to focus on the phase of development and associated conflicts known as the "female Oedipus complex." As we immersed ourselves in the study of this complex, it struck us immediately that the term "female Oedipus" is a blatant oxymoron. Since then, we have come to believe that much of what has been written about the Oedipus complex cannot be applied to females at all, and that "female Oedipus complex" is a misnomer.

Hence our dilemma. If we give this universal developmental phase a more fitting name, no one will recognize our topic. But if we *don't* tackle the process of renaming, we will be condoning misperceptions about female development that the current name perpetuates.

Freud's first published use of the term *Oedipus complex* was in 1910 (p. 171, n. 1), although he formulated the concept in his mind a dozen years before. He thought that both boys and girls were initially "masculine" in their psychosexual development, and that femininity for girls was a secondary construction. These early phallocentric ideas complicated and skewed the understanding of the so-called female Oedipal phase. Freud outlined a course of

1

development by which the little girl, to achieve entry into the so-called triangular Oedipal phase, had first to relinquish her inborn masculinity, and change the aim (active, "phallic"), the object (her mother), and the erotogenic organ (her clitoris) of her initial masculine sexual drives.

Early on, some psychoanalytic voices raised questions about this formulation. Karen Horney's papers (1924, 1926) presage current thinking about female development. She noted the male bias and the observer distortion in Freud's theories. She described the importance of early vaginal awareness, which Freud had denied. She suggested that a girl's wishes to be a man could best be explained as a defensive flight that warded off unconscious Oedipal fantasies and concomitant fears of genital injury in heterosexual intercourse. She also asserted that penis envy was not primary to girls' sexual development but secondary to a fear of genital injury. Horney challenged theories that understood the wish for a baby as compensation for the lack of a penis; she insisted that the wish for motherhood was primary for girls and that the so-called "flight from womanhood" noted by early psychoanalysts was influenced by the very real cultural disadvantages of being a woman. Horney attacked many of the major assertions of early psychoanalytic theories of female development, yet these assertions adhere to the theories to this day.

Thus, Horney was an early proponent of many of our current ideas about a "primary femininity" for girls and a forerunner of contemporary feminist and cultural criticisms of Freudian theory. Her additions and criticisms were particularly relevant to our focus in this book: gender identity, sexual orientation, love relationships, unconscious fantasies, superego formation, neurotic conflicts—the issues at the center of the female Oedipal or triangular complex.

A gradual but powerful movement away from the early psychoanalytic theories of women has been gathering speed since Horney's time. Anecdotal evidence, developmental research, and accumulated clinical findings have all challenged the traditional psychoanalytic understanding of the triangular phase in girls. Psychoanalysis and allied fields have produced a large body of literature on this topic over the last fifty years. The titles of these articles and books characteristically include such words as *reexamination, reinterpretation, reversal, rephrasing, repudiation, reformulation, rewriting, replacement, rediscovery, revision,* and *refutation.* And now the time has come to put forward a cohesive *re-explanation* of the triangular developmental phase in girls.

Unconscious triangular conflicts have always been an important focus in psychoanalytic treatment, and they still are, despite today's theoretical and technical upheavals. In this book we will attempt to integrate recent findings on female psychology into a coherent formulation about this nodal point in development. We will try to demonstrate how crucial transformations in psychic structure and fantasy formation occur in this phase that spans approximately ages three through six and how their later reflections in adult character can be traced back to the early years.

The imprint of this stage of development can be seen in the characters, personalities, and conflicts of the adult women who come to us for analysis and psychotherapy. According to Jacob Arlow (1963), it is during the triangular phase that crucial and idiosyncratic unconscious fantasies are formed into hierarchical structures that exert an insistent influence on mental functioning throughout later life. Clinical examples of unresolved conflicts from this stage abound: women who are forever attracted to unavailable men; women who are submissive and self-effacing, even masochistic; women who characteristically inhibit rivalrous feelings towards other women; who cannot achieve; who suffer work inhibitions; who live in and through their husbands and children—even, today, in young female adolescents who enact these conflicts in counterphobic or exhibitionistic sexual behavior.

For purposes of discussion, we will attempt to distill some of the characteristic dimensions of this female complex into the chapters that follow: the entry into triangular phase; the change from dyadic to triangular object relations; the feminine presentation of certain universal conflicts, including conflicts over separation and homoerotic impulses; the role of aggression and defenses against aggression; female superego development and the way it "resolves"; the role of the female body and female sexual pleasure; and finally, the manifestations of triangular conflicts throughout the female life cycle. We will try to take a fresh perspective on clinical material in each of these areas. Our principal sources of data are clinical—the psychoanalyses and psychotherapies of adult women. Consultations with child analysts about their clinical experiences with little girls at this stage and a wealth of material from supervised cases have enriched our understanding.

We will propose an alternate paradigm, which we feel fits the story of women better than the myth of Oedipus, and we will call it the *Persephone complex*. Other writers have proposed different myths and stories, and we will describe and explicate those as well. Our goal is not to insist on our choice of story, nor to impose it rigidly as a model and mold for psychoanalytic thinking. We are looking for springboards into better understandings of the triangular situation in women.

While the term "female Oedipus" remains convenient and familiar to psychoanalytically interested readers, we object to it on multiple grounds. First, its very construction—the name of a man and the limiting adjective "female"—suggests that the essence of the complex is masculine. This language reflects the emphasis in psychoanalytic theory on masculine development as the touchstone against which female development is measured and from which the feminine is derived.

Second, practitioners too often project automatically what they have learned about the male Oedipus onto clinical material presented by females. This tendency leads to distortions, blind spots, and expectations that the dynamics for males and females in the triangular phase are identical.[1] Thus, while a concept such as the "female Oedipus" appears to help to organize material in a meaningful and parsimonious way, this very organization constrains our thinking and ultimately encourages less accuracy than more. A common lexicon enhances communication, but as William Grossman (1995) astutely put it, a useful theory to some extent narrows the field of observation even as it directs attention to relevant observations. "As we know, chance favours the prepared mind, or as an old witticism says: 'I never would have seen it if I hadn't believed it'" (p. 888). Finally, we believe that the unnamed—or the hidden, as the female triangular phase has been under a male name—remains obscure and mysterious. We will examine in greater depth the question of language and its influence on theory and thinking.

Over the years, as we have presented our ideas about an alternate paradigm for the female triangular situation, we have observed a tendency toward immediate dismissal of such an idea. In spite of the evidence that they are incorrect, our old paradigms resist change. Any alternative model for the female triangular situation presents a struggle for analysts, male or female. Their objections cluster around two themes. First, if the Oedipal myth is to be replaced with another, then mustn't this replacement mirror the Oedipus story? Thus, we are bombarded with such questions as: Where's the punishment? Where's the aggression? Where's the dramatic adventure and active initiative taken by the female? We ask in response why female development must necessarily produce the same dynamics, defenses, or experiences as male development. There is the frequent demand that the story portray a female protagonist at an idealized best—brave, assertive, independent, an "equal" of a male hero.

Second, we are asked, "Why must we have a myth as a paradigm at all?" These critics argue persuasively that any given single story may reflect a singular cultural tradition—Oedipus and Persephone, for example, are both exemplars of paternalistic Western civilization. Intelligent voices insist there are many models for female development, depending on the cultural and historical context, and that to try to fit a psychology of women into any single story may be both reductionistic and culturally biased. While we are sympathetic to this thinking, we feel that there is heuristic and clinical value in *considering* a new paradigm for the female triangular clinical situation. We leave it up to our readers to judge its usefulness and validity for themselves.

The clinical analytic process can be adversely affected by a lack of sensitivity to uniquely female dynamics. One of our goals in emphasizing female triangular development is to initiate a change in the way we understand and work with our female patients in relation to this phase. In our reading of the psychoanalytic literature, and in our attendance at conferences and clinical workshops, we find that the Oedipal complex refers preponderantly to males. And so we acknowledge yet another goal—to restore balance by presenting the story as we see it for the more than half of our patients who are females.

Whenever possible, we will not use the term "Oedipus" or "Oedipal" in reference to females, except in quoting or paraphrasing other writers or in a historical context; otherwise, we will use the terms "triadic," "triangular," or "Persephonal."

Note

1. This was Freud's original hypothesis, which he ultimately rejected.

CHAPTER TWO

~

Female Oedipus: An Oxymoron

We are now obliged to recognize that the little girl is a little man.

(Freud, 1933, p. 118)

In his analysis of his own dreams, Freud uncovered an intense love for his mother and a murderous jealousy toward his father. Steeped as he was in classical mythology, he saw a parallel between his discoveries from his dreams and the Greek story of Oedipus. He named this nexus of feelings—love for one parent and rivalrous hatred toward the other—the *Oedipus complex*. Freud subsequently came to believe that the Oedipal myth carried universal truths, and he made it the cornerstone of his new discipline of psychoanalysis.

The myth runs as follows: It had been prophesized that the son of King Laius and Queen Jocasta would kill his father. This curse was set in motion by a homosexual act committed by King Laius, who abducted and raped Chryssipus, the son of Pelops. Hearing the prophecy that he would die at the hands of his son, Laius commanded a shepherd to bind the baby's feet and leave him on a mountain to die. But the shepherd took pity on the infant. Instead of killing him, the shepherd gave him to a childless couple who raised him as their own son. When Oedipus became an adult, he heard the prophecy that he would kill his father, so he fled his home to keep it from being realized. In his travels, he met a stranger at a crossroads. The stranger was King Laius, but neither man recognized the other nor was aware of the relationship between them. Laius ordered Oedipus to give way and Oedipus refused; a fight ensued and Laius was killed. Oedipus then proceeded to Thebes, where he solved the

riddle of the Sphinx and so won the hand of Laius's wife Jocasta (who, unbe-
knownst to both of them, was also his mother). They had four children.
When a famine threatened to destroy the land, Oedipus sought a reason for
the gods' seeming displeasure. Oedipus summoned the old shepherd who told
Oedipus his true history. With this insight, and full of despair, Oedipus
blinded himself with Jocasta's brooch; she hung herself. He banished himself
to wander the earth with his faithful daughter Antigone by his side.

This story has been applied to both males and females as paradigmatic of
a crucial stage of emotional development and the constellation of conflicts
and motives that stem from it. A central task for all children, around four or
five years of age, is to come to terms with the new meanings attached to the
triangular relationships that form in a family among mother, father, and
child. In this chapter, we will summarize the early psychoanalytic formulations of the female child's experience of the triadic situation.

The Application of These Insights to the Female

In his first full delineation of the Oedipus situation in *The Interpretation of
Dreams* (1900), Freud assumed that the triangular situations of girls and boys
were perfectly parallel. Some years later he reiterated: "As you see, I have
only described the relation of a boy to his father and mother. Things happen
in just the same way with little girls, with the necessary changes: an affec-
tionate attachment to her father, a need to get rid of her mother as superflu-
ous and to take her place" (Freud, 1916b, p. 333). For a while, he seemed to
leave the matter at that.

After his case study of Dora in 1900, Freud was preoccupied for a while
with an important series of papers on metapsychology. Still, he continued to
write about female development. In "Three Essays on Sexuality" (1905), he
said that the sexual life of men had become accessible to research, but that
that of women "is still veiled in an impenetrable obscurity" (p. 151). In their
notes to the important paper "Some Psychical Consequences of the Anatomical Distinctions between the Sexes" (1925), the editors pointed out that one
result of this sense of obscurity was that it led Freud to make the erroneous
assumption that women's Oedipal situation could be taken simply as analogous to that of men. In the "Three Essays on Sexuality" (1905), Freud advanced the idea that the sexuality of little girls is "wholly masculine" and
maintained that their leading sexual organ was the clitoris, which he perceived as a defective "masculine" organ.

In 1908, in *The Sexual Theories of Children*, Freud introduced two new concepts: the girl's envy of the penis, and the castration complex. At this point

he still assumed the little girl's sexual development to be just like little boy's. Her "masculine" libido, he thought, is aimed at first at the mother. When she discovers the difference between the sexes, however, and that she is "deficient," she feels a deep resentment toward her mother for not providing her with an adequate sexual organ. Freud believed that in order to find her way into the "normal" Oedipal complex and heterosexuality, the girl must relinquish and then refocus her original sexuality in three ways: in sexual organ, aim, and object. She must abandon pleasures from the "masculine" clitoris (in favor of the vagina, but only later in puberty); she must give up a phallic, active masculine orientation for a more passive feminine one; and finally, she must renounce her original sexual object, the mother, and turn her attentions to the father instead. What drives these developments, according to Freud, are the girl's discovery of sexual difference and her envious wish for the penis.

Thus, he describes for girls a tortured path into the triangular phase, since the feminine attachment to her father can develop only after the relinquishment of her inborn masculinity. With this elaboration, Freud implies that there is not, in fact, a complete parallel between the Oedipal situations of boys and girls, since they enter the triangular constellation by different paths.

In "Some Character Types Met with in Psychoanalytic Work" (1916b), Freud delineated further the psychological consequences of the girl's penis envy: wounded narcissism that leaves a permanent scar; a lasting sense of inferiority; persistent jealousy as an enduring character trait; and a deep resentment against her mother.

In 1919, with the publication of "A Child Is Being Beaten," Freud returned explicitly to the subject of female development. He admitted to a real dissatisfaction with his previous assumptions that the development of males and females were analogous: "The expectation of there being a complete parallel was mistaken" (p. 196). It was in this context that he noted differences in the pre-Oedipal developments of girls and boys. Yet shortly afterwards, in 1921 ("Group Psychology and the Analysis of the Ego"), he reiterated his original idea that the Oedipal situations of boys and girls were analogous. And in discussion of the development of the superego (1923a), he stated that the dissolution of the Oedipal situation leading to superego formation was the same for both sexes.

Soon after that, he abandoned the idea that the development of boys and girls were analogous. A new thesis began to appear when theory was linked to new clinical observations. A complete reassessment of his views about the development of girls appeared in "Some Psychical Consequences of the Anatomical Distinctions between the Sexes" (1925). Freud had now concluded that the dissolution of the Oedipal complex was different for males and females. He saw castration anxiety as the motivation for resolution of the Oedipal complex and development of the superego. The boy's fear of castration led to a definitive development of the superego and resolution of the Oedipal complex. Girls, however, lacking penises and therefore intense castration anxiety, were without a strong incentive to achieve these advances. Their superegos were therefore "weaker," and resolution of the Oedipal complex was extended, ambiguous, or never accomplished at all. In this paper, Freud also suggested that the individual's inherent bisexuality was implicated in the subsequent vicissitudes of the Oedipus complex, determining whether the outcome would be identification with the father or the mother.

By 1924 Freud had acknowledged that his insight into developmental processes in girls was "unsatisfactory, incomplete and vague." In "The Dissolution of the Oedipus Complex" (1924), he gave an account of the girl's Oedipal situation that stressed the fear of loss of love as the powerful motivation for the formation of the girl's superego and the resolution of her infantile genital organization. While Freud at that time saw fear of castration as an *internal* motive for the formation of superego in boys and the breaking off of the Oedipal ties, he believed that girls were motivated instead by external threats of loss of love or rejection within their families and from society. The Oedipal complex of the female was depicted as "much simpler than that of the small bearer of the penis" (p. 178). It is noteworthy that Freud recognized the fear of the loss of love so apparent in little girls in this phase, a dynamic motivating force that we also stress. However, rather than perceiving this as intrinsic to the complexities of the triadic situation for the girl, he dismissed condescendingly the importance of his own observation and described the situation in language that implied the superego of girls was inferior to, or weaker than, that of boys.

In "The Question of Lay Analysis" (1926b), Freud's doubts and uncertainty about the adequacy of his theory of female development emerge again: "We know less about the sexual life of little girls than of boys. But we need not feel ashamed of this distinction; after all, the sexual life of adult women is a 'dark continent' for psychology" (p. 212). Part of the problem was that Freud's view of the female triadic situation seldom included more than the wish to take her mother's place and the desire for a baby from her father. As he saw it, the wishes to possess a penis and to have a child remained strongly cathected unconsciously in the girl's mind to the exclusion of other concerns.

In "Female Sexuality" (1931), Freud's most important addition to his formulation of the female Oedipal complex was the discovery, based on fresh case material from women colleagues—Lampl de Groot, Deutsch, Bonaparte—of the strength and duration of the little girl's pre-Oedipal attachment to her mother. Although he had given an excellent example some years earlier, in "A Case of Female Paranoia Running Counter to Psychoanalytic Theory of the Disease" (1915), of a girl's strong tie to her mother and its role in the functioning of her superego, he had not incorporated these observations into his later theories about female superego development. In 1931, Freud saw in the girl's strong and abiding tie to her mother a virtually unending pre-Oedipal attachment, and a weak motivation ever to move beyond it.

In fact all the early psychoanalytic theorists (see below), and some later ones, have been impressed by the strength of the girl's attachment to the mother and the concomitant anxieties about loss of love and loss of the object. This observation, however, did not fit readily into pre-existing theory and was consistently taken as evidence of the strength of the pre-Oedipal maternal attachment. We argue that *typical development for girls became pre-Oedipalized, that is, pathologized, in traditional psychoanalytic theory.*

Freud's final view of female Oedipal development occurred in the essay "On Femininity" in 1933. Here Freud declared that the application of his findings from clinical work with men to women had been mistaken. Also in the same year in "The New Introductory Lectures on Psychoanalysis" (1933), he reiterated that the girl remains indefinitely mired in the Oedipus phase. Her attachment to her mother is dissolved only by hostility toward her—hostility arising, in part, from the fact that the girl continues to hold the mother responsible for her lack of a penis. "A hate of that kind may become very striking and last all through life" (p. 122). Freud makes clear again his view that for boys, the Oedipus complex develops and resolves "naturally from the phase of this phallic sexuality" (p. 129), while for girls it is the outcome of a long and difficult path and is a secondary development. The girl is driven by hostility and envy from her original choice of mother as love-object toward her father as a haven or refuge. Then, in the absence of castration fear, there is no motive to dissolve the Oedipus complex. "Girls remain in it for an indeterminate length of time; they demolish it late, and, even so, incompletely. In these circumstances the formation of the super-ego must suffer; it cannot attain the strength and independence which give it its cultural significance, and feminists are not pleased when we point out to them the effects of this factor upon the average feminine character" (p. 129). For girls, castration precedes the complex, and hence the Oedipal complex is a "secondary" structure. For boys, in contrast, castration destroys the complex and gives birth to the superego. Thus, boys have stronger superegos than girls.

Here in *The New Introductory Lectures*, Freud also expressed the firm belief that a girl's wish for a baby represented the wish for a penis. A girl's doll play was dismissed as "not in fact an expression of her femininity" (p. 128), but identification with the mother in terms of substituting activity for passivity. That is, the girl actively behaves toward the doll what she experienced passively at the hands of her mother. Freud speculated that the girl's behavior reflects her "intimate object relationship" with her mother. The girl's observed fears about loss of her mother or her mother's love were understood as pre-Oedipal anxieties by Freud and his early followers.

Other Early Contributions

It is striking that Freud's colleagues in their writing on female development did not focus on the female Oedipal complex but on the concept of the castration complex. That is to say, they focused on what they felt was missing in the female. The little girl was seen as a "garçon manqué"—a deficient boy (Freud 1933). For example, Karl Abraham (1922, 1924), an influential contributor to theories about women, emphasized the castration complex as crucial to female development. He described the ways in which women played out unresolved penis envy and castration complexes in trying to assume the masculine role, or in vindictiveness toward men.

As clinical evidence about the Oedipal situation in males accumulated, Freud's notions of correctness of his theory of the Oedipus complex and of its universality gathered conviction. Many of Freud's contemporary female colleagues supported his ideas about women, and these ideas became codified despite the efforts of some early dissenters such as Horney and Ernest Jones who addressed problems in the theory.

Horney, for example, pointed out the cultural determinants of the female's feelings of inferiority. Horney was one of the first psychoanalysts to describe how women have taken in society's biases and insistences of their inferiority. "Women have adapted themselves to the wishes of men and felt as if their adaptation were their true nature" (1926, p. 326). According to Horney (1924) and Lucile Dooley (1938), penis envy is a reaction to, and not an impetus for, Oedipal development. Horney saw it as secondary to Oedipal disappointment: inevitable, but transitory. Following the father's perceived rejection of her Oedipal wishes, the girl may react by a regressive identification with him. Although such a reaction of penis envy does give rise to the clinical manifestations described by Abraham, it is defensive. A second source for penis envy, she suggested, is the girl's guilt about her forbidden wishes. Conflicted, infantile fantasies of a sexual relationship with the father give rise to fears of being mutilated and consequent defensive wishes to have a penis. Thus, Horney's outline of female development, especially in regard to the Oedipal period, differed significantly from Freud's.

Horney, along with Dooley (1938, p. 38), upheld the notion of a primary femininity. While she did not use the term explicitly, she advanced such a concept in her argument that a little girl's sense of being inferior was not primary, but acquired and culturally reinforced. Horney also argued that a girl's reproductive urges did not necessarily stem from a compensatory substitution of a baby for a missing penis but via identification with her mother. In many of her ideas Horney anticipated contemporary psychoanalytic writings about gender and femininity.

Horney (1928) indicated that marriage promises women fulfillment of early wishes stemming from the Oedipal phase, but disillusionment inevitably ensues. Hostility and frigidity are often consequences of conflicts from the Oedipal period that get played out in marriage. The outcome is reinstitution of the Oedipus complex in which the alienated spouse ends up in the role of the child in the mother/father/child triad.

Similarly, Jones (1922) believed that the so-called masculine position in women, as described by contemporaries such as Abraham, reflects a retreat from disappointment with the father, and that femininity is innate. In opposition to Freud's theories, Jones (1935) postulated symmetrical Oedipal situations for the two sexes. He asserted that girls' Oedipal attachments develop spontaneously out of innate feminine urges, analogous to the masculine urges of boys that impel them toward *their* Oedipal objects. Because of disappointment and guilt over their Oedipal longings, girls may temporarily take flight into a phallic position.

On the other hand, Helene Deutsch (1925) supported Freud's views about early female development and accepted the view that the girl's wish for a child is secondary to the wish for a penis. Otto Fenichel (1931a) agreed with Freud in his emphasis on the importance of pre-Oedipal influences, such as the enduring ties to the mother, in the female Oedipal phase. With Freud, he thought that the decisive disappointment that leads to the girl's entry into the Oedipal phase is the mother's failure to provide the girl a penis.

Jeanne Lampl de Groot (1927) stressed the importance of "the negative Oedipal phase." For Freud, the negative Oedipal stage preceded the positive stage and grew out of the early phallic phase. It encompassed the girl's active sexual pursuit of her mother as love object and her competition with the father, along with a desire to give her mother a baby—that is, the reverse of the positive Oedipal stage in which the love object is the father. (Accordingly, the negative Oedipal complex in boys—sexual feelings for the father—does not precede the positive Oedipal complex.) Lampl de Groot, with a few clinical cases as evidence, supported this view. Later psychoanalysts have found no evidence for the regular occurrence of this sequence and argued that there is an early phallic narcissistic phase for both sexes, followed by the Oedipal phase proper (Edgecumbe and Burgner, 1975), or that both "negative" and positive stages occur simultaneously. We agree with this latter view.

Melanie Klein had a very different, and fruitful, view of the Oedipal complex, a view that has been very influential in psychoanalytic thinking. Klein (1945) asserted that it arises early, in the first two years of life, as a consequence of frustration at the breast and is shaped by the primitive introjective and projective processes of the mind. Kleinian theory did not rely on contrasting routes and motivations in males and females. Both boys and girls are impelled "naturally" into the Oedipal situation and their primitive fantasies about the primal scene: "In my view infants of both sexes experience genital desires directed towards their mother and father, and they have unconscious knowledge of the vagina as well as of the penis. . . . Under the sway of fantasy life and of conflicting emotions, the child at every stage of libidinal organization introjects his objects—primarily his parents—and builds up the super-ego from these elements (p. 78)."

As Klein (1945) saw it, these primitive processes provide dynamic explanations for the girl's "Oedipal" fears and her guilts and rivalries toward her mother, very different from those proposed by Freud and his followers. She presents the case of Rita, who was tormented by the fear that she would lose her mother's love or suffer retaliation from her for her sadistic fantasies. These derived from oral frustrations as well as observations of the primal scene. Kleinian ideas do not lead necessarily to the idea that wishes to be a mother rest solely on compensation for penis envy. Klein suggests that because of projected hostile fantasies, little girls may come to feel that their mothers will destroy their capacities for future motherhood.

Melanie Klein's theories helped to illuminate girls' triangular conflicts by highlighting hostile fantasies and their projection. We recognize and agree with the criticisms of the Freudian group (See A. Freud, 1965 and R. Tyson, 1991.) that Klein placed the Oedipal complex too early, thereby telescoping the conflicts she observed backwards into early infancy. This timeline may confound emerging triadic conflicts—that is, the early stages of the Oedipal complex with the earlier processes of mental development during which whole objects are still being established. Nevertheless, her penetrating look into the dynamics of early Oedipal conflicts provided a corrective to a developmental perspective skewed by its phallic preoccupation and its linear sequencing.

Following Klein, Hanna Segal (1974) described the infant's dawning awareness of the important link that exists between the father and mother; in her view this is the perception that sets the stage for Oedipal dynamics. Following Klein, Segal believes that the Oedipus complex evolved from very early, with the infant's fantasies of a relationship between part objects—penis and breast—which evolved into ideas about the relationship between the parents as a whole object, ideas that are influenced by these earlier fantasies. Segal (Britton et al., 1989) also clarified that for Klein, "pregenital" does not equate with "pre-Oedipal." That is to say, even before genital primacy, in the Kleinian theoretical viewpoint, Oedipal fantasies and conflicts abound. The acuteness of the child's ambivalence, the predominance of oral trends, and the uncertain choice of the love object characterize the Kleinian view of the very early stage of the Oedipal complex.

As this brief outline demonstrates, Freud's writings about the girl's triangular or "Oedipal" situation were marked by theoretical dilemmas and compensatory oscillations. As he struggled to build his theories of the psychology of women and of female development, he constantly changed his mind, voicing his own doubts about "murky obscurities" and "dark continents." He began with the error of declaring female and male development to be analogous, and the triangular situations for females and males consequently mirror images of each other. When he developed a more comprehensive view based on correctly identified differences, he floundered again. Trapped in his use of male Oedipal dynamics as the norm, only by theoretical contortions could he force his acute observations of the female to conform to these notions. Girls' entry into the Oedipal situation was convoluted, and they could not get out of it "correctly" or in a timely manner. Held to a masculine norm, women appeared abnormal, terminally narcissistic, morally inadequate, and forever tied by hostility to their mothers.

Freud's use of the word "attachment" was another source of error and confusion. We think that his attribution of "pre-Oedipality" to the girl's attachment to her mother contributed a great deal to the derailing of early attempts to understand triangular development in girls. Freud could understand clinical findings of the girl's strong attachment to her mother only as a pre-Oedipal fixation. He was too hampered by the constricting notion, based on his model for boys, of what the Oedipus complex must be. In contrast, we have argued in previous work (Holtzman and Kulish, 2000) that *fear of loss of love of the mother is part and parcel of the girl's triadic conflicts.*

We feel that Freud's use of language regarding female development and sexuality must be recognized as an important derivative of his unconscious fantasies about females and their genitals. Words such as "unsatisfactory," "incomplete," "vague," "impenetrable," "obscure," "gaps," "dark," "veiled," and "stunted" appear frequently in his writings about women. We will take up the question of language and how it affects theoretic and clinical understanding about women in more detail later. (See Freud, 1925, p. 244, editors' footnote.)

The genderizing of the superego according to the presence or absence of a penis in our view has distorted and obscured the psychoanalytic understanding of the development of morality. In our experience, the absence of a penis does not mean the absence of the structure of the superego, of the sense of justice, or of the symptomatic manifestations of these—obsessional neuroses, guilt, etc. The superego and guilt are subjects of a later chapter.

Since these early formulations, very little has been added to the picture of the female Oedipal complex, despite the tremendous outpouring of new psychoanalytic thinking on female development and sexuality. Even those writers who have focused on the female Oedipal complex have not moved far from Freud's framework. Nagera (1975), for example, has given a careful and very detailed exposition of the female Oedipal complex, negative and positive, that reinforces and elaborates Freud's original formulations. Charles Brenner (1982) made an attempt to reformulate the female Oedipal complex, but he too resorted to older conceptualizations centered around castration anxiety. Phyllis Tyson (1989) is one of the few writers who has put a more contemporary look on the Oedipal situation for girls by discussing it in the context of development of female gender identity and object relations.

The Need for Reexamination

What then are the areas of the girl's triangular or "Oedipal" complex that call for reexamination, in the light of contemporary psychoanalytic thinking? The first is the *entry into the triangular situation*. The discovery of the difference between the sexes, penis envy, and the turning away from the mother in disappointment and rage are no longer accepted as satisfactory explanations for the developmental step of entry into the triangular phase. We (Holtzman and Kulish, 2000) have emphasized the importance of separation issues for the girl in her entry into the triangular situation. We have also argued strongly that this development should not be characterized as a *change* of libidinal object for the girl from mother to father but rather as the *addition* of a libidinal object.

A second area that calls for reexamination is the *role of identification with the mother*. The importance of the girl's primary femininity in the sense of her identification with the mother was not appreciated by Freud, in its important influence on the girl's desire for a baby and to take the mother's role.

A third important consideration concerns the *dynamics of the triangular situation itself*. The shapes of triangular object relations are different for boys and girls, and aggression and competitive strivings are expressed differently as a function of these differing dynamics.

Fourth is the *important issue of the resolution of the triangular situation and the formation of the superego*. The notions that girls can never resolve the triangular situation and that their superego development is therefore compromised is untenable. We disagree with the notion that castration anxiety is necessary for this resolution, and even for mature superego development. All of these points will be discussed in the following chapters.

A fifth area calling for reformulation involves the female body. Throughout his formulations of the female triangular phase, Freud emphasized what the female lacks. Nowhere were there ideas—now falling under the umbrella of "primary femininity"—about the *role played by the female body in the triadic phase in terms of what it has*, and not what it lacks.

CHAPTER THREE

~

Myths and the Female Triangular Situation

A myth is, of course, not a fairy story. It is the presentation of facts belonging to one category in the idioms appropriate to another. To explode
a myth is accordingly not to deny the facts but to re-allocate them.

(Gilbert Ryle, *The Concept of Mind*, p. 8)

The psychoanalytic efforts to formulate the "female Oedipus complex" that
we outlined in chapter 2 confront us with two issues: Are the dynamics that
have been attributed to the Oedipus complex relevant to females? If not, can
paradigmatic myths be found that are better suited to the female situation?
But before we can address these two questions, however, we need to explicate
a more basic premise: The study of myth has been and continues to be a valid
and useful tool in the basic understanding of human motivations and dilemmas, most particularly a psychoanalytic understanding.

Myths

How does the study of myth contribute to the psychoanalytic understanding
of human motivations and dilemmas? Myths represent and convey profound
shared human truths; the anthropologist, Bronislaw Malinowski (1992), in
fact, suggested that myths are a part of the social order, and "maintain the le-
gitimacy of our social arrangements" (p. xvii). They function as active parts
of culture like commands, deeds, or guarantees. Through myths, humankind
learns to think and to fantasize in accordance with the mores of a particular

culture. Myths address culturally shared beliefs and conflicts, both conscious and unconscious; according to Don Cupitt (1982), they are stories of "archetypal and universal significance" (p. 29). They are commonly linked to communal practices and rituals. In the next chapter we will show how the myth of Persephone was utilized in widespread religious rituals in the ancient world.

Following Freud, psychoanalysts have used the study of myth as a window onto shared unconscious belief systems and the group imagination. Carl Jung (1934) pointed out that certain symbols appear again and again across time and culture in mythology, fairy tales, and religion. For Jung, the source of this symbolic material was the collective unconscious, a shared pool of experience that lies below consciousness. What he called *archetypes* are typical modes of expression that arise from this collective depth. Myth, like art, music, religion, and dreams, is for him a means of access to these experiences.

Joseph Campbell (1959) too believes that myth is indispensable, and his romantic version of Jung's theory has had vast popular appeal. For Campbell, myths show us that there is an organic unity to the mind and the world. This mystical view of the message of myth is shared by the Romantics. Campbell outlines four functions of myths: 1) to arouse and maintain a sense of awe and mystery; 2) to provide a symbolic image for the world; 3) to give divine sanction to social practices; and 4) to express the harmony and interrelatedness of all things mystical. Because of these overarching functions, he believes that myths will never disappear,[1] and cites *Star Wars* as an example of a modern hero myth. As a comparative mythologist, however, Campbell pays less attention to the differences among myths than he does to their similarities. He ignores the details of their plots or story lines, and in contrast to the psychoanalytic approach, is not interested in analyzing the meaning of myth in the life of a person.

Otto Rank (1914), one of the earliest psychoanalysts who studied myth, proposed that hero myths expressed socially and personally unacceptable impulses. For Rank, like Campbell, myths are codes that need to be deciphered and are to be read symbolically as representations of an unconscious part of the mind.

Jacob Arlow (1961), in the tradition of Freud (1900), Rank (1914), and Abraham (1909), is the contemporary champion of myth as a contributor to psychoanalytic understanding. "In the stellar cosmogonies of ancient mythology, for example, psychoanalysis sees writ large, in the heavens, projections of grandiose elaborations of the instinctual conflicts of childhood" (p. 372). Arlow went on to describe the relationship of individual fantasy and personal myth to shared fantasy and communal myth. Following Roheim, Arlow stated that mythology is a "culturally organized, institutional form of communal daydreaming" (1969, p. 36). Gaza Roheim (1950), a cultural anthropologist who became a psychoanalyst, brought myth to the forefront of psychoanalytic study. He believed that the mythology of a people is an indicator of their shared dominant conflicts.

Thus, Arlow and many other psychoanalysts have found value and meaning in the study of myth. We share their belief that myths carry shared unconscious meanings across cultures and times. We are particularly interested in the many myths about women—goddesses, witches, princesses, mothers, daughters (Neumann, 1955; Sjoo and Mor, 1975; Walker, 1983). Certainly, we have found that our clinical and theoretical understandings have been informed by the study of myth.

Myths and Fairy Tales

Since we will make great use of both myth and fairy tale throughout this book, we must say a word about the relationship of myth and fairy tale. According to Jack Zipes (1994),

> What we today consider fairy tales were actually just one type of the folk-tale tradition, the *Zaubermarchen* or the magic tale, which has many subgenres. The French writers of the late seventeenth century called these tales *contes de fee* (fairy tales) to distinguish them from other kinds of *contes populaires* (popular tales), and what really distinguished a *conte de fee*, based on the oral *Zaubermarchen*, was its transformation into a literary tale that addressed the concerns, tastes, and functions of court society (p. 11).

The fairy tale genre came onto the scene with the Grimms and Hans Christian Andersen by the beginning of the nineteenth century. Mircea Eliade (1963) stated that myth precedes the folk and fairy tale and has a more sacred function in communities and societies than secular narrative. Oral folk tales and literary fairy tales, however, convey mythic notions and motifs in camouflaged form. Myths and folk tales blended very early in the oral tradition: "myth narrates a sacred history; ". . . through the deeds of supernatural beings, it sets examples for human beings that enable them to codify and order their lives. . . . Consciously and unconsciously we weave the narratives of myth and folk tale into our daily existence" (p. 1– 4). For Eliade, the fairy tale, as it appears to be natural and eternal, becomes myth. That is, the classical fairy tale has undergone a process of mythicization. The author A. S. Byatt (2004) mused on the similarities and differences between fairy tales and myths. She follows Freud in stating that fairy tales are related to day-dreams and wish-fulfillment fantasies in which the questing self meets helpers and enemies. Myths are concerned with origins, the fear of death, and the hope for the overcoming of death in another world. Byatt feels that an important part of our response to the world of tales is governed by our instinctive sense that they have rules. Like with the games we love to play as children, we take pleasure and solace in these rules.

We will attempt to show in subsequent chapters how triangular conflicts, as derived by Freud from the myth of Oedipus, are indeed relevant in the lives of contemporary female patients. We consider these dynamics as central or paradigmatic to the female triangular stage: incestuous themes, for the same- and opposite-sexed parent; rivalrous competition with a third party; jealousy, murderous revenge on rivals; guilt about intense angers and sexual feelings; theories of birth; primal scene. We will trace myths containing these themes in various stories and tales which have been advanced as models for the female triadic situation. We will also assess the validity and fit of each of these tales for their explanatory value of this aspect of female development.

However, while we accept the importance of triangular conflicts, we reject many of the specific formulations about the Oedipal complex that have been applied to females. In our reformulation of female triangular dynamics, we adhere to basic psychoanalytic assumptions. Infantile sexuality and the long period of dependence and helplessness of the human infant are the basic soil out of which triangular dynamics for both boys and girls grow. The picture may differ among families and among cultures, but the unfolding of a passionate and many-faceted family drama is inevitable. A child, between the ages of two and a half and six, struggling with built-in sexual, angry, and dependent feelings, and the social pressures to control and shape them, will come to feel excited, frightened, jealous, guilty, confused, and full of fantasies and conflicts about the adults and the other children in its close proximity. And these fantasies and conflicts will influence the child's inner object relationships as well as its dealings with the outside world. We are arguing that the fantasies and conflicts about triangular issues are not necessarily the same for boys and girls.

According to Arlow (1961),

There is a hierarchy in the fantasy life of each individual, a hierarchy which reflects the vicissitudes of individual experience as well as the influence of psychic differentiation and ego development. To use a very static analogy for a highly dynamic state of affairs, we may say that the unconscious fantasies have a systemic relation to each other. Fantasies are grouped around certain basic instinctual wishes, and such a group is composed of different versions of different editions of attempts to resolve the intrapsychic conflicts over these wishes . . . With the passing of the Oedipal phase a certain degree of organization of the unconscious fantasy life takes place. The fantasy system tends to remain relatively constant as a characteristic feature of the organization of the individual psyche. This is another way of expressing what is commonly known in psychoanalysis as fixation (pp. 377–378).

He warns us, however, against a reductionistic reading of fantasy life,

I hope that no oversimplified conception of an orderly progression of fantasy formations will be inferred from what has been presented till now. Clinical experience, I have said, shows how various wishes from different phases of development are fused into one set of fantasy images, even as the fantasy is being experienced consciously (p. 384).

The developing child acquires the cognitive capacity to incorporate more and more objects within its mind and to deal with more complex interactions among family members. The child's inner world expands from the initial mother-infant dyad to more complex triadic relationships, and triangular conflicts and dynamics are the markers of this developmental step. The task of the triangular phase for both boys and girls is to work through the family drama with its attendant emotions, integrating an expanding inner world, and dealing eventually with the people in the world at large (P. Tyson, 1989).

Triadic dynamics, as they play out in adults, are the familiar stuff of love triangles and jealousies. Resolving triangular struggles means coming to terms with self-understanding, acknowledging one's past, and knowing oneself and discovering unknown parts of the self. The tragedy of Oedipus is that self-understanding and insight came too late. Robert Michels (1986) eloquently demonstrates how the Oedipal drama is a generic metaphor for the role of insight in development and psychoanalysis. We think this idea is true for males and females.

The Oedipus tale invigorated the understanding of central aspects of male psychology. So well did it do so that it was applied also to women's dynamics, but not always so successfully. The Oedipus myth is a story of crime and punishment, the fulfillment of sexual desire, and the struggle for power. Many writers, noting the similarities and differences in female and male development, have searched for another myth that could characterize girls' fears, fantasies, and wishes as succinctly as Oedipus does boys'. The myths of Electra, Antigone, Athena, and the fairy tales of Little Red Riding Hood and Cinderella have been prominent candidates. We will summarize the various contenders.

Alternate Models for the Female Triadic Situation

Electra

Agamemnon, king of Mycenae, has been fighting for ten years in the Trojan Wars. He sacrificed his first daughter, Iphigenia, to appease the gods and avoid defeat at war. While he is away, his wife Clytemnestra takes a lover, Aegisthus. Electra, the second daughter of Agamemnon and Clytemnestra, yearns for her father through the years and is enraged at her mother's betrayal of him. When Agamemnon returns from the war, Clytemnestra and Aegisthus murder him, and Electra urges her brother Orestes to avenge their father's murder. She does not perform the action herself. Aeschylus, Sophocles, and Euripides, authors of the three best-known dramas about Electra, all handle her future differently, seeing her sometimes as shamed, sometimes as blessed, sometimes as happy and fulfilled. In some versions of the myth, Electra marries a friend of her brother.

Jung introduced the Electra complex in 1915 as a female parallel to the Oedipus complex. Freud (1931), however, found Electra wanting as a paradigm for the female triangular situation. In "Female Sexuality," he wrote, "we have an impression here that what we have said about the Oedipus Complex applies with complete strictness to the male child only and we are right in rejecting the term 'Electra Complex' which seeks to emphasize the analogy between the attitude of the two sexes" (p. 229). He goes on to say here that it is only in the male child that the "fateful combination" of hate for the rival and love for the opposite parent exists. That is to say, he believed there was no *equal* complex for girls. For Freud, female development is a mere corollary to male development. (See Scott, 2005, p. 9.)

Sheila Powell (1993), a Jungian psychoanalyst, maintains that the story expresses the girl's anguish in relinquishing incestuous bonds and manifests the psychological problems of growing up and separating from her parents. She stresses Electra's terror and hatred of her mother, and points out that the story emphasizes early problems in the mother/daughter relationship: "It is perhaps the darker side of the myth of Demeter and Persephone" (p. 159). Powell finds Electra lacking as a positive model for female development, but nevertheless credits the story for showing that women can move beyond the dilemmas inherent in patriarchal structures. For Powell, Electra is a metaphor for a woman "caught in rituals set out for the hero" (p. 171). She characterizes Electra as someone who cannot think for herself and who collides with a patriarchal order in her feeling that only a man can change her world.

Jill Scott (2005), a scholar of German literature, argues that the myth of Electra has captured the modernist literary imagination and has replaced

Oedipus as a central source and model for art and literature. According to Scott, Electra's dilemma appeals to modern scholars as it counteracts the male-dominated culture of Oedipus. Artists such as the composer Richard Strauss and poets H. D. and Sylvia Plath have all woven works around Electra. She frequently serves as rallying point for modern arguments about the constraints of gender roles and the abuses of male power.

The psychoanalyst Doris Bernstein (1993) also examines in-depth the Electra story as a model for the girl's triangular situation. She points out that the Oedipus story describes a triangular love relationship, a rivalry between father and son for the mother. Similarly, the Electra myth is also concerned with the triangle of mother, daughter, and father—Electra hates her mother and loves her father.

Aeschylus presents Electra in two plays as helpless, envious of her mother's sexuality, and enraged that she prefers the man Aegisthus to her children. In this version, Electra is essentially a passive listener to her brother's designs. Sophocles emphasizes Electra's jealousy of her mother's love for Aegisthus, instead of for her. While she takes no active role in the deed, Electra is the driving force behind the matricide and is driven by her deep need for revenge. In Euripides' drama, Electra participates more actively in the plot to kill the mother by setting a trap for her. She is condemned to suffer shame and guilt for her role in the murder. The mother's bitterness and jealousy of Cassandra (Agamemnon's mistress) are set forth in parallel to the daughter's feelings. Bernstein suggests that Electra's love for her father is displaced upon her brother and emphasizes Electra's erotized masochism. She uses an example from the text in Aeschylus's *Libation Bearers*. Electra moans in self-pity, envy, and rage toward her mother, whom she calls a whore. The words throughout are full of blatant sexuality and raw masochism. Suffering seems to become a source of erotic pleasure and virtue.

However, in her search for a female myth that mirrored the Oedipus story, Bernstein eventually argues against the selection of Electra. First, Electra never consummates incest; in fact, she does not have a sexual life. Second, she herself never murders her mother. Third, she erotizes pain and wallows in masochism. Fourth, the father whom she idealizes abandoned her family, killed her sister, betrayed her mother, brought home a new mistress, and dethroned them all. Yet all of Electra's rage is turned, unnaturally, on the mother. Electra's idealization of her father could be understood as compensation for the pain of abandonment by the mother. In this, Electra denies the abandonment by the father.

Bernstein believes that the resolution of triangular conflicts is more difficult for females because unlike the male's identification with the aggressor (with Laius), "an identification with the early mother, without intervening identifications with her father, would resurrect threatening, re-engulfing regression" (p. 117). For Bernstein, identification with this early mother is basic to a girl's development. The very fiber of her identity is in conflict in this stage (p. 136). Although we agree with Bernstein that this story does not work as a model for triangular dynamics, we disagree with her view of the special vulnerability of females to regression and engulfment.

H. C. Halberstadt-Freud (1998) proposed Electra as a central paradigm for female development because of the importance of the mother-daughter relationship. Since the drama depicts a troubled mother-daughter relationship, she acknowledges that it is most applicable to girls who have troubled and hostile relationships with their mothers, and so in consequence idealize their fathers. Others who have considered the Electra myth include Daniel Dervin (1998), who also focuses on the Electra complex in terms of the girl's ambivalent love for her mother.

Antigone

Antigone was the child of incest begotten by Oedipus with his mother/wife Jocasta. After her mother's death, Antigone remained loyal to her father and accompanied him on his blind wanderings in exile. After Oedipus's death, her two brothers, Eteocles and Polynices, fought and killed each other. In one of the most familiar versions of Antigone by Sophocles, Creon, Jocasta's brother and the new king of Thebes, forbids Polynices's burial. Antigone defies Creon, buries her brother, and is sentenced to be buried alive in a cave. Her final act of defiance is to kill herself (Steiner, 1984).

Some analysts have considered Antigone to be Oedipus's female counterpart simply because she was his sister (and daughter). Others, however, have picked Antigone for reasons more intrinsic to her story. Nina Lykke (1993), a psychoanalyst, championed Antigone as signifier for a phase for girls. Lykke's particular interest was in clarifying the confusion that she thought Freud caused when he blurred the distinction between the pre-Oedipal and negative Oedipal situations in the girl. She distinguished the infantile symbiosis between mother and daughter from the triangular drama between the mother-lover and the father-rival during the negative Oedipal phase. In the triangular period, the mother is experienced as a separate independent other, separate from the girl in a dangerous and attractive sense, and whom the girl may chose as a partner. Lykke did not come to the conclusion, as Freud did, that girls remain in the pre-Oedipal phase longer than boys do, and she proposed a specific phase that comes between the infantile symbiotic phase and the triangular period proper. Lykke called this the "Antigone phase," which is similar to Lampl de Groot's "negative" Oedipal phase, or phallic/Oedipal phase. Lykke argued, however, against emphasizing the phallus to define the phase, in which the girl was characterized as behaving like a boy with her mother, loving her and fantasizing giving her babies. This "independent space" she dubs the Antigone phase, neither Oedipal nor pre-Oedipal, is marked by incestuous, erotic feelings for the mother.

According to Lykke, during the Antigone phase, which she applies only to girls, the symbolic significance of gender difference begins to register in the girl's mind. A third party, the father, has broken up the symbiosis between her and her mother. During this phase, the child's ideas about gender and sex are ambiguous.

We would not label the totality of the pre-Oedipal period "symbiotic," as does Lykke, but this is a matter of definition. Lykke's arguments are interesting, however, as she teases out the incestuous themes in the Antigone myth.

According to Lykke, Antigone defies the patriarchal law, a symbolic defiance of the father, Creon the king. Ellyn Kaschak (1992), a psychologist, also takes a feminist perspective in understanding Antigone. For Kaschak, both myths—Antigone and Oedipus—embody the family drama in a patriarchal society. Similarly, Natalie Shainess (1982) points out that Antigone's defiance comes out of ethical commitment, rather than rage. She uses this idea to challenge Freud's view that women have weaker superegos than men. Shainess admires the character of Antigone and holds her up as an inspiring ideal for women with appealing qualities of maturity, bravery, and independence. She suggests that the relative neglect of Antigone as a model for female development may reflect men's difficulties tolerating autonomy in females.

For us, however, the myth of Antigone is not strongly enough expressive of basic triangular themes to warrant it as a paradigm for that phase of female development.

Cinderella

The popular tale of Cinderella has been proposed as paradigmatic for the female triangular situation. Certainly, with its familiar plot of the innocent, good daughter persecuted by a mean stepmother and sisters and its happy ending with her winning the rich and handsome prince, it has had huge appeal to the imagination of many generations of little girls. According to Bruno Bettelheim (1975), it is the best-liked and best-known fairy tale. It is an old story; when first recorded in China during the ninth century AD, it already had a history. The tiny foot size as a mark of extraordinary virtue, distinction, and beauty and the slipper made of precious material are facts which point to an Eastern origin. The modern reader does not connect sexual attractiveness and beauty with extreme smallness of feet, as the ancient Chinese did, in accordance with their practice of binding women's feet. Bettelheim emphasized the themes in the tale of sibling rivalry and of wishes and virtue being rewarded.

Doris Bernstein (1993) championed the story of Cinderella in her search for "an image for successful feminine Oedipal development" (p. 159). Bernstein had rejected Electra and Antigone; Electra, because her relationship with her mother was essentially pre-Oedipal and Antigone, because of fixation to her family. She emphasized two versions of the many Cinderella stories. In the version by the Grimms (1972), Cinderella begins as a loved and happy child. Her mother falls ill, tells her daughter to "be good," and dies. As in most fairy stories about girls, the real mother is dead or absent in some way. Thus, her protection is gone. The father marries a woman who has two daughters. From this moment on, Cinderella is degraded and forced to do all of the heavy work in the house by her stepmother and stepsisters. Made to sleep on the hearth and to wear rags, she looks dusty and dirty and from this derives the name "Ash Girl." The father asks what gifts he should bring back for his daughters from a trip. The two stepsisters desire jewels, but Cinderella asks only for a twig. On her mother's grave she plants the twig, which grows into a tree where her wishes are fulfilled by a little bird. The king's son is to pick a bride at a ball. The bird equips Cinderella for the ball after the stepmother and stepsisters refused her wish to go with them. For three successive nights, Cinderella rushes home from the ball to hide from the prince whom she has enchanted. The prince finds the tiny slipper she has lost. He seeks its owner, and the stepsisters try to cut their toes to fit in it, but fail. Finding Cinderella, he takes her away to marry. In this tale, evil is punished: The pigeons peck out the mean stepsisters' eyes as they are on their way to the church.

Charles Perrault's version (1697) seemed to emphasize the daughter's dutiful suffering, as he "nicified" the tale for the French court. Cinderella did all the work in the household while her self-indulgent and selfish stepmother and stepsisters enjoyed themselves. It is a fairy godmother who helps Cinderella get to the ball by outfitting her and changing a pumpkin into a coach and mice into coachmen. In this version the slipper that fits none but Cinderella is glass. She marries the prince and forgives her stepmother and stepsisters. The triumph of good over evil is the central element of the manifest content. Cinderella is not enraged and vengeful, but loving and very good.

For Bernstein, Perrault's Cinderella "fits the model of the girl's Oedipus as an inversion of the boy's" (p. 172). Cinderella is totally good and innocent and accepts her lot in life. The mistreatment and deprivation she suffers is her "castration". She is "restored to completion by the arrival of her prince." Thus, Bernstein stresses the positive analogy in this story to the boy's Oedipal situation with the centrality of threatened castration. In comparison, the Cinderella of the Grimms is more resourceful and finds her way out of the situation with her request of the gift of the twig. Bernstein interprets the taking of the twig from her father as a "phallic" gift from her father, getting what she lacks. The parable is that the daughter must break that tie with her early mother, yet maintain the connection (the twig is planted on mother's grave) and participate in father's power (p. 174).

It seems to us that Bernstein favored this tale as a paradigm for the female Oedipal situation because of its intrinsic satisfaction and idealized picture. Evil was punished, and not forgiven. Cinderella is "restored to power and position" (p. 171) and evolved into a princess. At the end of this tale, Cinderella "has achieved her full feminine identity" (p. 179). We agree: as a fantasized good outcome—the girl achieves happiness, triumphs over evil rivals, and gets the prince through goodness, magic, and/or a little resourcefulness—the story of Cinderella cannot be beat. The story of Cinderella has been interpreted to represent the emergence of the girl's rivalrous relationship with her mother, the mother who stands between the girl and her father, frustrating her Oedipal longings. The father "betrays" her by choosing another woman over her—the remarriage. In both versions the daughter's rage is disguised and projected and emerges in the wickedness of the stepmother and stepsisters. We, however, feel that typical unconscious dynamics of the girl's struggles and conflicts of the triangular period—as opposed to only wished-for outcomes—are not captured completely by this romantic fairy tale. Incestuous sexuality is absent. In fact, sexuality is only given a hint in the future in the phrase "and they lived happily ever after."

Red Riding Hood

Bettelheim (1975) interprets the tale of Little Red Riding Hood as an Oedipal story, which splits two opposite feelings about the maternal object into two figures—wolf and grandmother, bad and good, sexual and nonsexual. Perrault's version begins with the grandmother making the girl a red riding hood and cap. The mother sends her to take goodies to the sick grandmother. On the way, she meets up with a wolf in the forest. The girl divulges where she is going, and the wolf runs ahead and gains entry to grandmother's house. The wolf swallows up the grandmother and dons her cap. He lies down in the grandmother's bed. When Little Red Riding Hood arrives, she is invited to join him in bed. She undresses and joins him and asks a series of questions: "Grandmother what big eyes, ears, and teeth you have." The wolf answers,

"The better to see/ hear/eat you with," and he eats her up. The Grimm brothers (1972) provide two more versions, which are essentially the same, with a few additions. Little Red Riding Hood is saved by hunters who cut her out of the wolf's stomach.

The fairy tale warns the girl of the dangers of her "Oedipal" conflicts. When the heroine strips and gets into bed with the wolf, the sexual meaning is clear. Note that Little Red Riding Hood helps the wolf to the grandmother's house. That is, she uses the wolf to get rid of the (grand) mother. (This is similar to the way in which Electra used her brother Orestes to rid herself of her mother, Clytemnestra.) At the same time, if the girl does not keep the maternal figure alive, catastrophe occurs. She is alone and abandoned.

In another version of this fairy tale, called "A Little Red Cap," Bettelheim (1975) explicated a budding sexuality, an exposure to sex, in which once again Little Red Cap gets rid of her competitor (grandmother/mother) and disavows responsibility for her motivations. He pointed out the many reversals in the tale and how a combination figure, male/female, appears in what he interprets as primal scene, which includes a child's fantasy of birth: The scene depicts the wolf's stomach being cut open, and grandmother is rescued. The good figure is the hunter who saves the child from the horrors of sexuality.

Lykke (1993) uses the story of Little Red Riding Hood as an illustration of the Antigone phase. She interprets the wolf in the story as a bisexual representation, a pre-Oedipal scary mother merged with a ferocious father.

For us, Little Red Riding Hood recalls aspects of the Persephone tale. The theme is again about a young girl who strays from her mother's side or is separated from her and thus puts herself in grave danger. Flowers, which are often symbolic representations of sexuality or the genitals, appear in both stories. In "Little Red Cap," it takes a male, the hunter, to save the girl. For both Persephone and Little Red Riding Hood, the moral is "If I stray from mother, the dangers I fall into are being devoured, in the sexual sense, abducted, and betrayed." In these common fairy tales or myths, it is the absence or death of the mother that brings the girl into danger and sexuality.

Indeed, Red Riding Hood depicts many central themes of the triangular phase for girls—straying from mother into sexualized trouble with a male; primal scene; disguised competition; and jealousy. However, its sexuality is fused with sadomasochism and its drama appears to us to be narrow in scope—childlike and domestic without mythic proportions.

Psyche

Psyche is another tale (Parada, 1997) that has overt links to the Persephone/Demeter story. The virgin Psyche is so beautiful that her older sisters and Aphrodite, goddess of beauty and love, are jealous of her. Aphrodite's son, Cupid, falls in love with Psyche himself, disobeying his mother's command to make Psyche fall in love with someone abominable. The lovers are parted as a result of Psyche's curiosity to see her lover. Psyche, bereft, wanders the wilderness looking for her lover. She works so well during the harvest that Ceres (Roman), or Demeter (Greek), takes her under her wing and advises her to try by "modesty and submission" to win Aphrodite's favor. Aphrodite sets her to perform a series of difficult tasks: one of which is to take to Persephone in the underground world a box in which to bring home some of her beauty. She is commanded not to eat anything or to look into the box on the way back. But Psyche once again cannot resist her curiosity and her desire to get some beauty for herself, so she opens Persephone's box. As punishment for her disobedience, she falls into an endless sleep. When Cupid sees this, he saves her by awakening her, then goes to Jupiter and pleads his case. Jupiter is moved to persuade Aphrodite to save Psyche.

We can see reflections in many of the favorite fairy tales—"Cinderella," "Snow White," "Sleeping Beauty"—in this story. The jealousy between an older woman and a younger girl characteristic of the female triangular story is apparent. Typically, the evil jealousy is shown to reside in the older woman or the sisters and not in the young girl. Like Cinderella, Psyche may finally get the man because she is obedient and good. She must "offer herself as a servant" to her rival Aphrodite in order to defuse the competition between them, although her curiosity and vanity almost bring her down. Carol Gilligan (2003) interprets this story differently. She sees Psyche as the epitome of an adventuresome woman who defies the patriarchal order and refuses to submit to the role of the beautiful object. We find this is structurally not a triadic story, although there are sexual and competitive themes in abundance.

Athena

The myth of Athena has also been proposed by Beth Seelig (2002) as a model for female triangular conflicts. Athena is a virgin goddess who envies all women. Bearing a spear, she was born fully grown from the head of her father Zeus and has never accepted a male as lover or mate. Athena is especially jealous of Medusa, who had once been so beautiful that Zeus had raped her in Athena's own temple. Seelig regards Medusa and Athena as two sides of the same personage—the virginal daughter of Zeus, and Zeus's sexual partner—and indeed Medusa and Athena are often depicted as a two-faced icon. Seelig argues that Athena's story depicts an Oedipal rivalry. The close relationship between Athena and her father Zeus and the competitive hostility she displays toward other females is suggested as a model of the female "Oedipal situation."

We agree that the myth of Athena does indeed depict clearly the conflicted hostility and competition among women, with a father figure in the foreground. Its drawback as a model of the triangular situation, however, is that Athena is a virgin who has not had sex, which is split off onto the figure of Medusa.

Themes of Father/Daughter Incest in Other Myths and Tales

Many folk tales and fairy tales are marked by open themes of father/daughter incest, specifically a father's wish to marry or consummate sexual relations with his daughter. The father's desire for the daughter is the other side of the female "Oedipal" story. The father/daughter incest implicit in the Persephone story (Hades is her uncle) is explicit in these stories. The Grimms took many of these lurid tales and excised or disguised the explicit incest, but Ashliman (1997) documented many of these stories and their variants in Indo-European literature. A common motif of these stories, according to Ashliman, is that the mother (usually on her death bed) gives implicit permission for the incest, asking the husband to marry someone fitting a certain description. As it turns out, only the daughter fits that description. The daughter, horrified by the suggestion, must use her wits to escape the union. Often in the end of these tales, the girl eludes the father and marries a prince.

Ovid's *Metamorphoses* (Melville, 1986) contains tales of incest and incestuous themes. One of the most striking tales is the tragedy of Myrrha. Myrrha, a princess with many noble suitors, is afflicted with an irresistible lust for her father, Cinyras. Feeling that there is no escape, she tries to hang herself, but is stopped by her old nurse. The servant, horror-struck by this secret passion, nevertheless pities the girl, and convinces the drunken Cinyras that a young girl his daughter's age loves him. Under cover of darkness she brings Myrrha into his bed. Ovid's poetic text pictures the scene:

> Her senses reel. The nearer to her crime,
> The more her horror. Would she'd never dared!
> Would she could steal away unrecognized!
> As she hung back, the old nurse took her hand
> And led her to the high-raised couch and said
> 'She's yours, your Majesty. Take her'; and joined
> The pair in doom. In that incestuous bed
> The father took his flesh and blood (p. 239).*

*87w from pp.239, 241 from "Metamorphoses" by Ovid edited by Melville, A.D. (trans) (1998). By permission of Oxford University Press.

Myrrha is impregnated, and the deceit is repeated nightly. Eventually Cinyras becomes curious, casts a light on the girl, discovers that she is in truth his own daughter, and tries to run her through with his sword. Myrrha flees for her life. Guilt-ridden and brokenhearted, she asks the gods to put her out of her misery. She is transformed into a tree, which forever weeps. Ovid's text comments on the incest:

> Those tears in truth
> Have honour; from the trunk the weeping myrrh
> Keeps on men's lips for aye the name of her. (p 241).

The tree delivers itself of the child of sin, a beautiful baby boy, Adonis.

This tale of father-daughter incest is striking in that the impetus and desire come from the daughter. More typically the guilty party is the father. Indeed, there is a whole group of stories in which the girl leaves her father voluntarily or provokes her own banishment in order to escape a too-intense Oedipal attachment. In "Beauty and the Beast," the Oedipal nature of the attachment is latent; Beauty volunteers to stay with the beast in order to save her father from its clutches. In the end, her virtue and sacrifice are rewarded as the beast turns out to be a handsome prince in disguise. The Oedipal figure is split into father/bad sexual beast and good, loving prince. In most of these stories the mother is dead or absent.

Conclusion

The period between ages two and a half to six, the triangular stage, is marked by incestuous conflicts and desires and their dynamic consequences. We are focusing on the course of this phase as it develops in little girls and appears later in grown women. Its excitement, its possibilities, and its dangers are described in many tales. Like the story of Oedipus, these describe a train of events that pull the protagonist inexorably toward a complex and sometimes tragic fate. And, as myths do, they take forms that reflect important aspects of human experience.

The stories outlined above can be read at many different levels. Clearly they can be seen as manifestations in fantasy of the enduring presence of incestuous desires. Feminists have argued that they also depict a sociological and historical truth: the frequent incest and abuse of power perpetuated on girls by their fathers. Contemporary psychoanalytic writings have emphasized the participation, unconsciously and subtly, by both parents and child in the triangular sexual complex (Greenberg, 2006). While a child may direct sexual impulses toward the parents, parents may equally elicit or seduce, consciously or unconsciously, the child into a desired role in a triangular drama. Clarice Kestenbaum (1983) has highlighted the father's role in the girl's Oedipal conflicts. Using fairy tales such as "Sleeping Beauty" to illustrate her points, she suggests that the father's frank expression of pleasure in all aspects of his daughter's femininity facilitates her successful transition into comfort with her developing body and its pleasures. Ruth Lax (2003) says that the father plays an important role in Oedipal development by unconsciously luring his daughter into a change of object from the mother, or responding to her in a sexual manner. Martin Bergmann (1992) gave the name "Laius complex" to the complimentary side of the Oedipal drama—the father's competitive and murderous urges toward his son. We feel that the triangular situation is a complex nexus of fantasies and relationships to which all parties contribute more or less, depending on the particular family and individual dynamics. It is reductionistic to suggest that the triadic drama is "caused" by the child's impulses, or the parents', alone.

Each of the myths we have described above captures some important aspect of the triangular story for the girl. None seems to fit the larger picture for us as well as the tale of Persephone, which we will present in the next chapter. None, including the Persephone tale, however, seems to encompass all the major aspects of the *triangular* phase and related conflicts—the rivalry, the balancing of loyalties, the importance of the girl's body and sexuality. Just as the tale of Oedipus does not encompass all aspects of male development, so too the tale of Persephone is incomplete. For us, what is most important is the understanding of the girl's unique triangular situation and not that we must fit the developmental and clinical data into any one paradigm.

Note

1. Tylor's Theory of Myth

   - Theory contained in his book, *Primitive Culture*, from 1871.
   - Myth and science are incompatible and the latter replaces the former.
   - Myth is a form of primitive science and a subset of religion, except for the hero myths which shape the customs and institutions of a society.
   - Myth is to be taken literally even if the gods started out as personifications of nature.
   - Myths are explanations of the effect that the decisions of the gods have on natural phenomena.

- Myths arise from intellectual curiosity and a belief in animism (i.e., that everything has a soul).
- Natural events are caused by souls and gods in primitive myth.
- Myth uses imaginative stories to explain the world—unlike religion.
- Weaknesses: Downplays role of imagination and overemphasizes kinship with science.

CHAPTER FOUR

~

The Myth of Persephone

They call me Daughter of Darkness, Pomegranate Girl, call me wanton,
say I yielded foolishly to some wild force surging through curled fronds
and came to harm because I could rest no more than Sibyls roused to
madness by Apollo's kiss. But there is more to bitter sacrifice than this.

(B. A. St. Andrews, *Persephone*, p. 494)

In the preceding chapter, we outlined the major myths that analysts have proposed as alternate paradigms for the "female Oedipal complex." In this chapter
we will present a more detailed account of the Persephone story and demonstrate how it can enhance our understanding of the female triangular situation.

The myth of Persephone/Demeter has permeated Western civilization to
a remarkable degree—in literature, poetry, art, and even music. Its evident
broad appeal rivals, if not outdoes, the Oedipus myth as a story that captures
the imagination, as we will demonstrate shortly. Persephone's story and its
variations have inspired scores of poets, writers, sociologists, feminists, histo-
rians, literary critics, and artists, as well as psychoanalysts.

We first became interested in the figure of Persephone while researching
the reaction of women to the loss of their virginity (Holtzman and Kulish,
1997). Several of our patients were preoccupied with virginity, and fantasies
about Persephone were prominent in their minds. One patient in particular
spoke of her long-standing interest in and identification with Persephone.
It was evident that this myth represented unconscious triangular conflicts
for her, too, and was deeply intertwined with her experience of them. Our

research into the myth led us to a study of the life and work of the writer Edith Wharton, who from early childhood was also fascinated with Persephone and incorporated the myth in many of her poems and short stories. Biographical material about Wharton's own life (R. Lewis, 1985) documented her considerable neurotic difficulties about sexuality and virginity. It seemed to us that for Wharton the Persephone myth represented "Oedipal" or triadic conflict, a theme that recurs throughout her work—for example, in the ghost story "The Pomegranate Seed" and in the novellas *Ethan Frome* and *Summer*. Many of Wharton's works contain triangular scenarios, in which two women compete for one man, and thinly veiled incestuous themes; and, as in the story of Persephone in her captivity by Hades, there are themes of communications from the underworld.

Once our attention had been drawn to the heterosexual, rivalrous, and incestuous aspects of this myth, a story of a girl's entry into adult sexuality, we began to study the variations and background of the Persephone myth. Our study convinced us that it is a far richer representation of female triangular conflicts than the story of Oedipus, a male.

The Persephone Story

The ancient myth of Persephone and her mother, Demeter, which can be traced back at least to 2000 BC, has been considered by many different kinds of thinkers as the most important myth about women and the mother-daughter relationship (Rich, 1976; May, 1980; Lincoln, 1991). It represents the central motif around which the Eleusinian mysteries were celebrated in the ancient world. Women, as well as men, participated and had central roles in these and other fertility rites, which honored the goddess Demeter (also known in the Roman civilization as Ceres, goddess of grain).

There are endless versions of this myth. The oldest and most complete is "The Homeric Hymn to Demeter" (Foley, 1994); we will refer to Foley's 1994 translation. The story goes like this: Kore/Persephone is the lovely young daughter of Demeter, goddess of grain and Zeus, king of the gods, who were sister and brother. Kore is gathering flowers in a meadow with other young girls. She is attracted by a particularly beautiful narcissus and plucks it[1], whereupon the earth suddenly opens and Hades, god of the underworld and death, abducts her into his dominions. No one hears her cries. (Some versions of the story make a rape more explicit.) When Kore next appears in the Homeric hymn, she is with Hades in the underworld: She is pictured as shy and demuring, reclining on a bed with Hades. It is important to note that prior to her abduction and presumably the loss of her virginity, the girl is known only as "Kore," which in Greek literally means "maiden." Afterwards, she takes on a new name—Persephone, queen of the underworld.

Demeter is bereft and frantic. She descends from Olympus to search the earth desperately for the girl, in her grief causing draughts and famines that will plague the world until her daughter is found. Disguised as an old woman, the goddess offers herself as a servant to a mortal family to care for their infant boy, Demophoon. Grief-stricken and mute, Demeter refuses food and drink. An older servant woman, Baubo (sometimes known as Iambe), teases her by lifting up her skirt and displaying her genitals to the despondent Demeter. Demeter laughs at this jest and comes out of her depression enough to eat and drink. We will explore this startling and little known but pivotal episode in more detail in chapter 9.

Zeus, moved by the catastrophe engulfing the earth, persuades Hades to release Persephone. But Hades "stealthily" tricks Persephone into eating a pomegranate seed (in some versions seven or several seeds), an act that undermines the bargain worked out among the gods. Persephone is to be released only if she does not eat in the underworld. When questioned later by her mother, Persephone says that she was compelled against her will and forced to taste the seed. (In other versions of the story the act of eating the pomegranate is variously and ambiguously interpreted as voluntary or involuntary, with or without the girl's awareness.[2]) In any case, having broken the injunction against eating in the underworld, she is now bound to Hades. In classical mythology, as in psychoanalytic theory, eating the seed symbolically implies sexual union (pp. 56–57).[3] A compromise is worked out between the gods by which Persephone spends two-thirds of the year with her mother and one-third of the year as queen of the underworld with Hades. This compromise is the ancient explanation of the origin of the seasons. Winter rules while Persephone is with her husband, and the earth flowers in spring and summer when she returns to her mother. The poem ends with Demeter's founding of the Eleusinian rites.

"The Homeric Hymn to Demeter"

"The Homeric Hymn to Demeter," composed in the late seventh or early sixth century BC in the period between Homer and Hesiod, was not written by Homer. Homeric hymns were short poems in epic style and meter that may have been originally designed as preludes to the kind of epic poems written by Homer (Foley, p. 83).

The author (or authors) of the Homeric hymn is anonymous, but undoubtedly male; still it puts the female experience at the center of its narrative.[4] In most of the Greek dramas, conflicts between the genders lie at the heart of the plot—consider, for example, *Oedipus* and *Antigone*. The Eleusinian mysteries, which were based on the hymn, accepted initiates of both sexes, but its rites had widespread female participation. The central religious mystery centers on female experience and emphasizes especially the relationship of mother and daughter. The cyclical narrative of the poem represents a female quest that differs significantly from the linear male myths embodied in such heroes as Odysseus. The hymn to Demeter has been interpreted as one (that is, the Greek) culture's attempt to come to grips with the human dilemma of death. Mother and daughter eternally separate and reunite in a seasonal pattern. The transcendence of death was embodied in the ceremonies of the Eleusinian mysteries (Foley, 1994).

Other Versions of the Myth

Later Greek and Roman art and literature offer many variations of this myth. This repetition is not unusual. Poets and artists often reshaped myths; in fact, in some cases the author assumed that his audience was aware of other existing versions (Foley, 1994). (For example, Cole Porter probably assumed his audience had knowledge of Shakespeare's *Taming of the Shrew*, on which his musical *Kiss Me Kate*, was based.) Persephone is mentioned by Aeschylus in *The Choephore*, indicating that in the fifth century BC the Greek audience knew her well.

Later versions tend to emphasize the origin of the seasons more than earlier ones do. Other important details are different as well. The Homeric hymn, compared to other versions, invites us to question how truthful Persephone is in her claim that Hades *made* her eat of the pomegranate. This detail is important to our argument that this ambiguity is suggestive of a girl's defense over her sense of sexual agency.

The Roman poet Ovid presents two versions in his *Metamorphoses* and *Fasti*. In Ovid, the theme of conflicts among the gods being displaced onto the mortal world is more prominent than in the Homeric hymn. In the *Metamorphoses*, for instance, it is Hades who sets the story in motion, and there is a reversal in that the chariot carrying Proserpina (Latin for Persephone) goes heavenward rather than underground.

Another treatment of the myth, this one by the fourth century AD poet Claudian, highlights the mother's desire to keep the daughter safe, which in his poem means protecting her from separating and entering into adult sexuality. In this version, Proserpina is beginning to feel sexual stirrings and the desire for marriage. She attracts suitors, so her mother sequesters her. The god of the netherworld seizes her nonetheless. But he treats her well and becomes a good husband to her. Still other variants include the Orphic versions with Ceres, many of which seem to give more details of local rituals of the early Eleusinian traditions than does the more epic hymn.

Background of the Myth

There is much evidence for an early cult of Persephone in Sicily. According to the Greek scholar Gunther Zuntz (1971), Zeus was believed to have given Sicily to Persephone as a wedding gift. Akragas is assumed to be the location of an early important cult of the goddess Persephone. There are remains at that site of a huge statue, presumably of a goddess, which has an aura of divine solemnity. According to Sicilian tradition, this was the spot where the earth split open to receive the lord of the netherworld with his victim (Zuntz, 1971). Ovid too seems to place the action of the story in Sicily more than does the Homeric hymn, which doesn't specify the setting.

Zuntz's scholarly work demonstrates how widely known and influential the goddesses Persephone and Demeter were across the ancient world and how many guises, traditions, and narratives are associated with them. However, the worship of female divinities predates these cults. According to Zuntz, the earliest divinity known to be worshipped by humankind was the mother, and the classicist James Frazer (1922) identifies Demeter as "Corn Mother" (p. 463).[5]

The worship in Greek religion of a pair of women is unusual. They are often seen as two aspects of the same deity; at times, Persephone represents not only the daughter of Demeter but also her lost youth. Laura Strong (2005) documents Persephone as one aspect of the triple goddess, "a powerful feminine archetype in which maiden, mother, and crone are seen as one" (p. 4). Robert Graves (1960), like Strong, argues that Kore, Demeter, and Hecate (a mysterious goddess often appearing as a witch) represent Maiden, Nymph, and Crone.

Readings of the Persephone Myth

Many scholars and writers, including classicists, feminists, sociologists, and psychoanalysts, have studied the myth. The classicist Helene Foley (1994) emphasizes the cultural-historical meaning of the myth, which describes the effect on women of arranged marriages and the ensuing separation from family. Bruce Lincoln (1991), a religious historian, interprets the myth as a scenario or rite of women's initiation. A theological Christian interpretation is furnished by Laurie Gagne (2002), for whom the Demeter-Persephone myth is about women's spiritual wholeness.

In *The Golden Bough*, James Frazer (1922) interpreted the Persephone myth in terms of the recurrent themes of dying and reviving, of death and rebirth. Persephone goes down to the underworld and rises from it again. Evidence for the importance of this theme is the ancient tomb in the vale of Enna in Sicily, magnificently decorated with these images from the Proserpina tale. Thomas Bulfinch (1979) writes of the agricultural allegory in which Proserpina represents seeds that are cast into the ground and then reappear. Another aspect of immortality appears in the Demophoon incident from the "Homeric Hymn to Demeter," in which the baby's mortal mother foils Demeter's intention of putting the baby boy into the flames to insure his immortality. Graves (1960) points out that in Ovid's version Persephone picks poppies, not narcissi, whose scarlet color promises resurrection after death. These images evoke the famous scene in Bergman's "The Virgin Spring" of life-water flowing from the spot on the ground where the young virgin was raped and killed. The theme of leaving the family is likened to death (Bulfinch, 1979). These cyclical themes of birth and rebirth impress us, too, in our search for a story emblematic of women.

The feminist Marianne Hirsch (1989) expresses our sentiments beautifully: "The cyclicity of the resolution, with which Persephone is to her mother alternately alive and dead, distant and symbiotic, offers an alternative to Oedipal narratives structured according to principles of linear repletion. The 'Hymn to Demeter' thus both inscribes the story of mother and daughter within patriarchal reality and allows it to mark a feminine difference" (pp. 5–6). Ruth Lax (2003) uses the Persephone myth to argue that the father has an active role in seducing the daughter away from the mother into the Oedipal situation.

Special attention has been given to the meaning of the pomegranate in the story as symbol of this cyclicity of birth and death. Winifred Lubell (1994), artist and mythologist, summarizes: "The pomegranate with its astonishing number of seeds and brilliant red juice has long been seen as a complex symbol combining womb or fertility with images of bloody death" (pp. 37–38). "Furthermore," Lincoln (1991) adds, "the red color evokes associations not only of mortal wounds but also of menstrual blood, the blood of defloration, and the blood of parturition" (p. 85). It is no coincidence, then, that pomegranates were the one food women were allowed to eat during the second day of fasting in the Eleusinian mysteries, nor that they were the food that bound Persephone to her womanly fate.

Many writers stress the importance of the story in elucidating other issues about women. The psychologist David McClelland (1975) argues that the myth exemplifies the feminine attitude toward power. From a traditional psychoanalytic view, Marylin Arthur (1994) sees in the myth a girl's renunciation of phallic strivings and acceptance of femininity. The mythologist Christine Downing (1989) argues that the Demeter-Persephone myth represents lesbian love, with its struggle between merger and differentiation between two women, recalling issues in early mother-daughter relationships. For Adrienne Rich (1976) there is no better representation of mother/daughter passion and rapture.

In an important psychological/sociological contribution, psychoanalyst and social researcher Carol Gilligan (1982) relates the myth of Persephone to her research on contemporary female adolescence, comparing the mysterious disappearance of the sense of self in female adolescents to an underground map "kept secret because it is branded by others as selfish and wrong" (p. 51). (We would add that this secrecy relates to the sexuality emerging at adolescence.) In a similar vein, Rosemarie Krausz (1994) interprets Persephone as portraying the voicelessness and invisibility of womanhood. For the feminist psychoanalyst Luce Irigaray, Demeter and Persephone represent femininity, divided by patriarchy (1991). She uses the myth to call for "the bond of female ancestries" to be renewed (1994, p. 104).

The followers of Carl Jung, who embrace myths so centrally, have paid much attention to the myth of Persephone. Jung (1967) suggested that Demeter and Persephone are archetypal mother-daughter imagoes. From their different psychological perspective, Jungians, like us, recognize the sexual and triadic nature of this story. However, they emphasize the important issues of separation in adolescence without necessarily linking these themes to the earlier developmental crisis we are trying to address. The Jungian Tanya Wilkinson (1996) sees in Persephone an elaboration of the archetype of the victim, and in Demeter, "anorexic depths of despair" (p. 36).

Virginia Rutter (2000) shares other Jungians' attention to mothers and daughters and embraces the myth as an inspiration to mothers trying to help their adolescent daughters separate. She reads the myth, as we do, essentially as a story of separation, loss, and return, and about adolescent girls' entry into the adult world of sexuality. Similarly, Clarissa Estes, a prominent Jungian psychoanalyst, using a pre-Hellenic version, sees Persephone as an active participant in leaving her mother on a quest to explore the world. The Jungian psychotherapist Kathie Carlson (1997), in her scholarly book on the Persephone story, also sees in the myth a historical commentary on the conquest of matriarchy by patriarchy. She argues, as we will, that it is not regressive for a girl

to maintain connection with her mother. She appreciates the varied interpretations of the myth, which she sees as complex and rich. Her book itself is
enriched by many works of art depicting Persephone and Demeter. For her,
the myth gives the inspiration that death can be overcome by reunion with
and transformation with the mother, and that even the most violent and deep
trauma can mean a renewal of the psyche.

Recent psychoanalytic writers from different perspectives (Spitz, 1992;
Estes, 1992; Young-Eisendrath and Wiedenman, 1987; Herman, 1989; M. W.
Donovan, 2005) also highlight themes of separation and reunion and the importance of the mother/daughter relationship in the myth. Another psychoanalytic writer, Susan Fairfield (1994), explains the universal appeal of the
myth in terms of pre-Oedipal separation-individuation issues. She presents
Kore as representative of the child of either sex who first experiences itself as
feminine in a primary maternal identification, and the abduction by Hades
as the paternal presence in early triangulation. We, too, focus on the separation themes in the myth, but we will argue in chapter 6 that the separation
issues are not simply precursors to the triangular phase ("pre-Oedipal" in psychoanalytic jargon) but are central to the phase itself.

Persephone in Art and Literature

Persephone and Demeter have served as inspiration for scores of literary and
artistic works, starting from the images of Demeter and Persephone that any
visitor to a major art museum will see in the marble sculptures and ancient
vases of the classical wing. In fact, we were amazed to discover the depth and
breadth of Persephone's allure. We can touch on only a few examples here.

There are many allusions in Shakespeare to Persephone. In *The Winter's Tale*,
the character of Perdita, torn at birth from her mother's arms in Sicily (scene of
Persephone's abduction) and raised in exile, evokes Proserpina in a speech:

> I would I had some flowers o'th' spring, that might
> Become your time of day; and yours and yours
> That wear upon your virgin branches yet
> Your maidenheads growing: O Proserpine,
> For the flowers now that, frighted, thou let'st fall. . .
> (4.4. 113–118)

Countless poets, earlier and later, have used Demeter/Persephone as muse.
Extraordinary examples, including D. M. Thomas and D. H. Lawrence, can
be found in Kossman's (2001) *Gods and Mortals: Modern Poems on Classical*

Myths. Other poets inspired by this story include Emily Dickinson and Louise Gluck, the American poet laureate. We quote Gluck's lovely evocation in "Pomegranate" of Persephone's eroticism:

> First he gave me
> his heart. It was
> red fruit containing
> many seeds, the skin
> leathery, unlikely.
> I preferred
> to starve, bearing
> out my training.
> Then he said Behold
> how the world looks, minding
> your mother. I
> peered under his arm:
> What had she done
> with color & odor?
> Wherupon he said Now there
> is a woman who loves
> with a vengeance, adding
> Consider she is in her element

In 1933 Stravinsky composed music for the ballet *Persephone*. A modern multimedia production called *Persephone* by Robert Wilson was performed in 2006 in East Hampton, New York.

Many women writers have been inspired by this myth and there is by now a significant amount of commentary on the Persephone myth, in literature. For example, Josephine Donovan (1989) demonstrates how the literary works of Willa Cather, Edith Wharton, and Ellen Glasgow all utilize Persephone or Persephone-like themes in their major works to represent in varying ways rebellion against the traditional women's culture of their nineteenth-century mothers. In Donovan's view, the explanation for why all these women chose this myth lies in the historical and sociopolitical context of their work; she does not see their embracing of this myth as a reflection of archetypes or their individual dynamics. Nevertheless, Donovan stresses the problems, especially envy, in the mother/daughter relationship which impede the process of separation. And, in accord with our central thesis, she alludes to Oedipal-stage separation issues in the story. In addition, Donovan suggests that there are clear allusions to the Demeter-Persephone story in the works of Virginia Woolf and Colette (p. 163).

In her examination of the problem of establishing identity for the female artists, Grace Stewart (1979) traced the themes and metaphors from the myth of Persephone in the works of several modern female writers, including Margaret Atwood, Erica Jong, and Doris Lessing. Stewart reads the process of individuation as central to the myth. And some feminist writings take Persephone as a spiritual inspiration. Victoria Weinstein (1996), for example, compares the trinity to triple goddess images and argues that goddesses have been denied a religious language of their own. Weinstein likens Persephone to Christ—a suffering and resurrected goddess, an innocent who endures the underworld before a resurrection miracle. She saves the world by bringing fertility, growth, and harvest back.

Persephone's compelling popularity over thousands of years and diverse cultures has convinced us that this myth expresses something meaningful about women and, more than that, something meaningful about human experience.

Persephone versus Oedipus

Several psychoanalytic writers read the Persephone myth, as we do, as an evocation of the female Oedipal complex. Here, too, many different points of focus are possible. Nancy Chodorow (1994b) notes Freud's emphasis on the girl's pre-Oedipal attachment to her mother and its carryover into the Oedipal period and comments that Persephone represents such a case: "torn from and always maintaining her attachment to her mother, Demeter" (p. 10). Tyson (1996) also speaks of the myth of Persephone as an example of a partial resolution of the Oedipal conflict, in which the girl feels she must take care of her mother.

Beverly Burch (1997), like us, proposed that the Demeter-Persephone myth describes the daughter's developmental crisis more aptly than the Oedipal story. She puts it beautifully: "The girl's early concerns seem less a pursuit of power and more a pursuit of relationships. She does not necessarily compete with her mother so much as she tries to hold onto her while she embraces the father. The daughter's interest in her father does not necessarily eclipse her interest in her mother. She wants both" (p. 19). These interpretations do not emphasize, as we do, the aspects of the story that provide a defensive covering for girls' experience of their sexuality.

We concur with these writers that the Persephone myth captures the female "Oedipal" conflict and its typical resolution better than the male-modeled Oedipus story does.[6] We emphasize in our argument four aspects of the story: first, its representation of the girl's loss of virginity and entry into adult heterosexuality; second, its dramatization of the themes of separation and rapprochement between mother and daughter, which we feel are central to the triangular situation and which we will describe in more detail in chapter 6; third, its depiction of a compromise formation to resolve conflicts over love, desire, and loyalty toward mother and father; and finally, its depiction of the clearly female themes of cyclicality, fertility, and pregnancy.

The tale of Persephone and Demeter is an erotic story. It begins with abduction and a seduction, or possibly a rape. Persephone may go unwillingly into the arms of Hades at first—as we have said, some see her straying from her mother willingly, attracted by the sensual unknown, but she is not so single-minded about leaving him; her ambivalence is manifest in the seeds that she eats, a symbolically sexual act in which she participates perhaps by trickery, but perhaps with intent. Demeter is the goddess of grain and fertility, brought out of her catastrophic depression by Baubo's display of the female genitals. Doris Orgel (2003), who has rendered the famous Greek myths into a series of books for younger readers, also renders Persephone as an erotic tale. Right after Hades has snatched Kore away, Orgel pictures a romantic interlude: "'Hush.' We'd come within a foot of the abyss. He brought the horses to halt and said, 'I'll tell you what I took you for: a goddess unsurpassed in loveliness.' I felt the color rising in my cheeks and turned my face away. 'No, look at me. You're even lovelier when you blush'" (p. 81).

The tale also depicts homoerotic love. Demeter's love for Persephone is passionate and intense. Foley (1994), the translator of the Homeric hymn, tells us that the Greek language of Demeter's lament for her lost daughter is that of an erotic love poem. She notes a passage that seems to emphasize eye contact between mother and daughter. "Normally in Greek poetry, such language is suggestive of erotic motifs: for the Greeks, love begins with the eyes" (p. 58). And when separated, Persephone and Demeter pine for each other with desire—with pothos—a word in Greek having sexual overtones (p. 131).

As in many stories about young girls, including fairy tales and myths, the tale of Persephone warns that leaving mother's protection exposes the girl to the dangers of sexuality; conversely, to become an adult and sexual woman, a girl must leave her mother's domain and enter her own. The change of name—from Kore, virgin, to Persephone, married woman—clearly represents sexual initiation, just as it does in our society. We think that the myth states several important psychic realities; the first is that a psychic separation is necessary for achieving the female adult role.

Another psychic reality depicted in this myth is how hard it is for girls to deal directly and openly with their sexual feelings and actions. Psychoanalysts and psychotherapists are aware of the guilt and anxieties that many women experience about sex and of the common defensive tactic of unconsciously disowning agency and responsibility for their own actions. Like Persephone, many women disavow their own desire, convincing themselves that they have been forced or tricked into sexuality.[7]

The third psychic reality that this story makes plain is the catastrophic consequences of severing too completely the bonds between mother and daughter. The triangular situation raises the dangers of direct competition with mother. In the myth, the competition between females is hidden, but it is discernable both in Persephone's disobedience and in Demeter's rage. Persephone comes into her own, seemingly without such overt competition; again she is forced into becoming a powerful queen of her own world. Even as she wishes competitively to take mother's place with father, a little girl certainly does not want to lose her mother. The Persephone tale finds a solution to such a dilemma: It allows her to keep her mother and have her father (uncle) too—to be taken as a *metaphoric* but not an ideal resolution of such conflicts.

We see the triangular situation for the girl—the ultimate psychological reality depicted in this tale—as a balancing of loyalties and relationships (Holtzman and Kulish, 2000; Kulish and Holtzman, 1998). The myth of Persephone is above all a female's story. Life, death, and rebirth are in the power of the female, and these are themes throughout the narrative, which dramatizes the cyclical nature of female experience.

The term "female Oedipal complex" is an oxymoron. We propose that the myth of Persephone and Demeter is a better fit for the female triangular situation, and better suited to name it. It tells the story of development as we have found it to be true for girls, which is that typically they do not wish to leave their mothers behind as they progress through their adult development and that they need that relationship to fulfill their most bounteous potential. Life demands separation, but it also permits reunion. In the next chapter we will argue that this name change is not superficial but crucial—as the story shows us, a change of name is a vital act of re-identification. It allows us to shed old and erroneous ways of thinking about girls and women and take on a new capacity to think about their development and lives in terms truer to their experience, to find stories of their own.

Notes

1. The narcissus that proliferates so easily is a symbol of fertility. Foley suggests that Persephone's attraction to the seductive flower demonstrates her readiness for a

new phase of life. Girls in myth are traditionally carried off while gathering flowers in a meadow (p. 127).

2. The ambiguity and variability in the telling and retelling of the story of the seeds in the different versions of the myth first suggested to us the idea of conflict and defensiveness around the question of the volition of woman's sexual impulses. Freud (1900) wrote that modifications, repetition, vagaries, and circumlocutions in dreams are evidence of censorship and conflict. Acknowledging the cultural, historical, and other reasons for variability in myth, however, we know that there is a danger in leaping to interpretation of myth as dream.

3. In psychoanalytic practice, the idea of eating seeds is a common children's fantasy of oral impregnation.

4. The poetess Sappho (Barnard 1958) gives us another rich glimpse into the female experience of the ancient world of women.

5. This is similar to an ancient Nordic tale of the daughter disappearing and reappearing from a divine corn mother.

6. Like the Oedipus myth, the tale of Persephone and Demeter has a central theme of incest. Demeter and Zeus are brother and sister who have a child, Persephone; Hades is the brother of Zeus and Demeter and hence is Persephone's uncle.

7. We have observed another common defensive tactic in contemporary young women who deny their sexual anxiety with a counterphobic promiscuity.

~

CHAPTER FIVE

The Changing Language
of Female Development

> But the truth of the truth about female sexuality is restated even more
> rigorously when psychoanalysis takes discourse itself as the object of its
> investigations.
>
> (Irigaray, 1985, p. 87)

In this book we have joined the scores of psychoanalytic thinkers of the last several decades who have tried to reformulate early psychoanalytic theories about female psychology and find ways of thinking about women that accord better with their experience. Specifically, we are attempting to reexamine and reformulate our theories about the female triangular situation. In addition, we are proposing a name change for this experience: from the "female Oedipal complex" to the "Persephone complex." This change of name is not simply cosmetic or superficial. There is a built-in relationship between language and thinking, or language and theory. It is our belief that if we are ever to revolutionize the way we think about women, we will also have to change the language we use to talk about them. The language we psychoanalysts use in our discourse about women has not kept pace with our reexaminations, even as these new ideas are more and more generally accepted. Indeed, many of us have argued that the further elaboration of newer theories has been impeded by our psychoanalytic lexicon, which continues to encourage psychoanalytic students to think in terms of ideas whose time is long past.

Over twenty-five years ago, Henri Parens and others (1976) proposed that the term "first genital phase" was more in keeping with his observations of a little girl's "dominantly feminine disposition" (p. 83) and should therefore re-place the term "phallic or phallic-Oedipal phase." Yet every new student of psychoanalytic development still comes automatically and unquestionably to speak of a normative "phallic phase" in girls' development. Similarly, while many psychoanalysts (for instance, Goldberger, 1999) have repeatedly argued that the term "castration anxiety" does not and should not apply to women, the phrase remains common in our clinical thinking about women. Its automatic usage skews our clinical thinking about female patients, blinding us to the manifold meanings of their anxiety-laden fantasies that do not involve a penis. The pleas of analysts (Bernstein, 1990; Kulish, 2000; Shaw, 1995, among many others) who have advocated a more general concept of "genital anxieties" for girls and women seem to have fallen on deaf ears.

More recently (Long, 2005), Parens called yet again for dropping the terminology of "female Oedipal" phase. We agree, on the grounds that this constant reinforcement of the idea of a "female Oedipus" has impeded our efforts to delineate what really happens in girls' development and obscures the ways that girls' triangular conflicts differ from boys' (Holtzman and Kulish, 2000). "Oedipal phase" should be replaced with the more generic term, "triangular phase" or "Persephonal phase," codifying in our language our recognition that "Oedipal" fantasies are a special case of a more general developmental crisis.

The psychoanalytic language of the female body needs attention as well. In general, it depicts female bodies and self-representations as a series of negatives, absences, and have-nots (Elise, 1997). For example, Rosemary Balsam (1996) has pointed out how the concept of the pregnant female body has been virtually erased from our developmental trajectory, annihilated by our devotion to phallic terminology and concepts. We need new categories to describe female experience. The French feminist Luce Irigaray (1985) poetically expresses her feeling that women's desire most likely does not speak the same language as men's desire: "Feminine pleasure has to remain inarticulate in language, in its own language, if it is not to threaten the underpinnings of logical operations" (p. 77). Although attempts have been made to introduce such new terms as "primary femininity" into our clinical theories, psychoanalysts still hold tenaciously to Freud's original descriptors—*penis* envy, *phallic* phase, *castration* anxiety, *Oedipus* complex—and have yet to adopt more appropriate ones. As always, resistance is revealing, and this stalemate affords us an excellent opportunity to explore the relationship between psychoanalytic theory and language.

Relationship of Language and Thinking

In this discussion we make two assumptions: the first and more self-evident is that language reflects our thinking. As the linguist Noam Chomsky has said, "language is a system for expressing thought" (2002, p. 76). Language can be seen as a means of communication, but this, he argues, is not its main function, which is to be a "mirror of the mind." A second and more controversial assumption is that language *restricts* and *shapes* our thinking and perception as well as reflecting it.

Contemporary gender research engages questions and controversies about the relationship between language and thought on many levels. Feminists argue that language perpetuates institutionalized gender biases. The science historian Evelyn Fox Keller (1985), for example, suggests that our most basic concepts of mind and science are constructed socially and imparted in language. Objectivity, reason, and mind are commonly associated with maleness; subjectivity, feeling, and nature, with femaleness (as in "mother nature"). For Bacon, nature was a bride to be tamed, shaped, and subdued by the virile scientific mind. Such socially shared metaphors perpetuate and privilege objectivity in science and dismiss as "unscientific" those methods, such as psychoanalysis, that make use of subjectivity.

In the literary field, women poets feel imprisoned in a tradition that denies them access to authoritative expression (Ostriker, 1986). Ralph Waldo Emerson (1982), for example, equated serious poetry with potent masculinity: "give me initiative, spermatic prophesying, man making words." Searching for her own language, the poet Alice Walker lamented, "Our mothers and grandmothers, some of them: moving to music not yet written. And they waited." Similarly, the poet H. D. in *Trilogy* portrayed a vision of a "Lady":

> she carries a book but it is not the tome of the ancient wisdom,
> the pages, I imagine, are the blank pages of the unwritten volume of the new.

Linguists Penelope Eckert and Sally McConnell-Ginet (2003) argue persuasively that language and its use are inseparable, and that, like gender, language is continually constructed in practice. Linguistic practices support particular gender ideologies and norms. Thus, biases encoded in language become perpetuated in practice. For example, calling a woman a "lady" may come to affect how she is treated and subsequently behaves. Robin Lacoff (1972) argued that women have a different way of speaking that both reflects and reproduces a subordinate position in society. As we are attempting to do here, Eckert and McConnell-Ginet asked how and why people change—or do not change—linguistic and gender-related practices. On the other hand, many have derided feminists' attempts to change attitudes through a change in language—from "chairman" to "chairwoman," for example—as trivial and/or ineffective.

But others take very seriously the idea that language shapes or dictates thought in a fundamental way. Orwell took it to an ultimate and chilling extreme in his great novel, *Nineteen Eighty-Four* (1949), in which the government, headed by Big Brother, develops a new language called "Newspeak" intended to eliminate undesirable ideas from the minds of the populace. New words are invented with very tangible referents or with political purposes while undesirable words are eliminated, and remaining words, such as "free," are stripped of unacceptable meanings. As Orwell described this new order: "A thought diverging from the principles of the new language should be literally unthinkable, at least so far as thought is dependent on words" (p. 310).

Working with notions originated by the anthropologist Claude Levi-Strauss, Jacques Lacan posited that language actually organizes the mind and the unconscious. Levi-Strauss suggested that myth and music are not merely analogous with language, but actually derived from language (MacCormack and Strathern, 1980, p. 3). According to Lacan (1968), the child's earliest attachment to the mother, the mirroring relationship or "imaginary," is necessarily disrupted by the father's presence. In the process of forming ideas about the internal world of object and self, the child submits to the laws of language, of the father, which fix meaning and impose symbolic law. Language inscribes sexual difference in vocabulary and syntax, with the phallus as the signifier of sexual difference. The social order is internalized in terms of difference and language; thus sexual difference, as inscribed in language, constitutes cultural structures and *not the other way around*. That is, language creates culture; culture does not create language. We cannot subscribe to Lacan's ideas about language. It seems to us that this in itself is an example of language subsumed to sexist purpose. He sees language as "the law of the father," but what about the countless people who think in terms of the "mother tongue"?

Language and Reality

Bonnie Litowitz[1] (Litowitz, 2002, 2003; Long, 2005), a linguist and psychoanalyst, argues that the psychoanalytic language is "more than a set of labels that describe phenomena; it is a conceptual framework for interpreting and creating those phenomena." She impresses on us the "power of language to create reality." (Litowitz, 2003)

She notes that "the Argentine poet Jorge Luis Borges (1972) made the same point when he said: 'A language is a tradition, a way of grasping reality, not an arbitrary assemblage of symbols.'" Borges's statement appears to be obvious when comparing distinct languages such as English and Hopi, as the linguists Sapir and Whorf (Whorf, 1940) have argued. (As you may know, they promulgated theories that suggest that the Eskimos' many words for snow facilitate the actual ability to perceive the varieties of snow. Their theories, we are told, have been disputed.) However, it also applies to specialized terminological domains within a language, such as psychoanalysis.

"For the most part, Freud used ordinary, everyday words (mostly German) to which he gave new meanings in an overall theoretical system" (Litowitz 2003). Litowitz cautions that we cannot change one or two (or more) of these words without calling the whole system into question. This is one reason, a powerful one, that we resist change in our psychoanalytic language.

"Every word is a point in a network of other words; a word's meaning is determined by its place and its relations in that network" (Litowitz 2003). For example, "penis envy," functioning as a compound noun in the system of explanation of female development, is different from "envy of someone's possession of a penis" as just one particular form of envy. In the former case the compound holds a certain place in a complex theory: it is the motivating cause for the girl's change in object from mother to father and for her entry into the Oedipus phase. In "Analysis Terminable and Interminable" (Freud, 1937), for example, it stands for a bedrock complex; once named in a woman's mind it becomes the limiting or final piece of the psyche to be understood in the unlayering of the unconscious. In the latter case, the phrase "envy of someone's possession of a penis" can stimulate a psychoanalytic inquiry into its meaning: What would a penis mean to the person who desires it? What problem or internal conflict would obtaining a penis attempt to solve? It is the answers to questions like these, not a static formula such as "penis envy," that delineate the *individual*, usually unconscious, fantasies that we search out in our daily practices. It is this appreciation of individuality that Nancy Chodorow (1994b) now advocates over broad generalizations about gender differences and object choice.

Litowitz suggests that "there is a tension in Freud's writing between his respect for the uniqueness of each individual's psychic organization and his desire for a universal. Although he argued most eloquently against any simplistic definition of sexuality, his theory of development bequeathed to us a network of myths and meanings" and an accompanying vocabulary, which for a long time constituted psychoanalytic reality. The power of theory is that, once instituted, it guides perception such that what we know from the theory feels more "real" than anything we experience ourselves. Even as perceptive and independent a woman as Marie Bonaparte—despite Freud's disapproval—undertook repeated and futile genital surgeries to reconstruct and relocate her clitoris, trying to reach the "mature genital stage of vaginal orgasm" prescribed by his theory (Appignanesi and Forrester, 1992), which we now know from Masters and Johnson is fictitious.

Michael Riordan wrote about the role of language in creating the reality of particle physics during the 1960s and 1970s:[3]

> The reality scientists know is the one that communicates: it is above all a shared reality. . . . Those ideas that capture the allegiance of a scientific community become—at least for a time—the objective reality of that field. This objectivity is not "the way things are," but the way they are understood and discussed by the great majority of its practitioners. . . . A scientific community resembles a vast collective "mind" (1987, p. 368).

"Our collective mind goes back to Freud, our collective father" (Litowitz 2003). His voice lives in the words we use, as do other voices from other discourses (Bakhtin, 1981). "These voices speak through us; they provide a shared understanding that resonates among us and ties us to our tradition. Cutting ourselves loose from past discourses, we risk losing psychoanalysis to biology or social psychology" (Litowitz 2003). What would a new language do to our sense of belonging to a psychoanalytic community?

"Our many dictionaries of psychoanalytic terms are really 'disguised encyclopedias';[4] behind every term lies a whole theoretical worldview. When a theoretical framework projects that a category such as "phallic stage" *should* appear in development, it can be found" (Litowitz 2003). The continued reality of its categories depends upon our continued reinforcement of them when we communicate with each other, and there is a building consensus that much of the way we have been talking about female development no longer captures "the way things are."

The Semantic Network of Psychoanalysis

To change the language of female development, we must appreciate the underlying semantic network that supports it and gives it meaning. Roy Schafer (1974) and others have pointed out that binary oppositions, based on the primary dichotomy of anatomical difference, have organized our semantic network as it applies to sexuality. Characteristics identified by Freud with maleness and femaleness, following age-old traditions, have taken on this binary quality: for example, active-passive, intellect-emotion, assertive-receptive. Once these characteristics are so defined, to identify them is to confirm and validate the categories to which they ostensibly belong. To the extent that maleness and femaleness seem absolute and dichotomous, each polar opposite is assigned an *a priori* set of exclusive (non-shared) features, while the features themselves are defined by the category and not the other way around. Deviations from a defined category require explanation by qualification; for example, the description of an aggressive woman as a "phallic woman."

Yet structural linguists (Jakobson and Halle, 1956; Chomsky and Halle, 1968) tell us that classification by binary features need not result in discrete or absolute categories, as it did so frequently with Freud.[5] In fact, according to linguists like Litowitz (Long, 2005), the virtue of a binary feature analysis is that it avoids discrete categories of absolute inclusion/exclusion based on a set of properties or features, allowing a greater variety of cross-classifications.

Litowitz elaborated a further problem with the binary oppositional sets posited by traditional psychoanalytic theory: One of the set of terms is "marked" while the other is "unmarked." "'Markedness' is a concept used in the study of language to describe conditions where one of a set of terms is articulated in terms of the other. The underlying, privileged term is said to be 'unmarked,' while the 'marked' term is measured against it" (Litowitz, 3003). The psychoanalytic view of sexuality has made 'feminine' the marked term, measured and defined in terms of the unmarked 'masculine'" (Long, 2005).

In marking systems, the unmarked category (in this case maleness) tends to go unnoticed; it is "unre*marked* on," as if it were "unre*mark*able." There are two problems with this kind of thinking. The first is the characteristics of the marked category (in this case "wo-men") are seen as a deviation from the unmarked template. The difficulties of explaining these differences and bringing them back into congruence with the unmarked "norm" leads to an understanding of women as problematic, and also to the "very circuitous path" Freud (1931) laid out, which further "marks" women as deviant in contrast with the straightforward development of men.[6] Girls need *three* shifts for successful development: from the inborn masculine to the "achievement" of a feminine "Oedipal" phase; in "leading sexual organ" from clitoris to vagina; in instinctual aim from active masculine to receptive feminine; in object choice from mother to father. The second consequence of this thinking is that a thorough psychoanalytic examination of masculinity—the unmarked concept—has suffered too.

If we were to try to construct a new language of female development, how can we avoid the pitfalls of binary and polar oppositions and markedness? According to current thinking and evidence, there is an early sense of femaleness in girls, a "primary femininity," from which feminine identity develops, which grows out of bodily sensations and from identifications with the mother (Elise, 1997; Tyson and Tyson, 1990). In proposing "primary femininity" to replace the older phallocentric view of a "primary masculinity" from which both males and females developed (and which a mature female must overcome), are we perpetuating dichotomous ways of thinking? And the concept of "primary femininity" poses problems in itself (Kulish, 2000). While it does "un-mark" femaleness, the idea of "primary" intimates an inborn biologically based femininity, rather than a complex psycho-social-biological developmental framework. Such an alternate conceptualization as "primary bisexuality," or two separate lines of development—a masculine and a feminine line (Mayer, 1995)—may not really free us from dichotomous categories, either.[4] As we propose a new language about the triadic situation, we are well aware that we may be creating new linguistic traps.

Litowitz (Long, 2005) and others (Chodorow, 1994b) propose that we can stay within our tradition and avoid binary systems by returning to the concept of a "polymorphous sexuality," that is, a sexuality that can take many forms as each individual compiles a unique composite of points along several continuous dimensions. This view, Litowitz suggests, would demand (1) that we determine what those dimensions are, taking into account how specific cultures determine values along them; and (2) that we articulate how individuals find their way along these dimensions. Her suggestions of non-binary, continuous dimensions of sexuality include: activity, objectivity, social connectedness, and aggression. Examples of choice points where conflicts or problems may arise include: establishing and maintaining object ties; expressing and regulating affect states; identifications and self-expressions; modifications in grandiosity and idealizations; separation/individuation; and managing triangular relationships. Thus, our specifically psychoanalytic approach would be to articulate the ways in which sexual solutions or choices express fantasies, defenses, and given meanings for our patients.

Examples of Psychoanalytic Language About Female Sexuality

The psychoanalytic lexicon is missing many terms and concepts when it comes to women and girls. There are very few words in this lexicon reserved for the female experience and image; to the extent that they differ from the "unmarked" norm of the male, they tend to disappear. Freud wrote that libido was masculine (1905), and Leon Hoffman (1999) has pointed out that psychoanalytic discourse still lacks concepts for female passion. Freud mistakenly insisted that children of both sexes do not know of the existence of the vagina, and the psychoanalytic lexicon "does not know" about female genitalia, either. For Freud (1926b), female psychology was a "dark continent" (p. 212). The number of references to the female genitalia as invisible is staggering. The psychoanalytic language of the female body is a language of lack—girls are "castrated," "the little girl is a little man" (Freud, 1933, p. 118), females are "lacking" motivation for development of the superego or sublimation, etc.

Kalinich (1993), in a critique of psychoanalytic theories about female sexuality, wrote of "the something that is not nothing" and how the notion of "nothing" stops our appreciating the complications of the "something." The naming of an organ, and the how and by whom and why it is named (or not named), and the nature of the name itself (or no name) will surely direct the fate of that organ as it is embodied within the imagination. Naming creates the possibility for the development of a mental image of the thing named. Silence compounds mystery and probably augments anxiety about organ functions. It probably also enhances guilt and taboos around touching the body and sexual sensation. Harriet Lerner (1976) described some implications of parental "mislabeling" of the female genitals. In many cultures, little girls are not routinely given a name for their genitals. In psychoanalysis, even when the clitoris is named, it is imagined as a stunted male organ, rather than a complete female one (Kulish, 1991). In Freud's works there are 48 instances of "clitoris" and 368 of "penis." The near excision of the clitoris from our lexicon mirrors the concrete and literal excision of the clitoris in female circumcisions across the world. It is a fact that the clitoris is the only organ in the human body that seems to have only the function of producing pleasure, and we can speculate that the motivations for clitoridectomy have to do with this. Non-naming reflects primitive and formidable fears of the female and female sexuality (H. E. Lerner, 1976; Kulish, 1991). How can we hope to help our patients with their fears and anxieties about their bodies if we have no language with which to speak and think about them?

Another noticeable silence surrounds pregnancy. In psychoanalytic theory, even the capacity for carrying babies was first conceptualized in terms of the male body: The girl's wish for a baby was traced to her perceived genital lacks—baby equals penis. Karen Horney (1924) asserted early on that a girl's love of her father and desire to have babies was an aspect of her primary femaleness and not a direct result of phallic jealousy, but psychoanalytic theory has not readily incorporated ideas like these. Our formulations rarely include descriptions that recognize and name the pregnant body and its imagery in the clinical situation. Even child analysts have not paid much attention in their writings to the details of children's reactions to their mothers' pregnancies.

Balsam (2003) presented the following vignette to illustrate this silence. She describes sitting in on a case conference in which a child analyst was recounting the insistent penis envy of a four-year-old patient. The girl was rageful about the birth of a little brother who was being highly celebrated by the mother—a common enough scenario—and was also communicating a recurrent feeling of helplessness about ever being "big enough." Curious, Balsam asked more about this theme and its possible relationship to reactions to the mother's pregnancy. The therapist answered, "Well, she didn't say anything much about her mother's pregnancy, but actually I was pregnant all during the time I saw her. Every week she used to take me to a bathroom and weigh me . . . she didn't comment on my body, but at the end of the therapy she said, 'When I grow up I'm going to be SOOO much bigger than you!'"

It is certainly plausible to wonder if hidden reactions to the therapist's pregnancy might be playing a role in this little girl's wishes to get bigger and to add something to herself—at least as much as her despair about not having a penis. How can a girl compete and have an image of growing up without including in her sensorium *some* body reference to the possibility of getting pregnant and out-sizing her mother? In work with adults, we find that memories about our patients' mothers' pregnant bodies emerge if we listen for the material and think about how they relate to their own body image problems. We see young women who go to extraordinary lengths to become much smaller than their mothers, and while not many young women *consciously* long to be bigger, fatter, and heavier in the belly than their mothers, isn't this a plausible wish? The longing for big breasts may be a point where such unconscious constellations emerge. Our phallocentric theoretical language trains us to think easily of the penis as something a girl can envy in her imagination, as an organ that is not hers. A pregnancy is something that she does not have either, but it is within her body trajectory, and it represents power at least as much as the phallus does. Why does psychoanalysis not give this metaphor equal time?

Traditionally, female interests in procreation have been explained away or formulated in phallic terms, as in this example from Anna Freud (1936). She described an incident of a little girl who compulsively lifted up her skirts to exhibit herself. Anna Freud interpreted this behavior as a defensive need to display the nonexistent organ, the penis: "Her envy and her wish for a penis took the form of a desire to have, like her brothers, something to display (p. 86). The girl then induced her family to come to admire something that was not there at all. 'Come and see what a lot of eggs the hens have laid!'" (p. 87). This is the familiar language of ego psychology and conflict theory, and many clinicians would quickly interpret such an incident in terms of "penis envy," or Brenner's "defense against castration and loss" (Brenner, 1982). But other interpretations for this behavior, influenced by contemporary theories about "primary femininity," might equally well come to mind. This child's display of "eggs" may have been referring to *feminine* attributes at least as much as to missing male attributes—that is, the future fecundity that her brothers would never have. Yet Anna Freud made no comment about babies or fertility. Early psychoanalytic theory referred to women's reproductive powers in purely compensatory terms: The baby is compensation for the absent penis. Other explanations for the wish for a baby might include positive identifications with the mother, pride in being able to bear children, and a non-phallic competition with males, who have no such capacity.

Donna Bassin (1982) calls for new language categories to describe female experiences beyond traditional roles and reproductive functioning—a bodily schema of a productive inner space that allows for "representations of woman's interiority and not her inferiority" (p. 200). She elaborates this concept of female inner genital space in an action-based schema of assimilation, parallel to the familiar developmental period in which the baby "mouths" its way through its environment. Based on the model of the mouth, the vagina can thus be represented as actively incorporative. Such a model might lead to other descriptions of female sexual experience and anatomy than just those of a passive receptacle.

Diane Elise (Long, 2005) explicates another area is which language skews our thinking about female development—the concept of the ego ideal. She argues that gendered ego ideals in male dominant societies such as ours are heavily influenced by phallocentric, value-laden cultural requirements that permeate language. Distorted and polarized images of "masculinity" and "femininity" tend toward caricatures such that these terms should usually be put in quotation marks. The sexes are divided into males, the "haves," and females, the "have-nots," promoting a problematic relationship to one's own gender for each sex and fear and animosity, envy and competitiveness, between the sexes.

The fact that feminine characteristics have been negatively correlated with psychological health is often overlooked. "Femininity" often refers to a set of traits held in conflicted estimation—traits, like passivity, for example, that are deemed socially desirable for females to convey, yet are not necessarily valued intrinsically. Elise challenges us to try to think of female sexual experience in terms different from those to which we are accustomed. What different quality would be conveyed if female sexual sensation were described not as diffuse or unfocused, as contemporary literature tends to put it (Bernstein, 1990), but as *extensive*?

Elise offers another example of how a newer, less value-laden language might help us to think differently about such experiences as "frigidity." Freud was the first to attribute frigidity to an overemphasis on the clitoris and to the masculinity complex—*too much* activity. Yet, clinical experience suggests that it often results from a need to avoid the self-perception that the vagina and the rest of the female genitalia are *actively* involved in the seeking of sexual stimulation and satisfaction. Such activity is positively recognized in men as potent and virile, but when applied to women's sexuality, it carries pejorative connotations, as in the idea of "voracious" female sexuality with its implication of regressive orality.

It is not only females who suffer from thoughtless phallocentrism; men may be straightjacketed by it as well. Phallocentric language sets up a sense of inadequacy and lack not only in females but also in males—even more insidiously, if less obviously. Michael Diamond (1997, 2006) refers to the "universal gender stereotype of men as active and potent—a phallic ego ideal in which impulses to penetrate and conquer illustrate the dominance in the male psyche of defensive phallicism." The acquisition of masculine identity has often been described not so much as an acquisition but as a disavowal of early maternal identifications perceived as weak—"a negative achievement" (Stoller, 1976). Many contemporary psychoanalysts and sociologists (for example, Chodorow, 1994a) have argued that males are generally forced out of an expressive-affiliative mode in our culture, which works hard to dislocate men from these crucial aspects of themselves.

Finally, our jargon impedes, limits, and directs our understanding in the theory of psychosexual stages and their unfolding. Adventitious findings from his child observational research led Parens to challenge Freud's (1925) assumptions that the castration complex thrusts the little girl into her Oedipus complex. The boy's castration complex brings his to a close. Parens and his colleagues (1976) did not see things developing this way in the girls they had been observing from birth and concluded that Freud's 1925 hypothesis could not be supported. Their findings also strongly discredited the belief that the wish to have a baby is a reactive compensatory phenomenon; this assumption was convincingly challenged by the remarkably powerful, what they felt to be "biologically driven," attitude toward babies that the researchers saw manifested in these and other girls.

Parens and his colleagues' ongoing study of aggression revealed a further finding that has a bearing on these issues. They found ample evidence of phallic aggression in three- and four-year-old boys. But, they saw sparse evidence of such "phallic aggression" in girls; on the contrary, they observed what they saw as a "femininization" of their aggression, which is especially evident in how they expressed their hostile impulses in indirect ways. Their findings are consistent with our work (Holtzman and Kulish, 2003), which suggests that for a variety of psychological and cultural reasons women and girls typically handle aggression in ways characteristically different from the way men and boys do.

Parens et al. came to the following conclusions: First, that having or not having a phallus does not determine the sexual nature, in both sexes, of this period of development; rather, it is the emergence of *genitality* that does. In addition, they did not find psyche organizing phallic aggression in girls. Second, the girl is carried into her first genital sexual differentiation, not as a re-action to penis envy as Freud's 1925 hypothesis suggests, but due to a biolog-ically programmed differentiation in her sexual drive, just as is the case for boys. As a result, they feel that the concept of the "phallic-Oedipal phase" is not applicable to girls and should be replaced by the more psycho-biologi-cally sound and generalizable term "the first genital phase." Parens and many others feel that this term can be applied with full justice to boys and to girls and recommend its use when speaking of children in general, and of girls in particular (Parens et al., 1976; Parens, 1990).

Narratives for Women

Let us now turn to the use of narratives in psychoanalytic thinking. There need to be narratives for female lives, as female eyes perceive them. The fem-inist psychologist Ellyn Kaschak (1992) pleads that women "must be able to tell and to continue to tell one another about their lives" (p. 88). It is clear that the story of Oedipus refers to a male model, that the term "female Oedi-pus" is an oxymoron, and that the very idea of it is based upon early and in-complete psychoanalytic concepts of female psychosexual development. We have proposed that the triangular period of developmental crisis and conflict for females be called the "Persephone complex," from the Greek myth of Persephone. We have found that psychoanalytic audiences are ready to think about our ideas of how the female triangular situation may be different from that of the male and need to be reformulated, but our suggestion that it be renamed has drawn intense opposition and resistance.

Litowitz (2003; Long, 2005) has argued that this positing of "a myth of her own" may be yet another manifestation of holding on to persistent opposi-tions: female versus male; earth/nature versus heavenly/supernatural; mortal-ity (that is, birth and death) versus immortality; below versus above; interior versus exterior; home and hearth versus war and politics. She, along with many feminists, insists that any discussion of myths/stories/narratives must address issues of discourse and power—who creates the myths and stories, and thus is speaking through them? They question whether any classical myth or tale arising from a patriarchal or particular cultural tradition can serve as a model for all women. What are the values myths are meant to reveal as "natural" or universal? For example, they argue that Freud's use of Oedipus made heterosexuality a "natural" outcome of development.

Pursuit of questions like these ultimately leads us to authors who call into question not just theory's relation to language but a woman's relation to language—and indeed, whether or not a language of female sexuality is even possible. These writers, mostly French women intellectuals and psychoanalysts (for example, Luce Irigaray and Julia Kristeva), have incorporated both the logocentrism of Lacan (who reads Freud through the prism of linguistics) and his phallocentrism. They accept his equation of the masculine and the symbolic, which leads them to seek femaleness outside of language: in the "beyond" of the maternal body, for example, and the excess or overflow inherent in "feminine *jouissance*." Among the solutions that these writers offer are a femaleness articulable only in the hyper-saturated meaning of *poetry* (Hélène Cixous, 1998); the willful *mutism* of the heroine in Jane Campion's *The Piano*, (who turns "you may not speak" into "I will not speak"); or such subversions of language as Anne Sexton's "Transformations" (1971), a reworking of the Grimms' fairy tales into a wisecracking Americanese that simultaneously modernizes and desentimentalizes them and turns the gender conventions inside out.

Conclusion

Obviously, we do not agree either with Lacan, that women are locked into a foreordained phallic linguistic, or with those of his feminist disciples who believe that women are locked out of language altogether. Clinical practitioners and theorists cannot rely on poetry or silence; thus we are seeking a new language of female development. That quest will require awareness of language and of its entrapments—of illusionary realities, binary absolutes, unmarked assumptions, and rigidifying biases.

Certainly, as psychoanalysts, we acknowledge the power of language both theoretically and clinically. A basic foundation of our work is the belief that giving our patients *words* helps them to control and contain affects, to manage the effects of trauma, to make the unconscious available. As analysts we have strong allegiances to our language. As we seek a new vocabulary we must be mindful that we need both terms that we can all accept as a way of understanding and communicating with each other and a theoretical framework in which those terms gain meaning.

As we have outlined above, many writers have suggested that we exchange terms like "castration anxiety," "phallic phase," and "phallic narcissism" for replacements with a neutral or female meaning: Instead of "castration anxiety," for instance, we might use "genital anxiety." We might drop "phallic phase" altogether and use "early genital phase" instead. We propose that "Persephone phase" or "triangular phase" should replace the use of "Oedipal phase" for females.

Lerner (1986), in her treatise on the creation of patriarchy, discusses the power of naming. In Genesis, for example, God gives Adam the power to name the animals and sovereignty over them. When God creates woman from Adam's rib, he gives Adam the power to name her. That is, a male gives birth to a female, and his authority to name her establishes his sovereignty over her. After the fall, Adam renames the woman Eve. The change in name indicates a change in status.

Similarly, the feminist scholar Agha-Jaffar (1952) points to the important issue of naming and renaming raised by the myth of Persephone. After her abduction and rape, Kore can no longer be referred to as "Kore," which meant "virgin" in ancient Greek, since she has lost her maiden status. Instead, she is called Persephone, a word signifying spring and reflecting the cyclical rebirth of nature, as depicted by Demeter's releasing the earth from its stagnation. The name change connoted this change in the girl's identity and status. It indicates her new and powerful role as queen of the underworld, a position that affords her the authority and respect that was denied her when she was merely Kore, Demeter's "slim ankled" daughter. At the beginning of the poem she lacks both voice and agency. When she emerges from the underworld, she is articulate and fluent, clear and confident in her speech—she has found her voice.

Thus, we propose renaming the female Oedipal complex and finally giving the female a story of her own.

Notes

1. We are grateful to our distinguished colleague, Bonnie Litowitz, Ph.d, a psychoanalyst and linguist, for providing us with the basis of this section on language and reality, and of the next section on the semantic network of psychoanalysis. We have paraphrased and, in some cases, quoted verbatim her unpublished presentation, "A case study in the relationship to the theory to language" as part of a panel on the changing language of female development at the meetings of the American Psychoanalytic Association in Boston, June 21, 2003. Long (2005) reported the summary of this panel.

2. Borges, p. 8, as quoted in Litowitz (2003).

3. Eco (1984) p. 68, as quoted in Litowitz (2003).

4. "We have to fall back on the everyday language of the larger culture. We have little choice. So we borrow words like 'quarks' or 'flavor' or 'charm' or 'color' and apply them in completely new ways . . . these are words plucked from the thin air of

everyday discourse and redeployed in this subatomic realm. Any 'meaning' these words carry comes mainly from their repeated use and elaboration by the whole community of practicing physicists. . . . But by the end of the 1970s, quarks were hard physical entities as 'real' as the electrons used to ferret them out. Form had become substance" (1987, p. 368).

5. To take an example from phonology, sounds are determined by a distribution of features, some shared and some not shared, which determine all sounds in the system. This allows many more classifications than just the binary categories of "vowel" or "consonant."

6. Other examples where marked-unmarked distinctions apply include heterosexuality, race, and culture.

7. Two separate lines would replace Freud's two sequential phases (1931): the first of a "masculine character"; the second, "specifically feminine" (cf. narcissistic lines of development in Kohut, 1971).

CHAPTER SIX

~

The Girl's Entry into
the Triangular Phase

> The little girl needs a psychic place of her own to get used to the turbu-
> lent desires, fantasies, fears and unaccustomed body signals welling up
> from within. But while she wants to feel she can shut the door on
> mother, she also has the seemingly contradictory wish that from the
> other side of that closed door mother approves.
>
> (Nancy Friday, 1978)

The girl's entry into the triangular phase of development represents a major
developmental milestone. In this chapter we will outline some of the important factors that contribute to this maturational event. We will focus on the
distinctive role of separation anxieties that emerge during this transition into
the triadic phase and will present two cases that illustrate our ideas clinically.

In Freud's early formulations of female development (1925), which we described in chapter 2, the girl's path into the triangular "Oedipal" phase is a
tortured one, from inborn masculinity to a hard-won femininity. Freud believed that in order to find her way into the "normal" Oedipal complex and
heterosexuality, the girl must relinquish and then refocus her original sexuality in three ways: in sexual organ, aim, and object.

We disagree with Freud's assumption that girls must make such radical
changes in their sexual feelings, aims, and objects. First, the original "sexual
organ," by which Freud meant the clitoris, is never renounced in favor of the
vagina later in development. Research has clearly shown that little girls
know of the existence of their vaginas and experience pleasurable sensations

in their vagina and clitoris and that sexual sensations in the vagina and the clitoris are indistinguishable in adult women (Sherfey, 1966; Masters and Johnson, 1966). Second, the aim of the sexual drive (by which Freud meant active or passive) for women is neither "masculine" nor "feminine" and is expressed both actively and passively.

In this chapter we will focus on the third of these supposed changes and argue that the entry into the triangular situation for girls does not necessitate a *change* in object from mother to father, as Freud proposed, but an *addition* of object. That is, girls retain their desires toward their mothers, while they add other objects—male or female. This point is often missed, because girls' sexual attachments to their mothers are very often camouflaged by their attention to male objects.

Review of the Literature

In reviewing the literature on the entry into the triadic phase, we will focus on those arguments that we believe have relevance for the issue of change of object. Over the years, many psychoanalytic writers have questioned the sequence of female psychosexual development as originally laid down by Freud, which we have summarized in chapter 2. A long series of psychoanalytic work, based on clinical and observational research, has challenged this sequence as erroneous and skewed (Chehrazi, 1986). To begin with, the timing of children's discovery of sexual difference is much earlier than Freud thought—at around eighteen months, not three or four years of age (Kleeman, 1975). The discovery that was thought to trigger the chain of events that leads to triangulation would occur several years before the Oedipal phase commences. Secondly, the role of penis envy in girls' development has been extensively rethought and reformulated. While many analysts since Freud have observed penis envy in their clinical practices, from the beginning they have disagreed about its *primacy* and its *role* in the girl's change of object and the initiation of the Oedipus complex. Early on, Karen Horney (1924) asserted that the girl's inferiority complex and penis envy were secondary and culturally based. Jones (1933), too, argued that the girl's "phallic phase" was essentially defensive. Many others through the years have offered rich clinical understandings of the role of penis envy, but from very different developmental perspectives than Freud's (Lerner, 1976). Most clinicians (Moulton, 1970) have linked penis envy to problems between the girl and her mother and conceptualize it not as an inevitable or necessary cog in a stepwise schema but as a passing experience of childhood.

We agree that penis envy may become prominent or fixed if particular forces within the family constellation, such as favoritism toward males or problems in the mother-daughter relationship, reinforce it. Janine Chasseguet-Smirgel (1970), for instance, focused on the anal-sadistic struggles between mother and daughter that nourish the girl's fantasy of mother's controlling and castrating powers and her defensive idealization and envy of the paternal phallus. Rhoda Frenkel (1996), in an article expressly dealing with object choice in women, presented clinical material from women and girls that persuaded her that penis envy is pathological and does not contribute to a shift in object choice to father. In one influential paper, William Grossman and Walter Stewart (1976) examine the concept of penis envy, emphasizing the need to analyze the meanings and functions of penis envy, when it appears, rather than reflexively taking it as "bedrock." We agree and argue that *in "normal" development, the psychological consequences of penis envy that Freud originally described would more likely impede triangular development than advance it.*

On the other hand, many analytic traditions still cling closely to essential aspects of Freud's ideas about the course of female development into the triangular period. Like Freud, Lacanians place importance on the concept of a change in object. The French analyst, Marie-Christine Hamon (2000), posed the question "Why do women love men and not their mothers?" as the title of her book. The question itself reveals a theoretical assumption: that girls start out with their mothers as primary objects so that there is a need to explain how they end up desiring their fathers. Hamon traced all the early psychoanalytic contributions to the change-in-object question and evaluated them through a Lacanian lens. A defining issue for Hamon is how different theorists deal with the girl's "castration." For Hamon, the necessary change of object that she takes as a given occurs when the girl recognizes her mother's and her own castration, acknowledges her father as the bearer of the phallus, and so submits to his law. "The primacy of the phallus, for the girl as well as for the boy, is what determines the separation from the mother and the turn to the father" (p. 39).

Others have questioned the inevitability of the sequence described by Freud and further elaborated by Humberto Nagera (1975), in which the girl is supposed to go through a so-called "negative Oedipal" phase, that is, a period of first loving her mother as a phallic boy might before she turns to her father in the "positive Oedipal" phase. According to Anna Freud, the "negative Oedipus" complex represents a normal homosexual phase in the life of both boys and girls (1965, p. 196), but Rose Edgecumbe and her collaborators (1976) doubted whether a negative Oedipal phase is a necessary step in normal female development. They found that a "negative Oedipal constellation" may actually be considered an arrest at, or a regression to, the pre-Oedipal phallic narcissistic level, which is characterized by dyadic object relationships.

Homoerotic Issues: The Homoerotic Triangular Situation ("Negative Oedipal" Phase)

We do not endorse the traditional psychoanalytic theory that female triangular development follows a linear progression from first a "negative" to a "positive" phase. (We also think the term *negative Oedipal* is doubly unfortunate when applied to women. It reinforces the projection of female development onto a background of primary masculinity, and, although the term "negative" was originally chosen to evoke the idea of a photographic negative, it forges an undesirable link between homosexuality and badness.) As children enter the triadic phase, emerging sexual feelings are directed toward both parents; homoerotic and heteroerotic desires emerge simultaneously. A child may have possessive or sexual fantasies about one parent and be jealous of the other at one moment and vice versa the next (and these fantasies may be expressions both of a wish and of a defense against it). Ruth Fischer (2002) put it this way: "Ties to each parent develop in tandem, not sequentially" (p. 278).

These ideas were voiced many years ago by Helene Deutsch (1944) in an important but little-noted passage about the bisexuality in the girl's triangular situation: "It is erroneous to say that the little girl gives up her first mother relation in favor of the father. She only gradually draws him into the alliance, develops from the mother-child exclusiveness toward the triangular parent-child relationship and continues the latter just as she does the former, although in a weaker and less elemental form, all her life. Only the principal part changes; now the mother, now the father plays it" (p. 205).

The themes of oscillation in the Persephone-Demeter myth—the cycle of seasons that reflects the shifts in Persephone's alliances with her lover and her mother—can be seen in the alternating attentions bestowed upon loved parental figures in the triangular situation. But while the girl's shifting identifications are clear in the myth, it is also clear that this is a cycle, not a progression. Hirsch (1989) argues that by the conclusion of the hymn Persephone has moved through the girl's typical oscillation between mother and father into a firm commitment to heterosexuality and a deep-rooted identification with her mother (pp. 101–102). But Foley (1994) suggests that "the Hymn commits Persephone more to accepting than to embracing heterosexuality" (p. 131).

Contemporary Psychoanalytic
Understandings of Object Choice

Contemporary psychoanalytic thinking adds further substance to the argument that sexual object choice in females cannot be understood as simply a matter of a change from mother to father. Many writers (Arlow, 1980; Young-Bruehl, 2003; Harris, 2005) stress such complicating factors as the multilayered nature of internal objects, the concept of bisexuality, and the role of multiple identifications in gender identity and object choice. Jacob Arlow showed that internal object representations are conglomerates of many earlier object representations and that the final point in any individual's choice of love object—male or female—is not the entire story. Pertinent to the subject of change of object, according to this line of thought, the girl's sexual object choice of father may be built up of many earlier object representations and identifications, including maternal ones. Similarly, Elisabeth Young-Bruehl described the many and varied permutations in which internal objects are layered or blended from disparate identifications—with siblings or with parents, which can become manifest as male or female but are inevitably bisexual (pp. 204–205).

What we have been saying is that an individual's object choice represents a composite, or compromise, whether or not it results from a heterosexual, homosexual, or bisexual orientation. The little girl, in loving her Daddy, does not give up her Mommy. She tries to retain both in some fashion. In the case of a woman's heterosexual object choice, she typically remains close to her mother and identifies with her. Her choice of husband may very well be a compromise— the manifest picture being father/male, but an impression of the mother lies underneath. Cases of a paternal object choice that masks or contains the maternal object are very familiar and frequent to most analysts. Similarly, the man's choice of an Oedipal object, mother, may contain or mask the pre-Oedipal facets. In individuals who are consciously and overtly bisexual in their object choices, switching from male to female loves, this amalgam is deconstructed.

The Girl's Transition into Triadic Object
Relationships from the Earlier Maternal Dyad

As we have indicated, penis envy as the prime motivation for the girls' entry into the dynamics and relationships of the triadic phase has been questioned by many psychoanalysts. Other motivations have been postulated:

1) An innate propensity to experience the primal scene. The Kleinians, and those closely influenced by them, have offered different theories about what

impels male and female children into the Oedipal drama (Britton et. al., 1989). For them, the Oedipal situation rests on a primitive unconscious awareness of the primal scene, which they consider to be known to the child much earlier than Freud posited. Thus they have no need to put forward a complicated explanation of how the girl finds her way into the Oedipal situation; it is in her mind from very early in her life. For Melanie Klein (1928), primitive Oedipal fantasies colored by oral sadism make their appearance in the first two years of life and are intensified and fueled by inevitable frustrations with the mother. This very early stage of the Oedipal complex is characterized by acute ambivalence, uncertainty, and oral trends. Hanna Segal (1974) noted the rudimentary dawning of Oedipal dynamics as the infant becomes aware of the important link that exists between the father and mother. Such primitive fantasies in themselves give the dynamic force to triangular conflicts. The power of such primitive fantasies about the primal scene is undeniable, but we question whether they are inborn. Rather, we think that the *capacity* for fantasy is innate. Moreover, the presence of such fantasies, innate or not, does not strike us as a sufficient explanation of the shift into the triangular "Oedipal" period. We do think that the primal scene acquires new affects and meanings for the child during the triadic period, who now more fully appreciates the differences between the sexes and generations (Kaplan, 1991).

2) Innate biological pressures. There may be hormonal or other inborn drives or gendered differences in the brain that might turn an individual to seek a sexual object of one sex or the other; perhaps some sort of social-evolutional explanation propels a person toward heterosexuality and propagation of the species. As far as we can fathom, in spite of exciting advances in research, solid scientific evidence for such biological influences remains elusive (Kirkpatrick, 2003). Elisabeth Young-Bruehl (2003) reviewed the research on the biological domain and concluded that none has yet yielded anything that resembles a causal explanation for homosexuality or heterosexuality, but that biological factors do seem to have an influence upon object choice in as yet non-specified, indirect ways.

According to this thinking, a little girl is propelled into the triangular phase by biologically given and "normal" sexual leanings towards a male. A long-standing psychoanalytic argument—Freud's "anatomy is destiny"— would suggest that a girl's body inclines her toward yearnings to be penetrated, or to have babies, by a male.

3) Cognitive factors. Cognitive development allows for the capacity to represent psychically relationships that can include or exclude the child and that have three dimensions. Contemporary infant research has documented that even from the beginning the infant can differentiate mother from father, and those two from different adults in her world. As cognitive development proceeds, more complicated understandings of the world help to move the child into the triangular situation and allow her to develop from it. Eugene Mahon (1991) argues that the successful navigation of the Oedipal phase relies on cognitive development, from a perceptually bound, preoperational view of the world to a new conceptual operational view, a la Piaget. Mahon uses the acquisition of number concepts as an example. In preoperational thought, six baseball bats are bigger in number than six toothpicks; conceptually, however, the numbers are the same. A six-year-old who sees the world from a conceptually operational view will realize, "All penises regardless of size are members of a conceptual category penis; in a way I am the equal of my father" (p. 630). Presumably, therefore, the six-year-old will be able to use such thinking to deal with the competition of the Oedipal conflict. Harry Brickman (1993), writing about neglected cognitive factors in psychoanalytic theory, concludes that the Oedipus complex is a culminating point cognitively as well as emotionally along a continuum of triadic experience. Marcia Cavell (1998) argues that the acquisition of "propositional thought" (the capacity for symbolization of a third object) is necessary for triangulation, and Robert Tyson (1991) emphasizes that triangularity rests on the child's attainment of differentiated internal objects. Ronald Britton (1989) asserts that the child's acknowledgment of the parents' relation with each other creates a triangular space in which thinking can occur. In this argument, acceptance of the reality of the primal scene promotes cognitive development.

   4) Bisexuality. In this argument, everyone is born with bisexual potentials, but in the course of development homosexuality is typically submerged. Strong societal forces guide children to performance of heterosexuality and suppression/repression of homosexual impulses. Thus, a girl's entry into triadic phase is a marker of a recurrent reinforcement and encouragement by her environment of the idea of her eventual role as mother and heterosexual partner. Along the way, her homoerotic interests are discouraged, negatively reinforced, and repressed. This idea was proposed by the cultural theorist Judith Butler (1995). She based her arguments on her understandings of Freud's 1917 "Mourning and Melancholia" and his early theories of psychosexual development in which heterosexuality, for men and women, is attained only after a complicated and difficult developmental pathway. Butler elaborated the idea that this laborious and uncertain accomplishment of a tenuous state of heterosexuality is constantly warding off a repudiated homosexuality. An eternally unmourned and unmournable state of being results, which is eventually covered by same-sex identifications and a conventional, shaky heterosexuality.

Rosemary Balsam (2007) observed that Butler's formulations do not take into account the significance of aggression toward the lost object in Freud's theories of mourning. Balsam reasoned that attachments to same-sexed objects are not necessarily foreclosed and forever mourned—that girls *add* the father as an additional object to the internalized maternal object. Nancy Chodorow (1994b) in a brilliant set of essays argued that both heterosexuality and homosexuality should be viewed as compromise formations, and that "normal" heterosexuality cannot be taken as a given, that needs not to be unwrapped and understood.

This idea of an original bisexuality can also be seen among a long string of psychoanalysts (Bryan, 1930; Freud, 1937; Stoller, 1972; Parens, 1980; Deutsch, 1982; Elise, 1998). Parens, for example, described a basic inborn bisexuality and neutral genital libido, from which "heterosexual libido deriving from primary masculinity and primary femininity" differentiates (p. 110).

Contemporary psychoanalytic thinking about how objects are internalized is also relevant here. In the psychoanalytic literature there are many examples of girls raised by single mothers who nonetheless develop internal representations of their fathers based—in part—on what has been communicated to them consciously and unconsciously by their mothers or other adults (Gill, 1991).

5) *The role of the father.* Many psychoanalytic writers cite the important role of the father as "the third" who intrudes into the maternal dyad and thus stirs the first experiences of triangularity. Ernst Abelin (1971) and Lawrence Brown (2002) have posited that triangulation has an earlier sequence, when the father first breaks into the original dyad and becomes a "third" for the infant of whichever gender. Brown proposed that there is a separate developmental line for triadic relationships. Following the Kleinian view, he accepted that early awareness and inner representations of the parental couple give rise to an early stage of triangularity and conflicted relations. Thus, even in what has been called the pre-Oedipal period, there exist primitive internal representations of father and mother.

Sallye Wilkinson (1993) spoke of a "dress rehearsal" for the triangular situation, as little girls try out blossoming sexual fantasies via masturbation first during the pre-Oedipal period. Wilkinson followed the work of Thomas Ogden (1987), who emphasized the need for a transitional experience for the daughter to participate in an erotic relationship with another, without giving up the mother as subjective object. The girl can love the father in the mother, which is to say, the father's representation in the mother's mind. The mother, in this way, allows herself to be loved, in playful fantasy, as a transitional object or substitute for father. The little boy in moving into the positive Oedipal stage, in which his mother is the desired object, can participate in a sensual, loving relationship with her all along.

Ruth Lax (2003) added another twist to the explanation of the girl's turn to the father, stressing the father's active role in seducing or drawing the girl to him. This is another motivational pull into heterosexuality in the triangular period for the girl.

Feminists (Irigaray, 1985; Ramas, 1985; Gilligan, 2003) insist that the so-called female "Oedipal" complex is an artifact of the patriarchal order. In this kind of thinking, the father imposes his sexualized power over his daughter, making her his object and preparing her for her role as submissive wife and child-bearer.

6) *The role of the mother*. It has been thought that a mother's sexual attitudes toward men are also communicated unconsciously to her daughter in many complex ways (Ogden, 1987). In an evolving and complex body of work, Jessica Benjamin (1988) has elucidated the problem of the acquisition of feminine desire. Early on, the girl may internalize the mother's object of desire—the father—as her love object. Diane Elise (2007, in press), in articulating "the failure of triangularity," cites the need for the mother to offer her daughter an image of maternal sexuality for identification: "Why is it not the Oedipal mother who furthers the daughter's sexual development, by introducing maternal genital sexuality, her relationship to the father (or female partner), such that an erotic couple is presented to the daughter" (p. 22).

Thus, both parents are thought to play a role in influencing their daughters into the triangular, "Oedipal" phase, communicating their expectations and desires consciously and unconsciously. Adrienne Harris (2005) describes the emergence of aspects of gender and desire as a complex interpersonal process: "Brought into an intense embodied responsiveness and contact with the material world, caught up in the conscious and unconscious reverie of parents, prenatally already an object of intense fantasy, a child finds the experience of self within a relationship in which he or she is already seen and 'recognized,' and in some particular way this construction will draw on some parental ideas and fantasies about gender" (pp. 180–181).

Separation

Our own speculations about girls' entry into the triangular situation derive from the work of other psychoanalytic thinkers, such as Nancy Chodorow (1978, 1994a), Ethel Person (1982), Beverly Burch (1997), and Elina Reenkola (2002). All these writers emphasize the ramifications for triadic development that come from gendered differences in patterns of early object relationships: In the typical family constellation, the primary object for both little girls and little boys is the mother, on whom they are dependent for nurture and care. In the so-called "positive Oedipal" stage, the parent of the same sex becomes the rival. For little girls, that is the mother. Unlike boys, then, their competitive feelings toward the same-sexed parent challenge their security in ways that present a major dilemma. Girls must find a way to balance their sexual interests toward their fathers with their need for security with their mothers.

In separating psychologically from the same-sexed person, in learning how to balance their sexual impulses toward their fathers with their dependency needs toward their mothers, and in finding subtle ways to express rivalrous feelings toward their mothers (see chapter 7 on aggression), girls may become particularly sensitive to issues of intimacy and to interpersonal relationships. Supporting research indicates that girls' interests and values lead them more often into interpersonal domains rather than the typical abstract or spatial/motoric preoccupations of boys (Gilligan, 1982; Robbins, 1996).

When young women first enter the world of adult heterosexuality, their mothers are on their minds (Holtzman and Kulish, 1997). Feelings of regret for the loss of childhood and separation from mother are common accompaniments of this initiation of the loss of virginity. This clinical finding adds support for the idea that for the girl in her entry into genital sexuality, there is an addition of object, not a change of or renunciation of object. She holds onto her mother as she finds a new kind of relationship with a man (or another woman). At the same time, she experiences anxieties about separating from or losing her mother.

The boy can simultaneously perceive his mother as nurturer and sexual object, but it is harder for the girl to perceive her mother simultaneously as nurturer and sexual rival. The boy's positive Oedipal yearnings are therefore not as fraught with fears of her loss. He may renounce his sexual longings for his mother out of fear, but he is not required to give her up as caretaking object. Enduring dyadic needs for nurturing may be easily masked by triadic Oedipal desires, leaving castration anxieties to show more prominently. But for the little girl, the fact that her rival is also her primary caregiver gives a greater weight to object loss and separation issues in the triadic picture.

Whether the mother is the *object* of erotic feelings or the rival, the girl can feel equally threatened by her disapproval and loss. Sexual interest directed toward the mother during the triangular phase can often disrupt the girl's inner sense of security about her continued care and acceptance.

What Freud (1926a) called the typical dangers of childhood psychic life—loss of the object, loss of the love of the object, castration, and superego disapproval via guilt and/or punishment—were thought to delineate and define a developmental chronology. However, as Charles Brenner (1982) and, more recently, Edward Nersessian (1998) have suggested, these calamities are in-

extricably interwoven with each other. Although they may appear in sequence during development, as Brenner points out, they become so interwoven that they cannot be artificially separated (p. 94). For this reason, we
feel that it is misleading to assume that different anxieties are necessarily related to specific levels of development. That is, separation anxiety and fears
of loss of love and loss of the object are not necessarily pre-Oedipal, and castration anxiety is not exclusively characteristic of the Oedipal period.

Anxieties around separation characterize the feminine triangular situation; to the extent that these are automatically schematized as early or pre-
Oedipal, it can be logically argued that girls tend to be fixated at lower levels of development than boys. We would argue that this view is wrong both
theoretically and clinically.

These childhood dangers, as they emerge clinically, cannot be readily cat-
egorized as representing any given level of development—pre-Oedipal or
Oedipal. Person (1988) pointed out that fears of loss of love, which are part
of the triadic Oedipal constellation for women, are often expressed in oral,
sometimes cannibalistic, terms. We agree that competitive fears can take
these forms because the object of competition is also the source of nurturing
and dependent gratification (pp. 265–288). By the same token, castration
fears are not necessarily characteristic of "later" developmental phases.
Galenson and Roiphe (1971), for example, observed that castration anxiety
occurs very early, pre-Oedipally. Others, such as Lisbeth Sachs (1962), have
argued that castration anxiety often carries very early pre-Oedipal terrors of
annihilation and separation. In our patients, we see the inextricable inter-
twining of castration and/or female genital anxieties with separation anxieties and triadic guilts. For example, the appearance clinically of fantasies of
a "cut-up" or "cut off" or "lost" part of the self are linked to the idea of a sev-
ered maternal relationship. That is to say, they can refer to separation—not
only to lost or damaged genital body parts.

Brenner (1982) writes that "passionate sexual wishes characteristic of the
Oedipal phase are most intimately bound up in every child's mind with object loss, that is, with the disappearance of one or both parents" (p. 103). We
feel, however, that these concerns around object loss or separation are especially pressing for little girls during the so-called Oedipal period. These differences between males and females do not necessarily reflect fixations at or
characteristics of differing levels of development.

We wish to emphasize that this idea has important clinical consequences.
It is infantilizing or demeaning to assume routinely that women's separation
fears are primitive or childish. In addition, attribution of separation issues
to the wrong level of development can produce a stalemated or endlessly

regressive treatment. Of course, pre-Oedipal issues around separation will intermingle with later separation material. The triangular separation issues we are focusing on, however, do not necessarily originate in or signal earlier separation problems. The separation themes and defenses that characterize triadic conflicts in women can be differentiated clinically from earlier material. First, they are frequently precipitated by important developmental steps in a woman's life—a first sexual encounter, going off to college, marriage, or a new career. Second, they are intertwined with rivalrous competition with other women, such as in a new job or a successful love affair. Above all, they appear in the context of triangular relationships—rivalries with mother for father's love (or vice-versa) or in other attempts to work out loyalties between two compelling loved ones. These relationships reflect internally differentiated self and object representations.

Case Examples

A Case of Mrs. L—Conflict about the Addition of an Object

Mrs. L was in her early forties. She had two adolescent children and had been married for eighteen years when she came for a consultation because she suffered from anxiety attacks and obsessive thoughts. She dated her anxiety symptoms to right after the birth of her second child, a boy, who she felt completed their family. She could not rid herself of what seemed inexplicable ideas that she had made a mistake in marrying her husband and that she should leave him. Running through her head were constant questions that perhaps somewhere there was somebody else she should have married—although she couldn't imagine being married to anyone else. She could make no sense of these symptoms. She loved her husband, and she thought that they were compatible, had good times together, communicated well, and had good sex.

Her symptoms diminished in psychotherapy. Discussions made clear to analyst and patient that Mrs. L really had no significant dissatisfaction with her husband or her marriage. She quickly realized that the symptoms must reflect some less apparent issue. The analyst and Mrs. L discovered a starting point for our explorations when the anxiety symptoms flared up after she got together for lunch with an old girlfriend who had been her best friend from high school. Mrs. L then recounted the story of her romance and marriage.

When they graduated, she and her friend went off to college, and Mrs. L's high school boyfriend entered a local technical school. Mrs. L would come home on some weekends to see him, but eventually she discovered—she did not remember how—that on the weekends in which she didn't come home, he was going to see her girlfriend and that a secret romance had been brewing for some time. When Mrs. L discovered this double betrayal, she was very upset, but what especially distressed her was the thought of losing her best friend. She launched an insistent campaign to maintain the friendship. It was around this time that she met her husband, who was several years older. She married him after a quick courtship, a month after the wedding of her girlfriend and her ex-sweetheart. She wanted to invite them to her own wedding, but her husband put his foot down against this. Nevertheless, she had remained friends with the girlfriend, who was still married to the ex-boyfriend.

That was the background of Mrs. L's flare-up in symptoms. She stated her belief that her husband was a much better match for her than the boyfriend would have been. Her husband adored her, and maybe this was her only complaint: that his devotion made her feel guilty and unworthy, given her obsessive thoughts.

Mrs. L's history was unremarkable. She felt loved by both parents and was successful in school and with her peers. She looked up to her older brother. Her father, very good-looking and a natty dresser, was very conscious of his appearance and proud of his good-looking children. During adolescence she dressed in the baggy and campy clothes that were characteristic of the era, but she recounted that her brother had given her a pair of high-heeled shoes for her sixteenth birthday, telling her how good she'd look dressed in sexier and more feminine clothes. From then on, as she remembered it, she wore skirts and high heels to school and felt very good about herself. The analyst's hunch was that her older brother was a paternal figure for her, as is often the case. In this instance, his interest in her looks and sexiness was charged with Persephonal/"Oedipal" significance and served as a positive stimulus in the development of a feminine identity. He was a kind of fairy godmother and Prince Charming, rolled into one.

The story of the boyfriend and the subsequent marriage certainly provide triangular "Oedipal" themes (both "negative" and "positive")—in the proverbial love triangle and betrayal. More striking, however, was that Mrs. L was less concerned with losing her boyfriend than her girlfriend.

At the end of adolescence Mrs. L was caught up in a triangular conflict. She wanted to keep her relationship with a beloved woman and also to have her own relationship with a man. It is also apparent that Mrs. L's object choice of an older man had incestuous, paternal, and brotherly components.

This was a short-term treatment, and the transference could not be explored in any depth. But Mrs. L seemed to relate to the analyst as a mentor or an older sisterly guide. In retrospect, the analyst suspected that Mrs. L may unconsciously have put her in the position of her older brother. What she came to understand was that she had married her husband for "the wrong reasons," as she put it—on the rebound, to deal with wounded pride. Still, she was convinced that her behavior made sense—both that he was a good and appropriate choice for her and that it was absolutely natural for her to want to keep her girlfriend. She acknowledged her feelings of betrayal, but it was the loss of the girlfriend that held the greater potential for hurt. The analyst lightly touched on the triadic "Persephonal" dynamics in her choice of her husband, and noted that whenever her reasons for her choice of her husband were discussed her thoughts would stray to her father. Thus, she gained some understanding that her obsessive thoughts about the man "she should have married" might relate to her father, indicating some insight into the triadic nature of her object choice. Mrs. L. left treatment satisfied with her life and her symptoms under control.

Miss R—Triangular Conflicts around Separation

In the following material there are images of cutting off a finger as a response to a pleasurable, but conflicted, experience, themes of a missing mother, attraction to a father figure, rivalry with a mother, and conscious and unconscious fears of bodily injury and separation as punishment for winning the competition.

The following session is from the second year of the analysis of Miss R, a young woman about to be married. She feels no strong passion toward her husband-to-be but feels that he is a good, comfortable, and appropriate choice. The session occurs just before the analyst's upcoming vacation. In the sessions preceding this one, Miss R had been speaking about how it would feel to be her dog, miserable and pushed outside into the wintry cold—away from desired warmth and closeness with her. She recounted a vignette about her hairdresser—"a bitch, beneath a nice exterior" . . . who had made the patient wait while she entertained a friend with talk about a party she was giving. "There she was behind me showing off and I had to wait." The analyst interpreted the patient's anger as being pushed away into the cold and being left behind while the analyst was off enjoying her vacation and private life. The patient became tearful and vented some of her hurt and anger at the analyst. This material appeared to be the typical dyadic reaction to a separation from the analyst.

When this session began, the patient was talking about her plans for her wedding and the analyst's upcoming vacation. The approaching wedding had re-evoked anxious beliefs and fantasies that her father was always more interested in her than he was in her mother.

"This is very close to my wedding," she began, "but I'm having these images that are just terrible—images about cutting tomatoes and cutting off the end of a finger. I think it was an image, but not a dream. I don't know. A terrible thing that gives me anxiety to think of, so I tried to think of a field of flowers." (Note the similarity of this imagery of a field of flowers with the setting of the Persephone myth.) "But every time I thought of that particular image I felt the pain of it. In my chest. It's like my whole self. A whole bodily feeling. How easy it is to lose the extremities. It seems like all is going so well now that it scares me. Work is going good. Bob [her fiancé] and I have a lot of new friends. Last night we went to dinner, with this guy and his date. I felt out of my league. I enjoyed the whole ambiance of the expensive dinner, but it all scares me. And then I come home and have images of cutting off my finger! It's like I can see the fruits of my efforts. I'd be the one chopping. It would be my finger. No one else would be responsible for it. It would bring me back to reality, the real world, and I would know this is the world I live in. This is a situation I could manage. As awful as it would be, it would be *my* hand and *my* problem." The analyst asked her to tell her more about that. "I don't know. It's like everything keeps getting better and better, and it seems very scary. At the dinner we were at it's almost as if people are taking me away from things that are familiar to me. It's like I really missed my mom. My parents were out of town this weekend. I wanted to talk to her. I feel pulled away then." The analyst asked, "Pulled away?"

"Pulled away from my mom. I now spend evenings with people she doesn't *know*. There's kind of loneliness in me. Maybe like the same thing when I went to college. When I went away I was there with all people my mom didn't know, and when we went to this dinner it's similar. I feel like I don't really belong, and I feel pulled away from what I feel is so comfortable. I'm becoming someone I'm not—in relationship to me. I don't know why I'm comparing all the time, but the whole thing makes me feel more alienated from my mother."

Miss R continued to describe how the other guy was in a different business from Bob—computers. It turns out that his first name, Jim, is the same as her father's. She commented, "It's really strange that it's the same name. I'm afraid of this guy because he is so sophisticated. . . . He's a real good catch but that bothers me because I don't want to feel that way—I'm engaged to Bob." Then she described how Jim, the guy with her father's name, said forcefully to his date at the dinner, "Taste this."[1]

"I was attracted to him but I don't like domineering men. Whoa—that reminds me of my dad a little because he can be that way. 'Take a bite,' he'd say. I'd say no.[2] He wouldn't force it, of course, but Jim's date, she'd do whatever the guy said. And it was like Chuck, my former boyfriend, who was also in computers. And this guy. . . . Wait a minute, I gave you the wrong name, the name I gave you, Jim R, is really a cousin of my Dad. The guy's name is really Tim R. I don't know why I called him Jim R—I used to have a crush on Jim R."

Her thoughts turned again to competition. This time she compared herself with Jim's/Tim's date (that is, the rival, the woman belonging to the father substitute). The patient said, "We both can't be good, we both can't be successful. It's like a seesaw. We both can't be up at the same time."

The analyst said, "This worry about alienation from your mother stems from your concern that you both can't be successful at the same time." The patient responded, "Well, I think that's true because we can never be together at the same level. Cutting off the finger is the same thing. It's like separating from a part of yourself. Like I could destruct and kill off a part of myself. Like if a little part of my finger was like my relationship with my mother and I cut it off. Maybe going to dinner with that guy last night, the four of us, is like a separation. Maybe it's also a separation from my fiancé, because I was really interested in the other guy. To be safely married to someone not as sophisticated as the other guy [and not as sexually exciting] is like my mother's world. If I step out of the world of my mom, I become disconnected. It's interesting and yet funny. With the same name as my Dad, this guy seems more dangerous, like dangerous new territory. I don't trust this guy. Or my cousin. They'd be condescending with me just like my Dad. It was exciting to enter into his territory but always humiliating."

The session had been preceded by separation material that appeared to be pre-Oedipal or pre-triangular and related to the mother/daughter dyad. It concerned two people, the parent/dog; hairdresser/client; and especially the analyst-mother/patient-daughter. It also engaged themes of early loss—being pushed out, ignored, and rejected. In the following session, this material then evolved into triadic—sexual concerns, in which the patient referred explicitly to the attempt to balance two different worlds. She contrasted the close-knit comfort of the mother and family with the world of excitement and forbidden sexuality. She clearly linked her father with the male relative with the same name as the father. The slip in the name demarcated the emergence of a conflict about an incestuous attraction with accompanying anxieties and guilt. Her anxieties about competitive rivalry with her mother led to fears of losing and being alienated from her mother and with being punished by having a part of herself cut off. The cut-off finger can be understood and interpreted in terms of castration, but this patient's associations alerted us to an additional and important meaning: that is, the loss of a relationship with the mother, as well.[3]

Miss R's two worlds concretely parallel Persephone's experience as queen of the underworld—the "world below," where she is mate to her uncle, Hades, for part of the year, but returns to be with her mother, Demeter, in the fertile "world above" during the other part. A balancing act is required to keep her mother's love and nurturance and at the same time to be sexual with a man. In this patient, competitive rivalry, incestuous heterosexual attraction and anxiety, and conflicts around loyalty to one parent versus the other are all present.

In the transference, a similar situation was of course developing. The patient talked about her competitiveness with the analyst, her desire to be just like the analyst and to possess everything the analyst had. Anxiously, she described a movie in which a young woman moves in with and wants to be like her new roommate. Eventually the character takes over the roommate's possessions, her lover—her entire life. The patient recognized herself in this character as her competitive and aggressive feelings emerged in fuller form.

Conclusion

As we have tried to demonstrate in our discussion above, in our view, much contemporary writing argues against the idea that women undergo a simple change of object in their entry into the triangular phase, and we have illustrated this more complex view in our case material. Our clinical experience tells us that the step of entering the world of adult female sexuality evokes one of the main dynamics of the triadic phase. Although these are separation anxieties, the girl's struggles with the conflict between keeping mother for security and nurture and her emerging sexual genital wishes toward the father (or the mother) are not "pre-Oedipal." Competition with the mother for her realm is seen as dangerous and fraught with fears of her loss.

Because genital activity for girls, in general, is met with by disapproval, erotic impulses turned toward either father or mother leads to fears of loss of the mother or her love and approval, fears that may become very frightening. In contrast, genital activity is typically more acceptable for males, although it may be accompanied by fears of a castration if the impulses are directed toward the mother. The loss of the mother is not at stake.

The entry into the triangular period is not, as Freud stated, represented by a change of object; rather, it is an addition of an object. The same-sexed parent—the mother—evokes loss of the object and loss of the love of the object, in tones that are triadic and different from males. The entry is intermingled with fears of separation and loss.

We do not know exactly what drives the entry into the triadic phase. Penis envy and castration fears are certainly not the push or pull into the period for girls, and probably not for boys. We can characterize this process, however, as multifaceted—biological, psychological, familial, and social. We have listed six possible influences on the entry into the triangular phase: an innate propensity to experience the primal scene, innate biological pressures, cognitive factors, bisexuality, the role of the father, and the role of the mother. No one component in and of itself provides a unitary and satisfactory explanation.

What are the psychic developments that signal entry into the triadic phase? These are the criteria we use to assess our clinical material for its triadic qualities:

1. There is evidence of the intra-psychic achievement of separateness of self and object and of the existence of whole internal objects.
2. There are maternal and paternal mental representations.
3. The individual has the cognitive and emotional capacity to comprehend, in some form, an adult relationship between the parents (that is, recognition of the "primal scene").
4. The individual has the cognitive and emotional capacity for "triangularity"; there is evidence of a mentalized three-party relationship—the parents (or parental substitutes) and the child.
5. Competition, rivalrous aggression, jealousy, and incestuous fantasies are prominent.
6. Genital sexual interest and curiosity are directed toward parental figures.

Notes

1. This is reminiscent of Hades' making Persephone eat the pomegranate seed.
2. Note the similarity to the eating aspects of the Persephone myth in which Persephone is enticed, fooled, or on her own eats pomegranate seeds—the forbidden fruit. It is this prohibited act which "seals her fate" and forces her to return each year to Hades in the underworld to reign as queen.
3. A cut-off member or part of a finger is an element which appears in many fairy tales, such as "The Enchanted Pig" or "The Little Mermaid." These two stories are both discussed by Bettleheim (1975). He attributed to these images the notion of a girl giving up a piece of herself (the hymen) in order to achieve a sexual or marital partnership. In addition, he suggested that it symbolized fantasies of castration, loss of a phallus. In our material we have a new finding. The cut-off part not only represents castration or defloration but also being cut off from the mother. Thus, in her mind the girl fears she will lose her mother in order to marry.

CHAPTER SEVEN

~

Female Aggression and Triadic Conflicts

Fighting is essentially a masculine idea; a woman's weapon is her tongue.

(Hermione Gingold)

"Mirror, mirror, on the wall, who's the fairest of them all?" With these words, a fairy tale queen expresses her competitive feelings towards all other females. When the magic mirror first gives her an unwelcome answer—that Snow White is more beautiful than she—the queen is consumed with envy and hatred of her ripening stepdaughter. She plots to kill her young rival with a poisoned apple.

Snow White, like the heroines of most such tales, is sweet, innocent, beautiful, and devoid of aggression. Angry impulses toward a rival woman are typically portrayed as evil and dangerous, emanating from an older woman, a witch, stepmother, enchantress, or evil fairy, not from the younger girl, who is cast in the role of victim. The older woman is the purveyor of powerful aggressive motives and actions. In tales about females that portray a triangular rivalry, that is, tales that might parallel the Oedipus myth, the protagonist is without overt aggression.

In this chapter, we will examine and explore the manifestations of aggressive impulses, including their absence and their disguises, in the female triangular situation. We will focus on the psychological influences on aggression, although we are mindful that sociological, cultural, and biological influences also contribute to females' attitudes toward and expressions of aggression (Bachofen, 1967; Warner, 1994; Hyde, 2005).[1]

85

Typically in stories about girls, aggression toward the mother figure is displaced from or projected onto others, or occurs by accident (Bettelheim, 1975; Palmer, 1988; Person, 1988; Dahl, 1989).[2] Some familiar examples are *Heidi*, Dorothy in *The Wizard of Oz*, Wendy in *Peter Pan*, Mary in *The Secret Garden*, and the princess in "Sleeping Beauty." Lady Macbeth and Electra use men as powerful instruments to carry out their ambitious or rivalrous plans for murder, which must be tempered and cleverly hidden. We have observed that when our women patients are involved in triangular Persephonal conflicts, their aggression may similarly be unconsciously inhibited, disguised, or externalized.

In tales about males, however, the protagonists' aggression is out in the open. Oedipus comes upon a man at a crossroads who will not yield to him. Not knowing that this man Laius is actually his father, Oedipus kills him. As the story unfolds, Oedipus unknowingly comes to rule Laius's kingdom, marries Laius's widow (his own mother), and has four children out of his incest with her. This was the tale of murder and incest that gave Freud his insight into infantile sexuality and the inescapable family drama that he called the Oedipus complex. The classic story of a triangle, a young man's sexual impulses toward the parent of the opposite sex and murderous rivalry toward the same-sexed parent, was universalized to apply to girls, as well.[3]

The female Oedipus complex is based on a male model and on outdated psychoanalytic concepts of female psychosexual development. We and others (Bernstein, 1993; Person, 1988) have argued that the Oedipus story does not adequately or accurately fit the typical triangular situation of females, as reflected in family dynamics, conflicts, defenses, or most pertinent here, the expression of aggression. If there are gender-related patterns of aggression characteristic of the female triangular situation, how can we understand them?

One possible explanation for such differences is based on the pattern of object relationships at the time the girl approaches the triangular Persephonal stage of development (Chodorow, 1978). Typically, the major caretaker is the mother, who now becomes the rival. In the boy's positive Oedipal situation, his rival is his father, who is not usually the major source of caretaking in the family. But the girl's blossoming sexual interest toward her father means she is faced with a conflict that threatens her basic security with her caretaker. The competitiveness and aggression that go with individuation and the growth of agency may feel exceedingly dangerous to a girl child when the nurturing object is her rival (in the "positive Oedipal constellation"), or the object of sexual impulses (in the "negative Oedipal constellation"). How to move forward and yet stay secure? Taking a view similar to ours, Elina Reenkola (2002) says of this situation: "This is a fateful com-

bination. The ambivalence of love and hate towards the mother arouses im-
mense guilt in a girl, having a powerful impact of the vicissitudes of aggression in women" (preface, xv). Diane Elise (1997) writes, "Not only can a
girl's anger get in the way of her relationship with her mother, her relationship with her mother (among many other contributing factors) can get in the
way of her anger" (p. 512). The typical situation for the little boy is fraught
with its own dangers, but they are very different.

Moreover, in the triangular situation in which the girl's rivalry toward her
mother is aroused, she can feel disloyal to "the hand that feeds her." Thus,
anxieties about separation from the mother are prominent. We feel that the
Persephone myth beautifully portrays the conflicts of the young girl as she
takes her first steps into the world of sexually competitive feelings. In previous chapters we have proposed that the story of Persephone demonstrates a
common unconscious defense against the acknowledgement of the girl's
sense of herself as a sexual agent. It is our thesis that the same dynamics of
sexuality that we see in little girls in the phase of triangulation hold also for
the expression of aggression.

It has been said, however, that the myth of Persephone is not analogous
or parallel to the story of Oedipus in regard to aggression. We have been
asked, "Where are the rivalry and rage toward the mother in Persephone,
compared to the rivalry and rage toward the father in Oedipus?" We agree
that female aggression is not visible in the myth of Persephone, except in the
vengeful retribution of Persephone's mother, Demeter, who unleashes famine
on earth until her daughter is returned to her. Aggression certainly does not
seem to mark the mother/daughter relationship between Demeter and Persephone. We argue that Persephone's sense of herself as an aggressive agent,
like her sense of herself as a sexual agent, is disguised and inhibited in this
story, as it is in the female triangular situation itself.

Review of the Literature on Aggression
in the Female Triangular Phase

It is striking how there is little in the psychoanalytic literature about aggression in women; even less can be found on aggression in the female "Oedipal"
or triangular situation. Themes of competition, castration, and aggression are
discussed regularly, however, in writings about the male Oedipal complex.

Many have written about general cultural prohibitions against the expression
of anger and aggression by girls and women (Bernadez-Bonesatti, 1978; Lerner,
1980; Nadelson et al., 1982; Bernay, 1986; Guzder and Krishna, 1991; Gabbard
and Wilkinson, 1996; Person, 2000). Both men and women of most societies

place negative values on women's aggression. In a discussion of the reasons for the general inhibition of female anger or aggression, Harriet Lerner (1980) suggests that this inhibition reflects women's fears of their own omnipotent destructiveness and separation/individuation difficulties in the mother/daughter relationship. Essentially her focus is on early, pre-Oedipal issues.

Paul Gray (2000) refers to the cultural inhibition of aggression in all vulnerable groups, including women, in a discussion of how best to facilitate the analysis of aggression: "It seems possible that an evolutionary process, cultural rather than biological (the latter would suggest Lamarckism), could contribute to the development in individuals of chronic, characterological defenses of the ego. This might restrain their conscious aggression, thus supporting survival in an otherwise dangerous environment" (p. 222).

On the other hand, many have argued that women's seemingly diminished aggression in comparison to men's is biologically based. (See, for example, Maccoby and Jacklin, 1974.) Based on recent observations in the behavioral sciences and neurosciences, Richard Friedman and Jennifer Downey (1995) have raised questions about the ubiquity of the Oedipus complex. They suggest that there is an innate, biologically determined tendency for *sons* to feel rivalrous, competitive, and aggressive toward their fathers, and vice-versa. Thus, this one component of the Oedipal complex for males, not necessarily connected with erotic desire, might be ubiquitous. (Presumably they would say that the ubiquity of an aggressive component does not hold true for females.) They argue that males are biologically more aggressive than females, citing evidence about rough-and-tumble play, a category in which sex differences have been consistently reported in most cultures, independent of child-rearing practices. By implication, therefore, the aggressive and competitive components of the Oedipus story would hold true more for males than for females.

There are other arguments too against the applicability of the Oedipal model to girls, especially with regard to its aggressive components. In one feminist view, Irene Stiver (1991) argues that Oedipal dynamics can best be understood in terms of patriarchal relationships: The major sources of anger in mother/daughter relations reflect the social reality of the mother's degraded and inferior position in the family constellation.

When aggression is discussed as part of the female "Oedipal" or triangular situation, it often appears in the context of female masochism. Jack and Kerry Novick (1972) report that beating fantasies in girls seem to arise in latency after resolution of the Oedipal period and therefore reflect defensive working over of Oedipal conflicts. They speculate that beating fantasies can be considered a "normal" part of post-Oedipal development that fosters the establishment of a feminine identity. Along similar lines that link masochism to the Oedipal conflicts of girls, Eric Plaut and Foster Hutchinson (1986) emphasize the masochistic, inhibited reaction of the girl to the Oedipal situation, in contrast to the more aggressive boy. Samuel Ritvo (1989) also stressed that aggression toward the mother may compromise that object relation and result in sadomasochistic tendencies in girls. Unfortunately, in our view, writings like these foster the misapprehension that "normal" female development is linked with masochism and passivity.

In one of the few direct articles on aggression in the female Oedipal phase, Sylvan Keiser (1953) discusses a manifest Oedipus complex in an adolescent girl. He noted that when the patient expressed the slightest disparagement of the mother, anxiety appeared in the absence of overt aggressive feeling. In this patient, defense against aggressive impulses toward the mother was especially intense because her father had died, so her mother was the only remaining parent, and her loss unthinkable.

Janine Chasseguet-Smirgel (1970) defined and described in the Oedipal situation specifically feminine positions that "have no counterpart in the males" (p. 96). One such feminine position is the aggression-based guilt of one specific moment in development: the change of the object from mother to father. The girl's attempts to resolve anal sadistic conflicts with her mother may give rise to idealization of the paternal object representation. The mother becomes the bad object; the father, the good. The girl may have difficulty in freeing herself from a particularly controlling mother, perceived as castrating to the father. Seeking haven in the triangular situation, the girl cannot really identify herself with this image of mother. Later, she may attach herself to a husband in a childlike dependency. (We think of Nora in Ibsen's *Dollhouse*.) Chasseguet-Smirgel wrote: "I have tried to show conflicts which oblige so many women to choose between mother and husband as the object of dependent attachment" (p. 134). Maria Torok (1970) describes similar conflicts around anal aggression that color the girl's Oedipal situation.

Chasseguet-Smirgel emphasizes the fantasy of castration by, and identification with, a castrating mother as sources of anxiety and guilt in the female triangular situation. Although her focus on the dynamics of one particular family constellation limits the general applicability of her theory, we agree with her stress on the problem of loyalty seen so typically in little girls at that period of development. As we see it, because of her conflicted loyalty toward the mother, the girl may defensively remain dependent upon her. We stress another source of anxiety—separation worries about the loss of the caretaker, who is the object of dependent attachment. For us, the loyalty and separation issues arise from this period of time itself and are not necessarily from a defensive outcome of earlier issues.

In her exposition of uniquely feminine aspects of the Oedipus complex, Chasseguet-Smirgel focuses on a specific form of feminine guilt and on a moment many speak of as particularly worthy of study, the girl's change of sexual object from mother to father. The motivation for the girl's change of libidinal object from mother to father in early psychoanalytic theory is attributed to anger and disappointment in her mother, as a "castrated" and degraded object (Hamon, 2000). For Thomas Ogden (1987), this change is best understood in terms of the development of object relationships: "The transition is not from one object to another, but from a relationship to an internal object (an object that is not completely separate from oneself) to a cathexis of an external object (an object that exists outside of one's omnipotence)" (p. 486). He suggests that the girl's discovery of the Oedipal mother's "externality" is experienced as a betrayal.[4]

In chapter 6, we have elaborated our argument, shared by more and more contemporary writers, that this process should be characterized not as a *change* of object but as an *addition*. Ritvo (1989), in a panel discussion on current concepts of the development of sexuality, commented that girls do not relinquish the tie to the mother but rather learn to deal with their aggression against the mother while retaining ties to her. In her discussion of the female "Oedipal" complex, Eva Lester (1976) said that the turning to the father "is not always accompanied by an aggressive flight from mother, although often antagonism and competition can be observed" (p. 525).

Phyllis Tyson (1989, 1997) and Otto Fenichel (1931b) also explicated the pre-Oedipal antecedents of girls' problems with anger in their relationships with their mothers during the triangular phase of development. Eleanor Galenson and Herman Roiphe (1982) have suggested that strivings toward separation are experienced as threats to the maternal bond.

Finally, sexuality and aggression are very much intertwined in young children's minds at the triangular stage of development. It is not yet possible to separate the patterns of regulation of aggression from libidinal issues (Herzog, 2000). The little girl's body, with its inner cavities and flowing sensations, must influence this interweaving in some way. Aggression, like sexuality, may be incorporated into the female body image and body ideal in keeping with bodily contours and inborn temperaments (Downey, 2000). The little girl may find more inward, interior ways to handle her aggressive and sexual feelings (Richards, 1992).

In this selected review, we observe an emphasis on the "pre-Oedipal" or pre-triangular influences on female aggression in the triangular period. We disagree with the automatic pre-Oedipalization of female dynamics in regard to aggression. We suggest that, even when aggression toward the mother is involved, the turn to the father represents an addition of object, not a change of object. We believe that the girl has a great deal of difficulty and conflict around her aggressive feelings, especially toward her mother. In a unique view, Maria Bergmann (1982) states that "clinical work suggests that the girl has a more difficult task in overcoming competitive wishes and hostility toward the mother than has the boy [toward the father]. I do not believe this to be a fact" (p. 197). We, on the other hand, are arguing the opposite.

Recent Research on Aggression in Girls

Researchers have lately become interested in the aggression of girls as it appears in school and social settings, giving rise to a spate of books and articles as well as consciousness-raising workshops at schools about certain manifestations of aggression.

In a feature article in the *New York Times* on aggression in middle school girls, Margaret Talbot (2002) described a class offered by a nonprofit organization aimed at helping girls be nicer to each other. Talbot talks about the harmful emotional consequences of exclusionary cliques, vicious backbiting, and scapegoating. Manipulations, exclusions, and gossip are described as the ways in which young girls channel their hostility. The psychologist Marion Underwood, who is quoted in Talbot's article, suggests that girls' valuation of intimacy and the sharing of secrets in itself gives them ammunition for gossip. Girls dubbed as "Queen Bees," "Alpha girls," or the "RMGs"—the "Really Mean Girls"—backstab and dump their friends. The rest of the female population is divided into victims, hangers-on, and messengers. Talbot's article describes the "intricate rituals of exclusion and humiliation" that fall into the category of "relational aggression."

According to research by Rachel Simmons (2002), girls express their anger in covert ways. "Yet I am arguing not that girls feel angry in fundamentally different ways than boys, but that many girls appear to show anger differently. Girls' aggression may be covert and relational; it may indeed be fueled at times by a fear of loss or isolation. That does not mean, however, that girls do not want power or feel aggression as passionately as their male peers" (p. 9). Simmons concludes, "Aggression may be biological but the face of aggression is learned" (p. 12). This kind of behavior frequently continues into adulthood.

The type of intervention in desensitizing groups that Talbot described above is based on research from the early 1990s, which contradicts older ideas that girls are not as aggressive as boys. Some researchers found that girls up to the age of four are as aggressive as boys and that social expectations force their behaviors underground or into other channels. We do not want to underestimate the social and sociological forces that go into these observations. Yet we think that an accurate understanding of female triangular conflicts provides a perspective that must also be taken into account. Little girls of four, at the height of the triangular period, must learn to negotiate and balance their loyalties between father and mother, and in so doing must often stifle their aggression, which then goes underground to protect their relationships with their mothers.

Observations from other sociological research suggest that girls' aggression becomes a problem once again in adolescence. This finding fits some psychoanalytic theories of adolescence as a period of revival of "Oedipal" or triadic dynamics in adolescence, with sexuality and competitiveness toward other girls being stirred up. In adolescence, when the social stakes become higher, there is an observed shift in the ways girls behave. Carol Gilligan (1982) writes that because girls perceive danger in the loss of relationships, aggression must become covert again—the crisis is "relational." Their aggression must be expressed in the roundabout ways that have been described in the social research.

In much of this recent research, there has been recognition of the manifest content of female aggression and the forms it takes, but not a dynamic understanding, which might provide more leverage. It may be that typically with little girls, aggression is inhibited only to fester beneath the surface and to reemerge at adolescence in these forms.

Clinical Material

We will now present four clinical examples of aggression connected with heterosexual triangular conflicts (two women competing for a man or a woman and a man competing for a woman) in four female cases. In all of our clinical material the triadic nature of the conflicts is evident and currently alive in the transference. The first two cases most clearly demonstrate the inhibition of aggression and competition toward a female rival—"who's the fairest of them all?" This feminine inhibition of aggression associated with Persephonal development is seen frequently in the treatment of female patients, especially in the earlier stages of analysis. In our clinical experience, only after considerable analytic work is overt murderous aggression toward the mother consciously tolerated, as in the third example. We have also observed such overt aggression in cases of extremely troubled relationships with the mother. As we reported in previous work (Holtzman and Kulish, 2000), inhibition of the sense of sexual agency in our cases has been notable. Sexuality and aggression are inextricably interwoven; we separate them only for purposes of discussion.

Case 1: Death of Mother and Inhibition of Aggression

Our first case is a woman whose defensive idealization of the analyst/mother functioned as a strong inhibitor of anger. Her mother died when she was five years old. In the following clinical material, fantasies about sexual pleasure with a man lead directly and immediately to thoughts about her mother's death. This sequence can be understood as the patient's conflicted unconscious linking of rivalrous, competitive, sexual feelings with the traumatic loss of her mother at the height of the triangular phase.

Miss M, a manufacturer's representative, is about to begin a five-times-a-week control analysis after a year and a half of three-times-a-week psychotherapy. Her presenting problems were depression and difficulties in her relationships with men. She also reported "wild behaviors," including drug and alcohol use, promiscuity, and impulsivity, which had started early in adolescence and continued up to her present age of twenty-nine. Miss M was the youngest in a family of five siblings. When she was five, her mother died suddenly. Her father remarried two years later. She invested a great deal of love and affection in her stepmother, and her siblings chastised her for not being loyal to their biological mother. During the psychotherapy it became evident to the analyst, but not to the patient, that the patient felt unconsciously guilty for her mother's death, as well as angry at her mother for dying and leaving her. Miss M's promiscuity seemed to be a cover for her desperate search for a mother via precocious heterosexual contacts.

The early therapeutic work began a process of true mourning for her mother. A very eager patient, Miss M expressed her desire to come often to analysis and her pleasure in coming. She told the analyst how much she loved her and what a wonderful mother she thought she would make. She stressed how intensely gratified she felt at being chosen as a control case. The following session took place shortly before the patient was to begin her analysis.

Miss M came in, breathless, coffee cup in hand. "I've been running around all day. Tomorrow we have the presentation. I have been all over the place. Thank God for coffee. I want to continue talking about what we were talking about yesterday—the idea of pleasure—not being able to enjoy it or tolerate it. Ron [the patient's old high school boyfriend] has asked me to go with him to a football game in a couple of weeks. I was talking to Mary [a much older sister] about it. A part of me wants to go with him. I think it will be fun, but a part of me doesn't want to go. I don't want to lead him on. I know he wants more from me. Also some of our mutual friends will be there. I really enjoy them. But I think they will really be annoyed if I am with Ron. They'll say the way Mary does, 'How can you be with him? Just leading him on, really not interested in him.'"

The analyst said: "Talk more about this idea of having pleasure and everyone commenting about it." The patient replied, "Yes, I feel the same way, I am worried that I will be leading him on and also don't want others to get upset . . . the whole idea of pleasure. Anyway, I will probably just get drunk, not to enjoy it."

To a series of queries from the analyst, the patient said, "Well, I think he will try to kiss me and I know I really enjoy it and then I also remember the time with Brian (another former boyfriend) in the van in the back. We were really kissing and making out. . . . It just feels like I can't enjoy it and if I am out of it, i.e., drunk, I don't have to take responsibility for it, for the pleasure. This is the problem: I'm thinking for some reason about my mom dying." (Note that the idea of mother's dying comes up in the context of guilt-ridden pleasure.)

Miss M started to cry. "Maybe . . . Mom used to make things pleasurable for me. When she died, I have to. . . . It is like I don't want to give up the idea of someone doing it for me, making it happen for me. . . . Well, thinking of this old friend, Donna, from the old church I used to attend, who sends gift boxes to me every year. Most of the time I don't even open them." The analyst asked, "What about not opening the box?"

"Well, anything from Donna would have the same message as my old church. It's the school of thought that says that things are predetermined. It's a Calvinist thinking, a belief in pre-determinism, heaven or hell. My dad believes in it, believes he is going to heaven. You can do whatever you want. So it's OK that he was such a jerk. I don't agree with it, the idea of being the chosen one. . . . I have this idea now that we make things happen for ourselves. I felt I would go to heaven but after my mother died I felt I would go to hell."

Here the analyst intervened perhaps too quickly. She did not follow the train of associations about going to hell. Instead she took up the idea of beginning the analysis and the patient's stated pleasure in being picked by the analyst as a control case. She suggested that the idea of being chosen was being triggered by the talk of starting analysis.

"Yes, I feel anxious, I know we have talked about it and I really want to do it but it makes me anxious. You know, when I was walking in today, I saw myself in the window. Here I was in a skirt, my hair pulled back, really looking like an adult, and I thought, 'I am one, I have to take responsibility.' But it makes me anxious."

The analyst said, "Perhaps there is a worry that there will be all sorts of needs and longings stirred up and I won't be able to help you and that I will leave you on your own to figure it out. Also it seems the idea of being 'chosen' is present. Perhaps feeling like the chosen one doesn't seem to feel so good. Perhaps you view my recommendation of analysis as your being the chosen one but it seems confusing. We can try to understand more of your confused and conflicted feelings."

Being "chosen" as a control case seems to have stirred up a myriad of feelings, fantasies, and anxieties for this young woman. She is gratified that she has been chosen by this new wonderful mother substitute, who may fulfill her longings for her lost dead mother. At the same time, there is a hint that being chosen might mean that other wishes or frightening sexual fantasies—to "make out" or even do more with a guy of whom no one approves—might emerge and be resented by the analyst/mother. It seems that the patient links such fantasies with punishment, the punishment of losing her mother. It is too early in the analysis to suggest that the patient may also feel unconsciously that her competitive strivings caused the mother's death. It is poignant and striking that the patient so clearly documents how her purity and goodness plummet with her mother's death, from heaven to hell.

To avoid guilt, the patient projects her anger and self-disapproval onto family and her friends, who she fears will "be annoyed" by her taking up with a former love. "Being drunk" is used as a defense against acknowledging agency over her sexual and aggressive wishes, and she doesn't perceive herself as "wanting something more." It is the male, Ron, who wants something more. Oral modes of protection and gratification also arm her against feelings of deprivation and anxiety, as when she brings a cup of coffee with her to the session. Inhibition and repression are sustained through action, substance abuse, externalization, and projection. This propensity toward action reflects the reality of early trauma—the death of her mother—in this woman's life. And the trauma of the early loss exacerbates her unconscious guilt and aggression, and her defenses against them, which appeared in the transference as idealization of a perfect mother.

Case 2: The Midnight Marauder

The following material is from the second year of analysis of a thirty-five-year-old married woman, Mrs. P, who has made significant strides in overcoming depression and self-depreciating behavior. Much work has concentrated on her strong, erotized attachment to her father and her problems in differentiating herself from a controlling but loved mother with whom she had strongly identified. She has been struggling with the emergence of dim memories from childhood that highlight her sexual feelings about her father, and possibly some sort of incestuous experiences—thoughts that are very unwelcome and terrifying. Nevertheless, improvements in self-esteem have allowed her to procure a new and very satisfying job and to buy a new house, one very different from the kind of place her mother would have chosen. Both the new job and the new home make her feel "more grown-up." Yet at the same time she feels pulled into feeling as she did as a child. She has been feeling very stressed.

In the week before the session to be presented, Mrs. P complained that everything seemed to be in disarray. In the session immediately before, she described an image from a dream: "I picture my dad on a ladder, kind of like a poster, with the title, 'Midnight Marauder.' He looks happy, good-looking. 'Midnight Marauder' brings a thought of him coming into my room in the dark."

Mrs. P began the next day's session by reporting that she had been contacted about a new and very prestigious position that paid double her current pay. She announced to the analyst that of course she would not even consider this proposal, so content was she with her current job, which was still quite new.

"Why not?" the analyst asked. The patient was quite taken aback at this, but then she began to speculate about what she might indeed do with more money and with other things she wanted in her life. "I didn't even interview, but I did meet with my current supervisor to tell her about this offer. It went swell. She did speak about a raise, but one that could not match the proposed salary. Talking last time did sort of open my eyes to thinking about what I do want. Or it would be so nice to buy things without worrying. I would like another degree—a Ph.D." Her thoughts went back to a couple of years before: She had investigated some of the Ph.D. programs in the area. She had even set out to speak to someone at the university with which the analyst was affiliated, but she had gotten lost on the way and never got to her appointment. Significantly, she had never told the analyst about these events.

With some exploration, it emerged that the patient felt intimidated by and afraid of the university. She said, "The people there are so much brighter, more competent. I feel like it's something about competition. And there are conferences and concerts there that I would like to attend, but I don't even think to get tickets because I assume I can't get them."

The analyst asked whom she knew from there that was so bright. The patient replied, "People who graduated from there seem better. It doesn't seem rational. I'm mad and disappointed how I blew off my college and my grades." The analyst interpreted, "You use a blanket of inferiority in your mind to keep yourself from competing—competing with me, getting a Ph.D. like me.

You probably connect the university with me, and feel inferior to anyone connected with it. You feel you can't compete with me."

Mrs. P replied, "I'm definitely not as good as you, or at least I feel that way. I feel that way about people from the psychoanalytic institute, especially."

Mrs. P was inhibited in procuring a more prestigious job, more money, and more education. The extent to which she needed to diminish herself, to "keep herself down," is clear. This material emerged with direct allusion in the transference to competition—becoming *equal* with, not necessarily better than, the analyst/mother. It is clearly related to the immediate context of emerging sexual material about the father, the good-looking "Midnight Marauder." Thus, the triadic conflicts, the fires of forbidden, sexual impulses toward the father, and the competitive desires toward the mother, must be put out with a blanket of inhibition and inferiority. Even the wish to become equal with, or like, the parent, seems to carry with it ominous rumblings of destructiveness.

Both of these patients commented on the experience of feeling and/or being grown-up. This phenomenon in and of itself speaks to the push/pull feeling and being on the cusp of the triangular situation. Once she is grown up, a woman can compete and take responsibility for herself, a position these two women intensely long for and yet fear at the same time. It means to them the loss of the early nurturing mother. In both cases the material is triadic. The cast of characters includes a young female, a desired male, and a disapproving or competing female or chorus of females. The female chorus whispers, "Don't lead him on" or "Don't be too successful"—or you will lose mother's love, mother's approval, or mother herself. Aggressiveness leads to loss.

Case 3: Killing Off Mother

Our third patient demonstrates a tolerance of aggression and some acknowledgment of agency, both as a function of considerable analytic work.

Mrs. A, a twenty-nine-year-old advertising executive, was in her fourth year of analysis. She was perceptive and psychologically sophisticated, and she made good use of her analysis, which enabled her to advance in her career. When she began treatment, she had been unable to work in a creative or effective manner. Analytic work had uncovered the unconscious competition and rivalry with her mother that had contributed to her work inhibition. In the session to be reported, some recent acclaimed success at work and the analyst's upcoming vacation were exacerbating Mrs. A's anxieties.

Mrs. A commented that it had been hard for her to get to the session because of the icy sidewalks around the analyst's office, and reported that she had hesitated before telling the analyst this. When asked why, she said that she was uneasy being critical of something about the analyst—that the side-walks had not been salted. The patient then began talking about how her mother put her down if she expressed any of her own aspirations, concerns, or criticisms. Her mother would do it in a "mean" way, which meant to Mrs. A that she had no right to such thoughts or feelings. The analyst pointed out that Mrs. A was intensely anxious because of her anticipation that the ana-lyst would be similarly "mean."

The patient replied, "I wanted to kill her." (The interpretation freed the patient to express direct murderous rage, but only in the past tense.) "Wanted to kill her?" the analyst said.

"Yes. I remember wanting to kill her. And I felt like a worthless, shitty, aw-ful person for feeling that. I remember her venom, her strength, and her power. I wanted to have the ability to wipe her out. I wanted to be the pow-erful one because I always felt so small. I felt there was no one to help me. Yet, the thing is, she would always be there. That's something. But there were times I remember very briefly when I wanted to obliterate, destroy, get rid of her. I wanted to be one up on her. This morning in aerobics, I did stretches, which I love. My stomach was bloated, which I can't stand because my mother had a big stomach. [Her mother had four pregnancies after the pa-tient's birth.] I was one up on her because I was young and pretty. How could I be that? I felt guilty about getting attention—something in our both being female. It's like maybe I could be more attractive to my father. The thought was scary that he would like me better. She would be angry at me. I would want his affection, of course, not his sexual advances. [Here there is a defen-sive negation of sexuality.] Mother was angry at me for being seductive and flirtatious. I wanted to get her obliterated and I used to fantasize I was father's favorite. But it's scary; how could I get rid of her? But I could be the prize daughter for my father. My mother, she was always there. *If I got rid of her who would take care of us?* But I do remember when I was three or four specifi-cally—how do I remember back so far?—sitting with Dad on the couch. I think what I remember is wanting to be touching him. I felt I was very, very special and thought, 'We don't need mother.' It was scary thinking that I had the power. I guess that's why I can't assert myself here and couldn't achieve— because it means that someone else gets destroyed and certainly would be an-gry at me."

"Is this what females go through?" she went on. "It's hard for me to expe-rience the relationship with you. It seems okay for you to be smart and have aspirations but that's not part of me. I expect you to put me down. I went and tried things but they never worked out. But I think that must have been wrong, to want to get rid of mother, and I must have realized it. Maybe I wanted Dad to touch me. I was afraid to tell him how close I wanted to be to him. He was a jerk, but being pretty was a good way to get his attention. But he was strong. But mother was always there. *What would happen if she really was gone?* I had that fleeting thought."

The analyst said, "What would happen?"

"Well, I needed her. She was the mom. I counted on her. She took care of me and my brothers and sister. Who would take over? Me? My little sister? And I just felt horribly guilty, inescapably, immutably awful, if I did get rid of her. I was bad, dirty, ugly to want to get rid of her, but I felt I hated her. Although I was stirred up . . . the way I was treated by her and her meanness back to me, I couldn't compete. She was bigger, stronger, and she was awful, and yet, because . . . I couldn't . . . I wanted to get rid of her. Scary . . . sexual toward my father? I fantasized maybe I was more desirable than she was. My father, as I talk all through this analysis, is a non-figure in my life. [Defensive negation again.] How come? He existed. I didn't talk to him. I walled him off. He's still walled off, and mother was unreachable. Maybe you can help me. It makes me want to cry. Then I don't know if others feel the same way. This is awful to feel this way. It's painful. [She's crying.] But I do, I feel sorry for myself but I don't like to admit it. Why do I have all this today?"

The analyst responded, "I think you wonder if I understand that this is related to my upcoming absence. You are feeling hurt and angry, even wanting to murder me and afraid I will retaliate, but you also want me back too."

Mrs. A said, "This is awful, painful. I remember feeling this same way when I was little—just devastated."

She went on to say that she was afraid that there was something she would do that would make the analyst stay away and something that the analyst would see—her ugliness. Then she said that her mother had the power to make her feel something like powerless: "I'll do something to alienate you."

The analyst said, "My leaving makes you feel just as powerless. Also you seem to have the fantasy that my leaving is related to something negative about you." Mrs. A ended the session by saying, "My anger and my hurt stain you, and you'll take that and you will be gone more. I'm frightened that you'll use my feelings against me."

In this session we see the emergence of material that has not been recalled previously: that is, the desire to kill the mother and replace her. This is directly analogous to the typical paradigm of the male; kill the rival off to replace him. Yet this material appeared only after many years of analytic work and interpretation of defense. It presented a picture very different from the inhibited woman who came into analysis. Even here, however, and this is our point, the competitive urge was intermingled with much anxiety about loss of the mother and the mother's love. The murderous rage was attached to fears of loss of nurturance and comfort from the mother. The patient almost undoes her anger as she expresses it, as illustrated by her feeling that she has no right to it. Clearly the material is triadic and competitive. The patient's assertion that she is younger and prettier than the mother/analyst is the answer to the wicked queen's question to the mirror in "Snow White"—*she* is the fairest of them all. The desires to have the man/father, to be pregnant and have a big stomach like the mother, and to be the favorite chosen one are evident.

But the patient also remembers her fear that she might be able to get what she wanted, that is, get rid of the mother/analyst. The warning, "be careful what you wish for, you might get it," is a common message in fairy tales. The expectation and fear of punishment should her competitive wishes be gratified shows her anticipation of the boomerang effect of such death wishes. Ugliness, instead of prettiness, she fears, will be the legacy of her murderous rage, and ultimately she will lose her mother. However, the analytic work continued its freeing influence, and the following session dealt with ambivalent transference feelings toward the analyst—love, admiration, and a desire for closeness alternating with derogation of the analyst's femininity and envy of her relationship with her husband. For example, the patient said, "It should be me going on vacation with your husband, not you. Why you? I'm younger and prettier."

Case 4: The Murderous Joke

Sometimes the rivalry can be more easily expressed by way of a joke. One patient reported to her male analyst that as she was driving to her session, she saw his wife crossing the street. The patient asked, "Doesn't she know that a yellow Honda could easily run her down?" Because much work in the analysis had been completed, the intense death wish towards the analyst's wife could be expressed, although defensively protected through the mechanism of humor.

Discussion and Conclusion

The above case material demonstrates how fears of the loss of mother and her love come to the fore for girls in the context of triangular erotic conflicts. We argue that this occurs not because the little girl has yet to resolve "pre-Oedipal" conflicts, and not, as psychoanalytic theory would have had it, because she has no penis and is therefore not motivated by castration anxiety. Separation from the mother and the threat of abandonment are central in the girl's triangular situation. The loss of mother is a major "Oedipal" or Persephonal punishment for the little girl. These dynamics are an important part of the period of triangulation, inherent in it, and not simply a carryover from earlier developmental phases. It is highly dangerous for a little girl to acknowledge and express her sexual wishes toward her father. She wants to be her father's chosen love and to outdo and replace her mother. Yet she needs to remain bonded to her caretaker and identified with her as a source of self-esteem. Homoerotic impulses, which also become highly charged in this phase, bring with them fears of aggression: anger at the mother for preferring the father or brothers, and angry jealousy toward rivals for mother's favors.

The more tenuous the mother/daughter relationship, the more difficult it may be for a girl to tolerate her own aggressiveness. For a little boy, the destruction and reanimation of his Oedipal rival is repeatedly expressed in active aggressive play. For a little girl, a more careful route must be traversed. Murderous aggression and rivalry must be denied or repressed. Thus, inhibition of a subjective sense of themselves as aggressive agents becomes a pervasive defense for women and girls (Hoffman, 1999).

Aggression, like sexuality, is an integral part of the triangular period. We challenge the view that it is disappointment with the mother for not providing a penis that propels the girl into the triangular period. We do not see disappointment or anger as the main motivating factors for developmental progression either into or out of the triangular situation; in fact, in coping with the conflicts of that stage, little girls may give up their subjective sense of agency over aggression and sexuality in order to preserve their relationship with their mothers. Unless the analyst is sensitive to the import of analyzing women's defenses against aggression, particularly the sense of themselves as aggressive agents, an analysis can be stymied. On the other hand, a focus on how female patients inhibit their unconscious competitive and aggressive wishes clinically within the psychoanalytic situation can lead to improved understanding and mastery of triangular conflicts.

Notes

1. We have not addressed the complex questions involved in psychoanalytic definitions of aggression. Parens (1980) has explicated different aspects of aggression: self-preservation, mastery, reactions of rage to displeasure, and destructive sadism.

2. An exception is in the story of Electra, taken by some as the female parallel to Oedipus. Electra is enraged at her mother, who has betrayed her father and had him killed. Electra does not carry out the murder and revenge but she prevails upon her brother Orestes to do the deed. Bernstein (1993) interpreted the rage and aggression

in the Electra drama as a reaction to mother's preference for a man ("negative Oedipal"). In Sophocles' and Euripides' versions of the story, Electra is masochistic, helpless, and envious and renounces sexuality.

3. Freud himself downplayed any rivalrous aggression felt by the girl toward her mother. For example, in 1931 he wrote the rivalry with the father in the female negative Oedipus complex is not very strong and is not in any way symmetrical with the boy's Oedipal rivalry accompanying his desire to possess his mother.

4. Following Ogden, Wilkinson (1993) described how the girl must renegotiate her loyalty to her internal, pre-Oedipal mother, while she begins to identify with the sexuality the external, Oedipal mother shares with her Oedipal father.

CHAPTER EIGHT

~

Superego and Triadic Guilt

The lady doth protest too much, methinks.

(Shakespeare, *Hamlet*, 3.3.239)

The Oedipus myth is a story of crime and punishment. The crimes are incest and patricide; the punishment is blinding, a symbolic castration. Thus, the Oedipus myth highlights a central dynamic of male psychology—feared castration as punishment for incestuous wishes toward the mother—and gives it a central place in the development of the superego in traditional psychoanalytic theory.

Our proposal of the Persephone story as a paradigm of the female triadic situation has been criticized because it lacks this clear connection between crime and punishment, so apparent in the Oedipus story. Is this true? And if so, what does it mean for the development of the female superego?

What are the crime and punishment in the Persephone myth? Is Persephone's crime straying from her mother's side, which leaves her vulnerable to sexual abduction? Is her crime joining in an incestuous union with her uncle Hades? Is her punishment the loss of the continuous relationship with her mother?

Oedipus uses the defenses of disavowal and denial against the recognition of the forbidden incestuous impulses in which he engaged. He remains consciously unaware of committing any crime. He himself is searching for the criminal, outside himself, who has caused the famine to ravish his land. He has no conscious notion that this criminal is himself.

For Persephone also, the incestuous act, rape or sex with her uncle Hades, is actualized. As we have suggested, her eating the seed or seeds of the pomegranate also symbolically represent the sexual act. We interpret the text to mean that Persephone utilizes the defenses of externalization and abdication of agency in order to escape from acknowledging her sexual desires and guilt for independence from her mother. Oedipus says: "I did not know I did anything wrong." Persephone says: "Hades made me do it; I would never on my own volition compete with mother or try to win the man. Do you think I have pleasure eating these seeds? This was not my desire. I was tricked, or I was forced." Out of guilt and fear, she denies her erotic and rivalrous impulses in order to maintain a close relationship with her mother. To keep a sense of goodness and safety she is willing to give up a volitional aspect of the self. This set of defenses that are directed against guilt is frequently found in the clinical work with females.[1]

In psychoanalytic theory, the superego/conscience is the mediator of guilt and morality. As we described in chapter 2, Freud linked superego structure to the resolution of the Oedipal complex. This linkage, in our opinion, has led to erroneous notions about female development in general and female superego in particular.

In this chapter we will review the thinking about morality in women and show why we conclude 1) that superego development for both males and females is not in fact determined by castration anxiety and its vicissitudes, and 2) that the superegos of females do not differ from those of males in such ways as early psychoanalytic theory posited.

Freud's Theories of the Female Superego

Freud concluded that what is ethically normal for women is different from what is ethically normal for men. The boy in the triangular period, motivated by the fear of castration, renounces his sexual desires for the mother. Here castration may be seen as retaliation for the boy's rivalry with the father. According to Freud, the girl, having no penis, does not fear castration and therefore possesses no strong motivation for giving up sexual strivings. Freud theorized that the female remains in the Oedipus phase far longer than the boy and resolves it more gradually, if at all. A woman's superego, he said,

is never so inexorable, so impersonal, so independent of its emotional origins as we require of it in men . . . [in] that they show less sense of justice than men; that they are less ready to submit to the great exigencies of life, that they are more often influenced in their judgments by feelings of affection or hostility—

all these would be amply accounted for by the modification in the formation of their super-ego which we have inferred above. We must not allow ourselves to be deflected from conclusions by the denial of the feminists, who are anxious to force us to regard the two sexes as completely equal in position and worth (1925, pp. 257–258).

Freud theorized that renunciation is necessary to the process of identification, which, he postulated, forms the superego; the girl having nothing to lose (no penis) therefore lacks the impetus for the renunciation. What Freud did not acknowledge was that the girl does have something very valuable to lose—mother, love of mother, and her own valued genitals. His conclusion was that girls end up with weak superegos. Many of these notions about women were preconceived, and theory about the superego was made to fit them. Harold Blum (1976) summarized these problems in Freud's arguments: "Freud's discoveries so important for the liberation of women and men from the tyranny of unconscious forces co-existed with other of his ideas which paradoxically outlined a masochistic and incomplete feminine personality. Those particular propositions of a diminished and deficient female psyche will bear fresh scrutiny. The female was then viewed as having a diminished and constrained libido, a weaker and masochistic sexual constitution, an ego with incapacity to sublimate and a tendency toward early arrest and rigidity, a relatively defective superego, and incomplete Oedipal and post-Oedipal development" (p. 169).

Subsequent Theories of the Female Superego

Since then, many psychoanalysts have countered Freud's arguments. Karen Horney (1926) argued that girls also have their own genital anxieties and therefore their own reasons for guilt and conflict. She described female fears of vaginal injury from the father's large penis. Similarly, Marie Bonaparte (1935) articulated penetration anxiety.

Following Freud in emphasizing the centrality of castration, Greenacre (1952) reversed Freud's conclusions. She found that women had a "fund of guilt" related to masturbation, which they fantasized had caused their "castration." As a result, girls struggle more intensely against their sexuality (Jacobson, 1965). As evidence for this point, many analysts report that female patients do not as readily talk about their sexual fantasies and masturbation as do male patients.

In well-known and influential psychological research, Lawrence Kohlberg (1973) postulated a six-stage line of moral development. He devised scales to measure position on various dimensions of morality, and on which females scored consistently lower than males. The content of these scales were based on notions similar to those conceptualized by Freud in that they utilized a masculine set of values to determine what was moral. Kohlberg defined the highest stages of major development as deriving from abstract understandings of human rights valuing the individual. A highly moral man, according to Kohlberg, identifies morality with abstract laws (such as the Ten Commandments). A woman, who would score lower on Kohlberg's scale, however, might have a more relativistic view, based on a sense of responsibility to others. Like Freud, Kohlberg has been criticized for using measures based on preconceived gender-biased notions of morality, so that his conclusion that females have a lower level of moral development than males was predictable. For example, Carol Gilligan (1982) discussed this issue at some length. Her research shows that in general females place more value on relatedness, and males on autonomy (Chodorow, 1978). Many others (Applegarth, 1976; Blum, 1976; Gilligan, 1982; Bernstein, 1993) have also challenged these scales.

From our point of view, another problem with such social research is that the data is based on conscious material; there is apparently no recognition of the notion that guilt can be unconscious. Psychoanalysts know that unconscious guilt provides strong motivation for many behaviors, particularly self-sabotaging, etc.

Martin Silverman (1982) speculated on some of observed gendered differences in superego in the latency or school-age period. "The superego development of girls and of boys differs in various ways because of developmental differences affecting control of aggressive and libidinal impulses, in the form and contents of the Oedipus complex, and the maintenance of narcissistic balance and self-esteem" (p. 217). These differences are played out later, he observed, as the female superego of school-aged girls is not as rigid, harsh, and imperious as that of boys of that age and is more effective in promoting impulse control. Like many other observers, he noted that girls are "more roundabout in their channels of attainment of satisfaction" (p. 220).

Adrienne Applegarth (1985) proposed several cogent arguments countering Freud's views of female superego development. She demonstrated in clinical material that both boys and girls may see the mother, as well as the father, as castrator. Therefore, she argued, there is an analogy between male and female superego development, and the superegos of both sexes are established by the internalization of the values of both parents. Applegarth delineated the unconscious complexities that, from a psychoanalytic vantage point, make assessment of superego strength so difficult. The equation of superego strength with the amount of conscious guilt present in any individual is questionable. In-depth clinical material enhances and sharpens such assessments.

One frequent psychoanalytic argument differentiating male and female superego is based on the belief that the strength of the superego is derived from the aggressive drives. If males do indeed have stronger aggressive drives than females, Applegarth conceded that there might be grounds for the argument that says there are resulting differences in the superego strength between men and women. However, the assumption of stronger aggressive drives can be questioned. While we think that the handling of aggression by males and females may differ, as we outlined in chapter 7, we are doubtful that such differences in defensive style contribute to differences in superego structure. We hear in these arguments echoes of the older notion (Jacobson 1965) that the superego is paternal and the ego ideal maternal, or the Lacanian notion that the father hands down the law. Phyllis and Robert Tyson (1990), in contrast, stressed the common elements in superego function and development in female and males in their identification with *both* parents.

Doris Bernstein (1993) has defined three attributes of the superego—strength, structure, and contents—and argues that it is not the strength of the superego that differentiates males and females, but its *contents*. This refers to the specific individual values held by an individual, exactly what is or is not allowed or prohibited. Many women, for instance, may value self-sacrifice in the name of their children and feel guilty for being "selfish"; many men would not allow themselves to inform on a comrade.[2] *Strength* refers to how efficiently the contents are regulated, and it is measured by how powerfully the contents are enforced. One individual may feel very guilty about cheating; another may let herself fib a little on income tax. *Structure* refers to the organization and inter-organization of the contents; which contents are related to others and their relative strengths.

Bernstein saw sources for strength of superego for females other than castration anxiety. The first was fear of and resurrected identifications with an omnipotent, early mother. These images threaten autonomy and individuation for the girl. Such images are re-evoked for the boy as well as for the girl, but the boy disidentifies with the image of the mother and therefore autonomy and individuation are reinforced. We find it difficult to follow and to agree with this reasoning, as a "disidentification" certainly does not rid one of unconscious ghosts. Moreover, this view gives a strongly regressive cast to the female psyche.

A second source of strength of female superego, Bernstein suggests, lies in the confusion of and diffusion between genitality and anality in girls. (See Salome, 1915; Richards, 1992.) All prohibitions of the anal phase become confused with or merge with genital impulses. Along these lines, Judith Kestenberg (1968), Edith Jacobson[3] (1965), and Phyllis Greenacre (1952) all observe that little girls seem to be cleaner and neater than boys, hence, they think, more controlled by guilt over anality. We do not necessarily agree that neatness is a sign of guilt, but rather it may signify compliance or identification with mother's ideals, for example.

The third source does come from castration anxiety, which Bernstein defines as the generalized sense of bodily harm for females—the "female genital anxieties," which she articulates in some detail (1993)—fears of access, penetration, and diffusivity.

In Bernstein's view, the *organization* or *structure* of contents is far more fixed and less flexible in men than in women. While this may be, we question whether there is enough evidence to make this claim. She used cultural stereotypes to bolster her argument—relying as an example on the major in the classic film *Bridge Over the River Kwai,* who too rigidly held to his standards, which meant he had his men build a sturdy bridge for the enemy. Bernstein also argued that superego *contents* are different for males and females and that content affects structure, thus women are more flexible than men. In countering Freud's theories, Bernstein repeated his mistakes, but in the reverse, claiming women's superegos are superior to men's.

Gilligan (1982), like Bernstein, also stressed the differences in the contents of male and female superegos. That is to say, women do not have weaker superegos, but rather may be concerned with different moral issues. The superego may fiercely demand that the female be pliant, pleasing, and non-aggressive, which may give the false appearance of weakness.

Gilligan also makes another point about the possible gendered differences in superego. She notes the developmental need to resolve ambivalence about the idealized object of the same sex, which arises in early childhood when cognitive skills are still immature. Thus, interferences in gender identity and superego development can arise. She believes that separation from the same-sexed parent is more confusing than from the opposite-sexed parent, and so the little girl's task is more difficult. We are not convinced by either clinical data or research that there are differences in resolution of ambivalence that are gender-based, which would lead to these proposed disadvantages in development for females. We acknowledge that differences in separating from a same-sexed versus different-sexed object may well lead to *differences* in development, but not necessarily more *difficulties.*

Sheila Hafter Gray (1996) offered a gender-neutral theory of the development of superego. She argued against the idea that a female's acceptance of "castration" relates in any way to the resolution of the Oedipal phase. She linked superego function to the development of healthy narcissism. In underscoring primary femininity, she asserted that there are "specific anxieties about genital injury in connection with her Oedipal wishes . . . which seem to operate to resolve the Oedipus Complex" (p. 27). Gray proposed a link, which she did not explicate, between faulty resolution of the Oedipal complex and inhibitions of intellectual achievement. Gray stated that psychoanalytic work with women on these issues is often ineffectual, but placed the major blame not on psychoanalytic theory but on a phallocentric culture. We would put this differently: We find it impossible to separate Freud's original theory from its cultural influences at the time (as it is impossible to separate *any* theory from its social context). Gray made some important points, but she, like others, was hampered by an adherence to older theory while making cogent arguments against it.

Thus, if control over drives, various manifestations of morality, and characterological conscientiousness are considered indicators of superego development, there is no evidence that women have *defective* superegos as was argued by early analysts.

Subsequent General Theories about Superego Development

Since Freud's original formulations, many modifications of the concept have been postulated. In reviewing the literature about the timing of superego formation, we find that many analytic theorists distinguish sharply between "pre-Oedipal" and "post-Oedipal" superego manifestations. At the time of the so-called Oedipal resolution, Freud thought, the superego emerges as a relatively new and autonomous structure, an internal regulator of behavior that largely replaces parental authority. He called earlier manifestations and processes of internalization "precursors" of the superego (Freud, 1940). Anna Freud (1936) and Parens (1980) also described such early "pre-Oedipal" superego components.

In contrast to this view of a structure which emerges from "pre-Oedipal" precursors, more contemporary psychoanalysts have proposed a more gradual process. An important spokesperson for this view is Robert Gilman (1982), who considers the superego, like the ego, to be a set of functions rather than a rigid structure. His developmental line is not genderized. He believed that beginning very early in childhood children make a stepwise process of multiple identifications that ultimately comprise the superego. Heinz Kohut (1971) supported a similar stepwise, gradual development of superego, as do Tyson and Tyson (1990). However, Gilman emphasized that the "Oedipal" period is significant in the creation of complexity and *enhancement* of the superego. He argued against an isomorphic relationship between "Oedipal" resolution and superego formation. According to Gilman, for example, many people with mature and fully developed superegos nevertheless manifest much Oedipal conflict. He also found that some patients whose main psychic organization is pre-Oedipal nevertheless manifest strong internal superego synthesis. He promoted the idea that earlier pre-Oedipal superego manifestations are actual superego formations, *not* precursors. He argued that if these phenomena are described as precursors they must be described as functions of the ego. Similarly, Renee Spitz (1958) referred to early superego components that are instinct-restraining forces. We are persuaded by Gilman's arguments, and find that their conclusions fit with our clinical experience.

Gilman, like Roy Schafer (1960), stressed the importance of identification with a comforting and nurturing parent, as opposed to identification with a feared aggressor, in the development of strong superegos and a mature personality. This idea, with which we concur, does away with the supposed differences between the superegos of males and females postulated in early theory. The desire to be liked and to be loved by a nurturing and loved parent is a strong motivation for superego development. This is true for both boys and girls.

The validity of the concept of the superego itself has been questioned in contemporary psychoanalytic thinking. (See *Psychoanalytic Inquiry*, 2004.) Dirk Fabricius (2004), for example, offers other ways to describe the phenomena encompassed by the older concept, such as the "inner normative system." Melvin Lansky (2004) deviates from the structural model in separating superego from castration conflicts, but nevertheless finds usefulness in a revised concept of the superego. He and Leon Wurmser (2004) strongly advocate the pragmatic value of keeping the term, which encompasses both the superego and ego ideal. For them, the superego manifests itself by the dynamics of shame and guilt and includes moral and ethical choices.

Joseph Lichtenberg (2004), like Gilman before him, presents evidence that the development of morality is a gradual process that entails continual additions and revisions of values and standards throughout infancy, childhood, and adulthood. He compares his doubts about the superego with those of Kohut (1971), who did not question the existence, timing, or origin of the superego but did question the emphasis on guilt in the problems of humanity. With the concept of tragic man, Kohut emphasized man's struggles with emptiness, shame, and humiliation over his struggles with guilt.

Jack and Kerry Kelly Novick (2004) amended and expanded the concept of the superego. They have proposed two systems of self regulation, an open and a closed system, which are related to superego functioning. In their model of narcissism, they contrast the "closed" system, which is unrealistic, sado-masochistic, and omnipotent, with the "open" system, which is competent, loving, and reality attuned. These two systems, representing alternative choices of conflict resolution and self regulation, are available throughout development. Connected to the closed system is a tyrannical and sadistic super-ego reflecting the conviction that the child is not external or powerful enough to control imperious wishes and demands. A cycle of harshness and suffering results in masochism, as the harshness of the superego is turned on the self.

The Novicks hold to the idea that conflict over incestuous wishes is encoded in the superego. The fate of incestuous wishes active in the triangular period can be manifested in different kinds of superegos. If the environment is collusive, seductive, or overstimulating, incestuous wishes may become omnipotent beliefs. Thus the threat of incest becomes incorporated into an omnipotent belief system and closed superego system. On the other hand, with a more benign environment, the child can differentiate wishes from realistic possibilities and develop an open superego system. The Novicks' theories are unique and especially clear. They are among the few who have detailed superego development in the triadic phase and integrated it with narcissistic issues.

James Hansell (2000) differentiates the effective superego and the "melancholic superego" based on the child's ability to internalize completely the caretaking functions of the parents. From a Kleinian perspective, James Grotstein (2004) describes two superego structures based on Kleinian ideas: the first develops from the paranoid schizoid position and the second from the depressive position. The first is formed from projective identifications. This earlier structure is related to "the law of the mother" and mediates greed, envy, and hatred. The second structure relates to the "law of the father" and mediates exhibition and competition. Similarly, Freud's patriarchal conception of the superego is based on the Oedipus complex. Grotstein then offers a more mythical origin of the superego—a composite entity comprising a trinity representing the father, mother, and child. We find that this thinking is unwarrantedly genderized; similarly, we do not agree with the earlier formulations that the ego ideal is maternal and the superego paternal.

Shame and the Ego Ideal

Hans Loewald (1962) differentiated the ego ideal from the superego along lines of narcissism. For Loewald the superego is the agency of inner rewards and punishments in respect to which the ego experiences contentment or guilt. It represents the internalized parental authorities, tied to the resolution of the Oedipal phase but modifiable throughout development. The ego ideal, an earlier structure, is a representation of a fantasy of recapturing the "original primary narcissistic omnipotent perfection of the child by a primitive identification with the omnipotent parental figures" (p. 264).

Jacobson (1965) described an earlier nucleus of the ego ideal in the girl than in the boy, which, although vulnerable to regression, could lead to the eventual constitution of a mature ego ideal and autonomous superego. Blum (1976) argued that the female ego ideal has a maternal core in origin and function, including valued representations of all aspects of the mother as well as selected paternal identifications. His thinking is in line with contemporary psychoanalytic theorists who suggest that multiple identifications—masculine and feminine—make up the ego ideal (Elise, 1997; Young-Bruehl, 2003; Harris, 2005). We would add that the idea that the "soft ego ideal" is maternal and that the "strong superego" is paternal sets up a spurious dichotomy.

The affect of shame has been linked more closely to the ego ideal rather than the superego. Many writers have attempted to distinguish shame from guilt, phenomenologically, developmentally, and functionally. The first systematic review of the two emotions was by Gerhart Piers and Milton Singer (1953). They believed that shame occurs when one fails to live up to one's ego ideal. Exposure, an aspect of shame, is a process "wherein one's failure is observed from the point of view of the internalized parental imago." They distinguished these shame experiences from guilt, which occurs when a boundary or rule set by the superego is transgressed.

Many others have conceptualized shame within the framework of narcissism and the self (Jacobson, 1965; Kohut, 1971; H. B. Lewis, 1971; O'Leary and Wright, 1986; Gilman, 1990). In summary, shame, in contrast to guilt, is more outer-directed, related to some perceived deficiency in the self, with an accompanying sense of being observed.

Gilman (1990) articulated the role of shame in the Oedipal period, alongside guilt, as a source of unpleasure and a signal affect. He reported a case in which the patient's shameful masturbation fantasies of being humiliated were related to incestuous and primal scene fantasies. Ana-Maria Rizzuto (1991) also wrote about the crucial connection between unconscious Oedipal fantasy and narcissistic humiliation and shame.

We see shame as an important aspect of triangular dynamics for both genders. The triadic phase inevitably produces feelings of rejection in not being chosen by either or both parents. Typically, the child feels little, deficient, squelched by a feeling of not winning the competition for the loved parent. Both little boys and little girls feel smaller and less powerful than their parents. These contents are frequently organized at this phase around perceived genital and other bodily deficiencies.

Irene Matthis (1981) pointed to the central importance Freud gave the feeling of shame to the psychology of women with his emphasis on the sense of shameful deficiency of their genitals. Matthis argued that a patriarchal society contributes to more vulnerable feelings of narcissistic shame in females. "The convention in our society, which Freud clarified, tells us that the boy is the complete person and the girl the incomplete one. . . . However, lack of something that you are supposed to have or know of but can never have or know, and which makes you have a defect, can only lead to constant shame, followed by different solutions constructed in order to hide or defend against it" (pp. 50–51).

Matthis presented an example of a little girl proudly exhibiting her "bottom" to the therapist as a natural and joyful act, which was immediately met with a rebuke from her mother. Here a sense of shame and fear of rejection is likely to take over the girl's initial pleasure in her body. We will return to the subject of female exhibitionism in chapter 9.

Our view is that there are no differences between males and females in the intensity or frequency of fears of humiliation. What we do find is that the *contents* of the fantasies and the perceived sources of the shame may differ according to gender, family context, and society.

Conclusions from the Review of the Literature

From this very brief review we offer the following points: 1) We argue that the development and structure of the superego cannot be differentiated by gender. In particular there is no supportive data, clinical or research-based, for the gender-biased notion that females do not have strong identifications or superegos. 2) In fact, clinical data relevant to superego development have not been sufficiently utilized in theorizing about the superego. 3) We do agree that the superego contents and specific identifications may be different between the genders. 4) The presence of a penis and castration anxiety does not determine superego formation. *Superego development and identifications do not necessarily rest on castration or genital anxieties of any type.* 5) In psychoanalytic discussions of the superego, it is important to differentiate between conscious and unconscious aspects of guilt. This differentiation is often missing entirely in attempts to "measure" superego strength and functioning. 6) We disagree with the traditional sharp psychoanalytic distinction between pre-Oedipal and post-Oedipal functions and the view of the superego as "heir to the Oedipus complex." 7) We think that superego development is not indelibly forged in the crucible of the triangular or "Oedipal" phase, but that important additions occur at this time.

Finally, we believe that all these arguments miss an important point. We question whether there is, ever, for either gender, "resolution" of the Oedipal or triangular phase.

Clinical Examples

To illustrate the clinically based rationale for our thinking, we present the following clinical examples related to female triadic phase conflicts and superego.

Adolescent Behavior

One example of what we feel is more uniquely female triadic superego function can be seen and has been often documented in the behavior of middle school and high school girls and described in the previous chapter. While bullying, punching, and other forms of overt aggression are the preferred outlets for boys in the school yard, girls often resort to cattiness, backbiting, secretiveness, and social exclusion to express their aggression and competitiveness. Girls are keenly aware of both "not wanting to hurt someone's feelings" and its opposite, the desire to exclude the other, as shown in some of the clinical material above. This need to exclude or hurt the other leads to the "bad girl" behavior that has attracted so much attention in the media recently. Such sadistic "relational aggression," as it has been dubbed, can become a cause for guilt in girls.

Case 1: A Dream of Abduction

A married woman in her twenties is trying to get pregnant. She has been struggling with a guilt-filled attraction to a married man who has a child. Recently they worked late and had a drink together. The patient is also anticipating an upcoming separation from the analyst. The material during this period is filled with guilt and self-recriminations and fears of punishment—she is afraid that she will not be able to get pregnant. Her guilt-ridden hostility to the analyst is externalized, and she fears that the analyst does not like her and will leave her.

We will report in detail a session two years into the analysis:

The patient begins, "Yesterday I was talking about my mother and men. And one particular man . . . I was certain they had never had an affair. But last night I had a dream in which my mother said she had intercourse four times with this man when she was twenty-seven. I was shocked. I said to her, 'I thought you never had done that.' She replied, 'I never said that. Your dad and I had an open marriage.'"

At this point, Mrs. A asks the analyst, "Is this true? I had never known this . . . I can't think of this. I always thought my mother was faithful. I remember when I was four years old, little and impressionable, relying on my parents for everything, guidance. I'm going to be twenty-seven next month.

In the dream we are intertwined. . . . I don't know where my mother ends and where I begin."

Statements like this can be read, and often are, as evidence of a permeable self-object boundary, a symbiotic, or pre-Oedipal manifestation. But patients with major problems of self and object boundaries in an analysis confuse their thoughts with the other, display a sense of fragmentation, and so forth. Mrs. A, however, seemed to hold a whole sense of herself. She displayed no other consistent signs of fears of merger or loose self/other boundaries. This statement can be interpreted as an unconscious wish to be her mother. She justifies her own guilt-ridden wishes to have an affair by projecting them onto her mother in this dream.

"It makes me scared. I don't want to be like my mother, but we are similar. I think I am like her maybe, to some degree. I like to deny I am anything like her."

Consciously Mrs. A insists that she does not want to be like her mother—a common cry of female patients, which we often understand as "she protesteth too much." In fact, Mrs. A battles against the intense unconscious desire to *be* her mother and take her place. Beneath the disavowal, we see a clear wish to take over her "mother's domain"—the sexual world. The theme here is an unconscious wish to be her mother and/or destroy her, and so have her father for herself.

The patient continues in this vein, "I have her beliefs. You can't trust anybody. Being a woman, you do not deserve too much. You can't expect your husband to be faithful, because you do not deserve it. If my mother really said what she said in the dream, though, I would feel betrayed." We see this feeling of betrayal as twofold—the mother's having an affair and thus loving someone else (a "negative Oedipal"/Persephonal experience) and a tainting of the ideals and standards set down by the mother who always told her to "do the right thing."

Mrs. A then remembers another dream in which her mother is abducted. There is a tape of the mother's voice on a phone. Her associations lead to the pictures of abducted children that used to appear on the milk cartons when she was a child. She was always afraid she'd be taken away to a strange place with no way to reach anyone or to be reached—held captive, tortured, sexually molested, or murdered. She was always afraid that if she didn't do the right thing this would really happen to her. To manage her fears, she would tell herself that if she were good and did the right thing nothing would happen to her.

Her use of magical thinking here is apparent. The manifest content of this second dream represents a reversal of the Persephone story: It is the mother, not the daughter, who is abducted. The patient immediately undoes the reversal with the revival of her childhood fears of punishment, which comes up in the context of her sexual interest in a married man and her female analyst's leaving. She fears that such incestuous desires will alienate the mother/analyst and cause desertion.

The patient goes on. She was always scared that people would leave and that she would never see them again. "What if it were my father who was abducted and I would never see him again?" she muses now. Here perhaps is the other side of the coin, the so-called "negative Oedipal" feelings of wishing her father would disappear so she could have her mother to herself.

"It all would be my fault. I could have prevented it if I had done something different. Panic. I'll never see her again. And the people who would torture her are people who don't care anything about you. They'd do mean things, just to be mean. And there was nothing you could do to make this better." (The mean torturer is also a self-representation.)

In a seeming change of subject, Mrs. A then goes on to talk about how she experienced meanness with her girlfriends. One summer when she was twelve she thought a group of girls were her friends. But, "they didn't make their intentions clear. They simply wanted to hurt me. They plotted behind my back. They all went to the movies together and they left me behind."

In order to appease her guilt, her own anger and rivalry are directed outward—meanness resides in *other* females. She will be left.

She comes back to the present—"I'm so upset about betraying my husband. Being an awful person. Am I as bad as I think I am? Part of me loathes myself. I think nothing bad would happen if I were better. I believe that I truly make things happen, or that things happened in the past, because I wasn't good enough."

Her association to the telephone in the dream is that she is feeling guilty about a call from the man to whom she is attracted. Realistically they didn't talk about anything except business. She really wants to deny or suppress the awareness that anything has occurred. She is afraid that something horrible, she feels, would happen as a result of the situation . . . a fear of betrayal. Then she talked about becoming "paranoid" at times, feeling that people are against her at work.

"Maybe I am difficult to deal with, but if I'm a strong person I can't be liked by everyone. If I were a soft-spoken woman I wouldn't get advanced anywhere. I'm sure I could tone down a little." (Her ambition and competitiveness frighten her.) "There's always room for improvement. Part of me thinks that what the boss is saying is garbage; the other part is scared." Her boss's evaluation of her had included a critical statement about her strong-mindedness. Her reaction to this is similar to the way she feels towards her mother—angry as well as castigated. She struggles with how to value or discard their criticisms. Under the aegis of superego prohibitions, she fears her ambitiousness. Her wish to be the mother and be the "boss" creates much conflict.

Her thoughts return to having been deliberately betrayed by the mean girls. "They dump you, or want to, but don't make their intentions clear. They plotted behind my back."

The analyst took up the transference anxieties about the coming separation—how the patient thought of the analyst as a woman who was friendly but also someone who did not make her intentions clear, and now is dumping her, plotting behind her back; and how the patient thought that it was her fault that the analyst was leaving—even though she knew that was not the reality.

"Maybe that's because I don't deserve to have good things anyway. Maybe you don't think I'm good enough. I have weaknesses."

"In what way?"

"All that I tell you. Like what happened with this guy."

"It sounds as though you feel that I would disapprove of anything relating to your sexual interests and attractions."

"Yeah. I feel so rotten. I don't know why you wouldn't feel the same. I just know that if my husband knew what happened he would divorce me. He's very conservative. And could never forgive me. It's the same feeling like in the dream. I'm going to lose my dad. He'll fall in love with a different woman. Always a fear. My mother said that men fall in love with different women, that they grow tired of a woman, and then they want someone who is younger. . . . I'm in my late twenties. I feel like soon I'll have my last good years."

Abduction of the father in this context reflects the threat that her father will be taken away by his love for another woman. The idea that men want someone younger is frightening to Mrs. A because she *is* the younger woman vis-à-vis her father. This idea both raises her hopes and frightens her (her mother might learn of her desires) and makes her feel even worse when she is not the chosen one.

The patient talks for a while about being excluded at a party; then she returns to her feelings about her father.

"In the end, though, it was my mom who he wanted to go out with every Saturday night." The analyst asked her how she felt about that, when she had imagined herself to be the favored one—even more than her mother. The patient answered that her feelings were very hurt. She did not like the feeling of being left out, of not being part of it. Death and destructive wishes towards her mother, now toward the narcissistically wounding and abandoning analyst, form the basis for this hurt and the wish to control.

The next day Mrs. A began by asking, "Should I tell you this?" and then went on to talk about secrets in the family and different ways she felt left out—"primal scene" themes. The initial question, very characteristic of her at this time of the analysis, implies a need for permission to speak, or perhaps a wish to be forced to speak, and thus abdicate responsibility for the guilt-laden wishes that were struggling to be expressed; that is, she begins looking for ways around a superego prohibition against her material.

Abduction and rape fantasies (which include white slavery, being forced into sex, taken into a different world) are common in women. These illustrate the externalization of responsibility and the use of projection. The bad man, the stranger or strangers are disguised and displaced away from the real object of sexual desire, who is the man near at hand, the father. In Mrs. A's dream, the mother is taken away, representing her wish to rid herself of her mother as well as her fear that the wish might come true. Immediately, however, the fantasy changes—now it is the patient herself who is frightened of being taken away, showing us the wish, its accompanying fear, and the fantasized punishment. With it appears a typical fantasy, a rape fantasy about being kidnapped and forced into a strange world that is consciously feared but unconsciously longed for—the fate of Persephone. In this way the patient defends against acknowledging agency over her own sexual desire.

According to Blum (1976) "fantasies of rape, of being masochistically abused while being excited, of sexual enslavement and surrender with mounting excitement are not uncommon in females' conscious erotic daydreams. Furthermore, the superego of the female adolescent also contributes to these fantasies which simultaneously represent sexual prohibition and punishment for forbidden temptation. Rape fantasies evade guilt over instinctual wishes. Some of these conscious fantasies are derivatives of infantile beating fantasies" (p. 167).

In this case there is also evidence of a "negative Oedipal" or "negative Persephonal" transference. When the predominant object of the girl's erotic desire is the mother (the "negative Oedipal"), the superego is no less active or intense. The girl fears the loss of her mother's nurturance, even though a homoerotic choice may carry hidden wishes to keep her close to mother.

Case 2: Punishment for Sexual Pleasures

Mrs. B began analysis as a depressed, phobic, sexually inhibited woman. She had spent years in a joyless and sexless marriage and had recently had a hysterectomy. She came from a strictly religious home. Her father, a judge, was stern and strict. She was kept under close control, while her two elder brothers were allowed more privileges. All the children were reminded frequently of the family's responsibility to keep up appearances in the community. In keeping with the family tradition, Mrs. B married a law student immediately after college—apparently an "Oedipal"/Persephonal choice.

She has an important screen-memory from the age of three, of dressing up with delight in her mother's clothes and painting herself with her makeup. When she paraded in front of her strict and religious father, however, he demanded that she take off her finery and intoned: "No daughter of mine will be a slut!" She was devastated.

Her mother was more permissive but apparently envious of and competitive with her pretty daughter. In her adolescence, struggling to separate from her mother, Mrs. B alternated between anxious reliance on her mother for guidance and slightly rebellious behavior, such as flirting with older boys. She was confused by double messages she received from her mother, who at times encouraged her to stand out so as to attract males but at other times criticized her harshly for such behavior.

When Mrs. B was about thirteen, she had a nighttime ritual of slipping paper notes under her mother's pillow. On these notes she would write "confessions" containing little secrets. As she looked back, Mrs. B realized that these so-called secrets were totally innocuous. They were confessions of minor misdeeds, such as skipping a chore or being a little late. We understand them retrospectively as a defensive maneuver around her superego: That is, she would confess little sins in order to prompt an instant pardon from her mother. She did a plea bargain with her conscience by owning up to lesser conscious crimes instead of more serious unconscious ones, with her mother as judge. These nightly confessions to her mother were akin to the diary-keeping of young adolescent girls. In Mrs. B's case, however, she had not yet separated enough from her mother to keep her thoughts locked in a diary, totally secret from her.

After Mrs. B was married, her mother accompanied her once to the gynecologist's office, and announced, upon hearing of her sexual difficulties, that *she* could count on the fingers of one hand the number of times she did not have an orgasm.

In spite of some gynecological difficulties, Mrs. B was able to have two children who were the joy of her life.

Thus, two factors in the patient's history contributed to her anxieties about sexuality: the mother's confusing competitiveness and the father's condemning severity. Entering the mother's domain of sexuality was associated with danger for Mrs. B.

Shortly after she began treatment, Mrs. B began to talk about her sexual difficulties. As she felt bolder, she decided to face these more directly and to try to resume sexual relations with her husband. After a session in which she talked of her resolve, she called her husband at work to tell him what she was thinking. He dropped everything to rush home to have sex. The next day they had sex again. On the following day, with no explanation, her husband announced that he wanted a divorce. In the subsequent months we came to understand this as a devastating repetition of her childhood rejection by her father. This series of events appeared to be a serious setback for Mrs. B's progress.

Difficult years followed, during which she hid out at home and avoided social contacts outside of family and work. Early on she talked of her resentment toward the men in her life—her father and brothers and her husband—and of her jealousy of their power and freedom. She wallowed in her sense of inferiority to men and was quite willing, indeed eager, to talk about "penis envy." In the third year of analysis, however, as she began to understand and overcome her symptoms, she began to show some interest in changing her lonely, but safe, existence.

She came to one session bemoaning how frightened she was of entering the dating scene. She declared that she felt she was walking around with a scarlet letter "U" for "Uptight" on her chest. The analyst remarked that the scarlet letter was not "U," but "A" for "Adultery." This infuriated her—she must have perceived the analyst at that moment as a judgmental parent (We think her mother). But in subsequent sessions she began grappling with new revelations and new insights. She recounted, for the first time and with great difficulty, the tale of an adulterous affair she had had early in her marriage, over which she had long suffered in secret. Next, she began to talk about her daughter, who had been born sometime after the affair. This child had a minor birth defect. She knew in reality that the child was her husband's, but she recalled that at the time of the baby's birth she had harbored painful fantasies that the baby was the fruit of the affair.

Soon after this, Mrs. B reported that she had gone to a parent-teacher conference at her daughter's school and had been aware of feeling defensive and anxious. As she talked about this experience in the session, a stunning insight came to her. She realized that she felt that her daughter was the embodiment of her sin and that the child's deficit was her punishment, her scarlet letter. She broke down sobbing in an intense mix of guilt and pain. In subsequent sessions, she also came to see that she felt her longstanding, painful, and humiliating gynecological difficulties were also punishments for this sexual misdeed, as well as for the childhood ones of masturbation and dressing-up. She came to understand that she unconsciously felt that she had had to punish herself for the affair by cutting off her sexual passions forevermore. "*It would not have been so bad if I had not enjoyed it!*" she cried.

She summarized her growing understanding: "So underneath I'm not uptight, but interested?" She began to remember how she felt very pretty when she was younger. She loved being the center of men's interest. She confessed that she enjoyed the feeling of power that her sexual attractiveness—and her sexuality—gave her over men. She said, "I think I feel this anxiety about what I suspect I might be. I might be a *very sexual woman*." She went on to talk of her fears of "going hog wild" if she were to let her inhibitions go. Perhaps she would become promiscuous, a prostitute, turn to kinky sex.

Inhibition and a feeling of inferiority had served as defenses against her own sexuality, which frightened her by its intensity, its triadic, incestuous associations, and its anal threat of getting out of control. Experiences such as the time her father called her a slut laid the groundwork for this little-girl feeling that her sexual impulses were unacceptable and bad. While she felt inferior as a female and envious of her brothers, the "penis envy" covered over other, and presumably more basic, fears she had about the wildness and intensity of her female sexual desires. It also hid from awareness her sexual and incestuous passion.

After this, Mrs. B dreamed of a going around and around on a Ferris wheel in an amusement park she had enjoyed as a pubescent girl. Her associations led to ideas of long lost pleasures, which the analyst interpreted as buried sexual feelings that reflected a primary and positive "sense of femaleness," to borrow Elise's term (1997).[4]

The intense guilt that Mrs. B connected with triadic incestuous desires exacted a severe punishment. Motivating her fear of punishment was a fear of rejection from both her parents and castration, in the sense of loss of female fertility.

Case 3: Identification with a Masochistic Mother

Mrs. C, a childless woman in her late sixties, has been in treatment for a number of years. Currently the analyst and the patient have been working with material related to her masochism, which was manifested in her relationship with her wealthy and bullying husband, a physician. She felt angry and demeaned by him, yet compelled to submit to his financial control of her. Over the years of their marriage he had given her limited money so that he could control her expenditures. She had recently learned that he had arranged for her to have what the family lawyer called a "skimpy" income if he should predecease her, one that would not allow her to live in the style to which they were accustomed and could easily afford.

She and her analyst had previously come to understand certain important aspects of her unconscious identification with her mother, who was the hard-working and long-suffering partner of her gambler father. The father was not an abusive or mean man but was an embarrassment to the family. Finances had always been an issue in Mrs. C's youth, as there had never been an abundance of money available, and Mrs. C remembered learning through religion and from her mother to "be thankful for what you've got and not look for anything more."

Clearly she identified with this stance of her mother, a so-called "virtue" that enabled her husband to treat her financially in such an egregious manner that even the family lawyer labeled it "improper" and balked at colluding in the husband's plans despite his insistence.

As Mrs. C was talking about this situation in one of her sessions, she said suddenly, and seemingly out of context, "So what has all of this to do with sex?"

The analyst, surprised, replied, "What did you have in mind?"

Mrs. C then told a story of how, when she was engaged to her husband, they visited his parent's home. He sneaked into her bedroom and rubbed up against her and she had an orgasm. She whispered to him that they should not being doing this because his mother might discover them. He laughed and said, "That's OK, my mother would blame you!" She was then, and continued to be, enraged at the notion that it was the woman's job to say no and to be blamed for being "the hussy," while men weren't blamed or restricted.

This material demonstrates a superego embodied as a maternal imago standing against this woman's sexuality. It appears in this session as a warning that her sexuality was dangerous and forbidden, and suggests that her masochistic compliance with her husband has been connected with such sexual prohibitions. She was "being" her masochistic mother and consciously complaining, but unconsciously enjoying this role.

Mrs. C continued to associate. Bathroom issues were very private matters in her family, she said, and that to her knowledge she had never seen her father or brothers nude (as if someone had asked her). She then began talking about how her husband wanted to have sex "according to a schedule" derived from a manual that said that at their age one should be having sex about two or three times a month. Wistfully, she said that her husband was not romantic, but that she had read and heard of all kinds of stimulating sexual fantasies in books. She tried to talk to him about these fantasies, but he didn't seem to want to discuss such matters.

The analyst asked the patient if she were aware of any fantasies of her own. She replied, "Within my own head. I can imagine them, but I don't want to talk to you about this."

The analyst asked about this strong feeling. The patient replied, "Suddenly I have an image of my grandmother and how she would respond. She'd probably faint. This reminds me also of my mother-in-law. She was very proper, super proper." She then recalled once being chastised by her grandmother with a "tsk tsk" when she was about five years old. Her grandmother had found the patient listening to music and bouncing her head rhythmically. She saw the disapproving look on her grandmother's face. She also recalled how she never really needed to be admonished because a slight look of disapproval from her grandmother or mother would be enough to inhibit any behavior. (Throughout the treatment, the analyst was aware of the deeply searching looks that Mrs. C gave her upon entering and leaving the analytic sessions.)

Now the analyst asked what she thought her grandmother disapproved of. Mrs. C thought this might have been a prohibition of masturbation. She continued with another memory of her mother, who "only used proper words" for bodily functions. The analyst pointed out to Mrs. C that her inhibition in talking about any of her intimate sexual feelings stemmed from her expectation that the analyst would respond just like all of the women in her past—with shock and disapproval of her thoughts and sexual desires and behaviors.

The patient thought it over and then said, "Well, I guess I can tell you. Here is one I have had for many many years and often still have. I am a queen, and I can pick who I want to please me sexually. I pick my brother or my father to watch me masturbate. I am attracted to men who look like them, very handsome with dark eyes and curly hair." She explained that in her fantasy, they would get excited and turned on, but she was in control as to whether they could satisfy themselves or not. Here we see her sadistic revenge on men, who are not the ones blamed for sexual impulses.

Mrs. C then talked about how sex is so different today compared to when she grew up. It wasn't talked about in her household. Her final comment in the session was "I guess it is not so dangerous to talk to you about this."

These memories of her grandmother, mother, and mother-in-law were clearly related to how difficult it had been for Mrs. C to talk about this material. It is evident that she had projected a stern and disapproving maternal superego onto the analyst. These feelings came up only after some years of analysis, and only then was she able to talk about her masturbation and masturbation fantasies.

This session was an important organizing moment in the treatment. The masochistic response to her husband, its link to early triadic sexual fantasies, and her unconscious masochistic identification with her mother all emerged together. This material can be understood as her compromise; she takes her mother's place in the triangular situation, but at the same time pays the price to her superego in her masochistic lifestyle. Thus she does not risk losing the love of a maternal figure—her mother, her mother-in-law, her grandmother, or her analyst. The appearance of uncensored incestuous object choices makes clear that the material is triadic. As analysis progressed, these harsh superego elements were deprived of the inhibiting power that had created such a strong resistance. Finally at this age and stage, she could begin to understand her inhibitions and her masochistic submission and move towards changes for herself and in her marital situation.

In all three of these cases, strong and intense superego conflicts and contents are focused on triadic configurations. The guilt over incestuous wishes and disloyalty toward the mother is clearly evident. All three of these women desire a man who belongs to another woman or is otherwise a forbidden object. In the first case, we see tremendous guilt over even the thought of forbidden pleasure. In the first and second, fantasies of adultery led to intense guilt and fantasies of punishment. These two cases manifest a common fantasy containing unique superego content for females—the specific punishment of being infertile or not being able to carry a child to termination. In the third case, early incestuous sexual fantasies, which had caused enormous anxiety and inhibition, were recalled.

We might argue that there are differences in the structural strength of the superego of these women; that is, the manner in which the impulses are contained. Clearly, there was a difference in the internal balance of forces, as only one of these intensely self-critical women, Mrs. B, allowed herself to act on her impulses; the others remained inhibited, even in their thoughts. Mrs. B's rage and sense of rejection toward her husband and all men in her life allowed her to disregard her superego admonishments and rationalize action. In all three cases, the feared punishment for transgression was the loss of a primarily maternal object. Mrs. A feared and wished that her mother would be kidnapped. She was concerned with doing the "right" thing. Mrs. B feared her family's disapproval and experienced loss through divorce. Mrs. B also experienced as punishment for "Oedipal"/Persephonal transgression a loss of fertility and sexual pleasure—in the broad sense, a kind of castration. Mrs. C's images of stern and disapproving mothers produced anxiety and inhibition of sexuality over the span of a lifetime.

Summary

In our work with women we have seen no gendered differences in structure, strength, and functioning of the superego. We believe that castration anxiety is not the necessary motivator for superego development for females; the central motivator is fear of loss of love and loss of the loved object, and not in an early and "pre-Oedipal" sense. But we are not certain that castration anxiety is the central motivator for boys, either. We agree with those who describe superego development as a gradual accretion of functions, acquired step-by-step through identifications and learning. We have found no differences in the process or function of identification for males and females.

On the other hand, we do think that there are gendered differences in *contents* of the superego. The content of girls' fears seems to concern the mother. We have seen that whenever the step into assuming active, competitive sexual activity is contemplated—from age three in fantasy or in young adulthood in reality—the mother is psychically present (consciously or unconsciously) and the daughter begins to worry about her disapproval or even her loss.

We do think that there are major gendered differences in the ways guilt is defended against and handled. What we frequently find in women clinically is the character type of a masochistic martyr. In these individuals aggression and competition with mother is so frighteningly forbidding that rage and sadism is turned back upon the self.

We have never encountered the caricatured "Jocasta superego" that enjoins Oedipus not to worry about sleeping with his mother. Freud (1900) noted that, "At a point when Oedipus, though he is not yet enlightened, has begun to feel troubled by his recollection of the oracle, Jocasta consoles him by referring to a dream which many people dream, though as she thinks, it has no meaning:" (p. 264) "But do not fear touching wedlock with your mother. Many men before now have so fared in dreams also; but he to whom these things are as nothing bears his life most easily.'" (Sophocles, Jebb trans., p. 100). Here Jocasta evokes the image of a seductress with a "weak" or compromised conscience, who wants her pleasures with a weak conscience.

We believe that an intense guilt about sexuality and competition with mother and fear of being caught at it, accounts for the tendency of women to inhibit reports of frank sexual and/or masturbation fantasies in the clinical situation. This inhibition becomes a real difficulty if the analyst, female or male, is seen in the transference as a maternal object. Even in this "postmodern" period of sexual revolution, where sex is displayed in talk shows and cinema, in the clinical situation girls and women are still uncomfortable revealing their sexuality in detail.

In conclusion, we argue that the superego is not the heir to the Oedipus complex, which rests on resolution of triangular conflicts. Nevertheless, the triadic phase stands as an important point in the timeline of superego development. It is then that the child must grapple with intense conflicts of, and consequent guilt about, sexual desire, death wishes toward rivals, and competition. In terms of object relations, it is a time for dealing with three objects instead of two, which requires a balancing act that must in some way engender guilt and anxiety. This is so for boys as well as girls.

Only when superego development proceeds optimally can girls traverse the conflicts of loyalty and the fears of loss of the object or loss of love of the object—the mother—without paralyzing their ability to deal with triangular complexities within the family and out in the social world and ultimately participate without inhibition in adult sexual relations. Failing such optimal development, detailed clinical attention to the analysis of strong superego prohibitions in females can remedy the incomplete development.

Notes

1. It should be noted that in this tale, as in many others, it is by leaving or separating from her mother that dangers occur to the girl. Ultimately through this separation, adult sexuality is achieved. In many stories the separation is portrayed by a physical separation, as in the Persephone myth. The necessary developmental separation that we are underscoring, however, is psychic separation. We do not mean the separation that marks the early pre-Oedipal stage in which the infant emerges from early symbiosis, through a stage of part objects, internally. Rather, we are referring to separations when the child has already a fully developed cohesive sense of self and object constancy.

2. A relatively uniquely female content of the superego concerns reactions to having given up a baby for adoption or having an abortion. These are almost always guilt-ridden secrets divulged in the analytic process. The fantasies are both conscious and unconscious around these life events. We have frequently seen that the dynamics are related to female triadic conflicts.

3. Jacobson concludes, along with others (Schafer, Blum), that the female superego is different from the male but not inferior, even if less rigid and punitive.

4. Here is a clear clinical example of the need for such concepts of primary femininity and ways of conceptualizing female passion. Otherwise, we would have been left only with the idea of the patient's penis envy, which in this case was used defensively to cover conflict-ridden sexual passion.

CHAPTER NINE

~

Baubo: The Female Body in the Triangular Phase

The girl in the positive phase of her Oedipus complex is a little woman, just as the boy is a little man, and the fact that she does not menstruate and produce ova is only parallel to the fact that the boy does not produce sperm.

(Daly, 1943, p. 156)

No girl's story can be complete without taking into account her experiences of her body, which inform both her triangular phase and her later development. In this chapter, we will focus on how the female body and genitals are depicted in the Persephone story and the related themes of sexual pleasure and exhibitionism. We will also examine the role of the female body and the physical and psychological experience that it engenders during the triangular period—the sexual pleasures, the bodily anxieties and fears of penetration, and the fantasies of pregnancy. In particular we will consider girls' identifications with their mothers' bodies and the triangular conflicts that may be expressed in masturbation and masturbation fantasies.

Baubo

The startling and pivotal Baubo episode (Foley, 1994, p. 12) of the Demeter and Persephone myth highlights many of these issues. Demeter has descended from Olympus and is frantically searching for her missing daughter. Grief-stricken, disguised as a mortal woman, she wanders over an earth devastated by a famine of her own wreaking. She offers herself as a servant to a mortal family to care for an infant boy, Demophoon. "Voiceless with grief," (p. 12) she refuses food and drink. But Baubo, an older woman in the household, lifts up her skirt in jest, displaying her genitals to the despondent Demeter. Responding to this gesture, Demeter laughs; she comes out of her depression and accepts food and drink.

The fascinating figure of Baubo (also called Iambe) appears in one form or another in all the versions of the Persephone myth. The gestures associated with her "ana suramai" or lifting the skirt, and "aischrologia" or indulging in indecent speech or joking became important women's rituals in the Eleusinian mysteries. In the context of this story, the display of the genitals, the sexual jesting, and the intimate communication between the two women represent female sexuality, expressed without negativity or restraint. The Baubo episode reinforces the feminine genital and erotic significance of the myth (Kulish and Holtzman, 2002).

Baubo is variously depicted as hostess, servant, nurse, and priestess; in all instances she is an important figure who brings Demeter out of her depression. Over the ages Baubo has been given form in countless inscriptions, poems, figurines, carvings, and rituals (Olender, 1990; Foley, 1994; Lubell, 1994), depictions that have been described variously as amusing, awe-inspiring, beautiful, troubling, and obscene. Three gestures associated with her appear repeatedly in ancient art: a frog-like squat (sometimes interpreted as a birthing position), upraised arms, and a lifted dress.

The very name "Baubo" is associated with a Greek noun for body, cavity, womb, vagina, or nurse; Baubo's icon is the vulva (Olender, 1990; Lincoln, 1991), and wherever she appeared she was associated with holes, entrances, or caves. Her Orphic origins, stemming from early Greek religious cults in the seventh century BC, preceding Greek culture, have been documented (Lubell, 1994, pp. 48–49). Baubo-like representations have been discovered carved into the walls of English and Irish churches of the twelfth to fourteenth centuries.

Baubo's gesture of exposure is the impetus for a detailed and scholarly study by Winifred Lubell (1994), who explores the history, meaning, and importance of this figure. She sees Baubo as representing the strength of the female: "Her power was the power of her body. She is a symbol of the nurturing and transformative energies of women, which combine with women's resourcefulness and laughter" (preface, xix). She is the embodiment of female sexual power and pleasure. Other Baubo scholars (Estes, 1992) with feminist interests have emphasized the importance of close relationships among ancient women, in

which they shared their concerns and laughter. "It is a chuckling, wry sort of humor, compounded of irony, compassion and shared experience between women" (Lubell, p. 12).

Interestingly, Freud (1916a) made special mention of Baubo in a piece about symbolic displacement, where he described the obsessive mental image of a patient: his father's facial features painted on a woman's naked abdomen. Freud likened this image to terracotta representations of Baubo with which he was familiar. In 1898 archaeologists discovered a strange group of terracotta statues in the remains of a temple of Demeter and Kore. These figurines were characterized by bodies of women with faces carved on the abdomens. Disproportionately large heads sit directly on top of the legs, blending into and replacing hips of atrophied bodies. Their lifted dresses framed the faces like a rings of hair. A sketch of such a figure appears in the margin of the paper in the *Standard Edition*.

Pleasurable Exhibitionism

We offer the following observation of such pleasurable exhibitionism from our own time. Janie, not quite two, is at the synagogue, where her official baby naming has been incorporated into her older sister's bat mitzvah. Dressed in a special party dress, white tights, patent leather shoes, and with a big bow in her hair, she is standing on the stage clutching her father's hand. A large bouquet of fragrant flowers, much higher than she, stands in a tall vase next to her. The rabbi is speaking, and Janie begins to fidget and look out at the large congregation. She pulls away slightly from her father, not letting go of his hand, to smell one of the large blossoms. The audience titters. Janie, more ostentatiously now, begins to smell each of the flowers, putting her little face deeply into the blossom and closing her eyes in apparent ecstasy at the fragrance. She is clearly enjoying herself and the attention, which is now all on her and not the rabbi. Suddenly she lets go of her father's hand, takes her skirt daintily in each hand, and twirls around in a full circle. She finishes off this maneuver by lifting her skirt up over her head, pushing out her pelvis, and displaying her ruffled panties to the delighted audience. Thus this tiny Baubo steals the show from her older sister. Her pleasure in the attention, in her sensual femininity, and in her joke on the solemn adult world is apparent. We contrast this observation with the one supplied by Anna Freud (1936) of a little girl lifting her skirts. Miss Freud's case (which we discussed in chapter 5) has become a classic example of a defensive reaction to "castration anxiety."

On a subsequent occasion over a year later, Janie lifted her skirt again. Her mother, who has gently told her not to, asked why she did it anyway. "To show Daddy and be funny," Janie replied. To appeal to her daddy and to defy her mother—the dynamics of the triangular phase are clear.

Psychoanalytic Theories of Female Pleasure

Early psychoanalytic theory had no place for the pleasure and delight in the female genitals as exemplified in the Baubo story and in Janie. Early accounts of the "female Oedipal complex" likewise neglected any attention to girls' sexual pleasure, which surely must be a part of the drama. Leon Hoffman (1996) has demonstrated that Freud did not have constructs for female passion. Since Freud, many psychoanalytic writers have addressed these issues, trying to formulate theories that allow for a basic developmental line of primary femininity (Hoffman, 1996; Elise, 1997; Kulish, 2000; Reenkola, 2002). Such a line would encompass an early awareness of the vagina, an appreciation of the female body, and an early sense of being female, all of which contribute to positive feelings about the self as female and capable of sexual pleasure.

Also missing from psychoanalytic theory is an adequate account of the female exhibitionism that is central to the Baubo episode. On the other hand, Freud was well aware of the importance of the body in psychological development during childhood. Bound by his Victorian and phallocentric attitudes, however, he did not develop any comprehensive understanding of femininity and the role of the *female* body in the girl's experience. The major role of the female body in his theory of the female Oedipus is in the first act of the drama—the motivating force of penis envy. What was relevant in terms of the girl's body was essentially its lack. We critique this conceptualization specifically in chapters 6 and 8.

Furthermore, conventional psychoanalytic theory has understood female exhibition, originating in the "phallic" phase, as a defense against castration anxiety and feelings of shame (Freud, 1923b; A. Freud, 1936), conceptualizations with which we disagree. Freud proposed that little girls, unlike little boys, whose phallic narcissism focuses on the visible and tangible penis, feel mortification at the lack of a penis and react with a compensatory narcissism that spreads to all other parts of their bodies.

> Shame, which is considered to be a feminine characteristic par excellence but is far more a matter of convention than might be supposed, has as its purpose, we believe, concealment of genital deficiency. We are not forgetting that at a later time shame takes on other functions. It seems that women have made few contributions to the discoveries and inventions in the history of civilization; there is, however, one technique which they may have invented—that of plaiting and weaving. If that is so, we should be tempted to guess the unconscious motive for the achievement. Nature herself would seem to have given the model which this achievement imitates by causing the growth at maturity of the pubic hair that conceals the genitals. The step that remained to be taken lay in making the threads adhere to one another, while on the body they stick into the skin and are only matted together. If you reject this idea as fantastic and regard my belief in the influence of lack of a penis on the configuration of femininity as an idée fixe, I am of course defenseless (Freud, 1933, p. 132).

Thus, according to Freud, the only affects that the female genitals themselves attract are feelings of shame and negativity. But that belief and the resulting ideas of anxiety-driven exhibitionism and penis envy do not do justice, in our view, to Baubo's raucous, joyous, and healing gesture. Baubo represents the concretization of pleasurable exhibitionism (Holtzman and Kulish, 2002).

Another example of such theoretical constraint was Freud's argument that little girls are not aware of their vaginas. He insisted that the vagina was discovered only in puberty; before that, a girl experienced sexual sensations only in her "masculine" clitoris. This theoretical proposition reflects a defense frequently found in boys and men—a denial of the reality of the vagina—and stemming from unconscious castration anxiety.[1] This male dread of female sexuality was first elucidated by Karen Horney (1932, 1933) and later elaborated by Janine Chasseguet-Smirgel (1976).

In traditional theoretical accounts of the triangular phase, therefore, there is no place for the girl's sexual pleasure, awareness of her genitals, or real appreciation of her body. Freud, in his focus on embarrassment, lack, and shame, ended up with a negative and distorted view of the story. Undoubtedly, the affect of shame frequently does accompany girls' and women's triangular experiences. But so does a primary sense of femaleness—girl's knowledge of what she has, and not what she does not have, and of her vagina and clitoris as sources of pleasure. We will now turn to a reexamination of the triadic phase of development, incorporating ideas of a primary sense of femaleness.

The Representation of the Female Body during the Triangular Phase

Long before a little girl reaches the triadic phase she has become aware of her body and has developed an early sense of femaleness (Elise, 1997). By the age of two, her core gender identity is solid; she knows she is a girl and is beginning to experience what her gender means for her—its limits and possibilities. By the time she is three, she has a solid body map, which includes a sense of her genitals and the pleasure they might bring. Contrary to what Freud thought, it has been documented that girls experience intense, erotic (vaginal) sensations from early infancy (Plaut and Hutchinson, 1986; Greenacre, 1952); genital self-stimulation has been observed in little girls before the age of two, somewhat later than in boys (Kleeman, 1975). With the entry into the triangular Persephonal phase, her sexuality becomes more genitally focused and intense. With her blossoming sexual feelings and her new capacities to appreciate the complexities of the interpersonal sphere around her, her fantasy life becomes richer and more complex. Already identified with her mother and her mothering functions, her interest in babies takes a new turn; now she wishes to have a baby *with* someone. Princes and princesses, babies, and fairy tale adventures fill her mind.

Masturbation Fantasies and Practices

The triadic phase serves as an organizing moment for unconscious erotic fantasies, which can then be expressed in bodily exploration and in masturbation fantasies and practices that are laden with erotic, incestuous wishes and with hostile rivalries and guilts. Masturbation, although conflicted, has adaptive functions during this time: "In the Oedipal period, masturbation encompasses progressive forces which prevail over the regressive pulls that have been activated by the anxieties of the period. It provides outlets for tension of genital and Oedipal wishes, and strengthens the awareness of self. Fantasies are object libidinal and have to do with attainment, conquest, and dread of retaliation" (Marcus and Francis, 1975, p. 24).

One typical masturbation fantasy that we encounter frequently in adult female patients is a variant of the beating fantasy, within which triangular wishes are disguised. One representative version is that a mean woman—a "Nurse Ratched" type, say (from *One Flew Over the Cuckoo's Nest*)—places the patient in the hands of a group of strange, often rough, men. When analysis deconstructs the defensive disguises, it can be seen that the father, who *is* known, has been split into many unknown men, and that the child has been *forced* into sex by the rival/mother. The child is portrayed without desire and therefore without competition or guilt. Her sadomasochistic interpretation of the primal scene is replicated in these scenarios, and the girl/woman/subject in these fantasies may be forced to exhibit her genitals or nude body, here too enabling a prohibited desire, this time to show herself and be admired. This exhibitionism cannot always be interpreted as compensation for a lack of a penis, as it frequently is in the literature (A. Freud, 1936). We agree with Virginia Clower's comment (1975) that in masturbation fantasies "Oedipal" objects often appear as onlookers, and Oedipal wishes are expressed in images of being admired or envied by parental figures.

Freud described the beating fantasy in 1919 as a masochistic expression of disguised incestuous wishes. Later psychoanalysts (Ferber, 1975; Bonaparte, 1953; Kris, 1956) have also linked beating fantasies to the "phallic Oedipal" period. Jack and Kerry Novick (1972), in their study of beating fantasies in children, concluded that the beating fantasies they observed in girls in latency clearly represented both Oedipal strivings in regressed form and punishment for them, as Freud described, but did not appear in the vague third-person form he found in adult patients. They traced a link between beating fantasies and the "typical" latency fantasies of family romance and rescue.

As is well known, the girl feels masturbation must be hidden because of guilt induced by such associated incestuous fantasies, fears of strong parental disapproval, and the belief that sexuality belongs to the mother. James Kleeman (1975) points out that a cultural influence over girls inhibiting masturbation has been largely neglected: the documented fact that the same mother treats her little girl differently from her little boy in terms of her response to their genital self-stimulation. In 1975 Clower observed that society views masturbation in boys as perfectly normal but disapproves strongly of the practice in girls.[2]

In contrast to males, whose erections betray them, the female's body allows sexual impulses to remain more hidden. Girls can masturbate without using their hands—not necessarily to avoid an "inferior" genital as Freud (1925)[3] indicated—but rather to avoid agency and responsibility and knowing ones own desire. Unconsciously they can get away with such masturbation equivalents. *And why not?* They can masturbate without their hands easily, so they do. Rhythmic physical exercise from playing games, sliding down ropes and banisters, and bicycle and horseback riding can all create strong sexual excitement, sometimes even to orgasmic climax. The complete genitalia, and not only the clitoris, are aroused and stimulated through such activities. Many females do not identify the feelings associated with such activities as connected to masturbatory behavior or sexual excitement until some sudden conscious understanding, or psychoanalysis, makes the link for them (Clower, 1975). Very often, women do not put words to, or name, masturbation and orgasm. An organ whose function seems to be to stimulate pleasure and masturbation, the clitoris, has gone unnamed in most societies, or worse, literally excised in ritual clitoredectomies (Kulish, 1991). Thus, the manner in which girls masturbate, its secrecy, is one way in which the sexual excitements of the incestuous triangular situation are different for little girls than little boys. Girls' anxiety about losing the love of their mothers means that such masturbation must remain a secret to others around them and even to themselves.

We believe that masturbation fantasies (conscious or unconscious) have a consistent core throughout the development, even across the life span. Women's beating fantasies can be lived out in real life in symbolic or derivative forms, as for example, in masochistic proclivities or lifestyles. (We are well aware, of course, that masochistic proclivities are supported and reinforced by societal pressures and patriarchal values.) The triadic object relations implied in these masturbation fantasies are enacted in everyday life in repeated themes. For example, a woman unconsciously arranges every situation in her life to appear to herself and others as if she is the forced victim. Like Persephone, she is "forced" to be queen. A familiar picture is a woman who is attracted only to men who are inappropriate or unavailable. Often embedded in these stories are hopes of eventual triumph—of winning over father's love and affection and taking mother's place. This is not to say that females are intrinsically masochistic or that men do not suffer from masochism also, but men more frequently play out their masochism by hiding it beneath sadism.

Secrets

As we have said, eventually Persephone does become a queen in her own right, but in an underground realm, away from the land where her mother rules. For the girl, sexuality cannot easily exist in her mother's presence. She hides her wishes, dangerous because of the potent and enduring childhood fears of loss of her mother or of her love. She must also keep secret any erotic impulses she may feel toward her mother, which would put their relationship on a different and dangerous footing. As the girl becomes aware of sexual impulses toward her father, she becomes aware too of competitive feelings towards her mother. This thrusts her into a major conflict, between the sexual attraction to her father and her love for, and dependency on, her mother. Sexuality, which is seen as belonging to the mother, must be inhibited and go underground. Fear of loss of mother as the nurturer motivates the girl's repression of sexual impulses. This is where the situation is different from that of boys. Boys may challenge or imagine destroying their fathers, but they will still have a loving mother to take care of them.

Kirstin Dahl (1989) has also emphasized the need for secrets from the mother as a component of the Oedipal complex. She suggests that the common witch/mother fantasy hides two secrets: one, the secret sexual yearnings for the mother, which are disguised by loathing; and two, the secret that the girl loves her father and in so doing is betraying her mother. Her Oedipal rivalry is projected onto the figure of the vengeful witch. Fairy tales and myths warn girls against acquiring sexual "knowledge"—as if, once armed with this knowledge, women will proceed to exercise their sexuality without constraint. Curiosity that leads to knowledge is forbidden. In the tale of Bluebeard, the heroine's curiosity about what lies hidden behind a forbidden door leads her into deadly danger. The Judeo-Christian tradition makes a direct link between knowledge and sexuality; the Bible uses the term "to know" a woman to mean sexual possession. Naming a thing gives one power and responsibility over it. Learning the strange dwarf's name gives the heroine in the Grimms' fairy tale "Rumpelstiltskin" power over him and allows her to keep her baby. The fact that girls are not given names for their sexual body parts weakens their sense of ownership and control over their sexuality (Kulish, 1991).

So girls may deny sexual knowledge, remaining "ditsy" to avoid their mothers' disapproval or society's punishment or their own superego guilt. Carol Gilligan (1991) puts it well: "Girls often use the phrase 'I don't know' to cover knowledge, which they believe may be dangerous, and the phrase 'you know,' correspondingly to discover what it is possible for them to know and still be connected with other people" (p. 11).

This need for secrets, we feel, is more characteristic of little girls during this period than of little boys. But girls also take great pleasure in secrets—in stories about secrets, like *The Secret Garden*, in sharing secrets with each other, in collecting and hiding precious things in secret little boxes and hideaways. This pleasure in secrets reflects the girl's pleasures in her body and its secrets, with its inner cavities and passageways and its mysterious sensations (Kulish, 2002).

Bodily Comparison and Competition

For little girls and boys, as genital erotic desires emerge more fully, the comparison of their bodies and their genitals with the bodies and genitals of the adults around them leads to feelings of inadequacy and other narcissistic concerns. As Irene Fast (1979) has suggested, young children's sense of their gender possibilities is limitless—they want it all. In this context penis envy may certainly arise, but so can breast and womb envy. The response from the immediate environment to these wounds will determine their intensity and whether or not they become symptomatic.

The girl's body becomes a vehicle of competition with her mother, as the boy's does with his father. She compares her body with her mother's. She wants to have babies like her mother or other women she sees, to have breasts, a big belly.

Psychoanalyst Rosemary Balsam (1996) has thrown light on the previously neglected topic—the meanings of the mother's body to her daughter. She presents clinical material that demonstrates the importance of the mother's body on a girl's perception of her shape, size, abdomen, breasts, buttocks, genitals, skin, and hair. The effects of these female-to-female comparisons and perceptions are apparent in the analyses of adult women and help to explain both the particulars of women's body images and also the pleasures and anxieties about them that we see so often in our clinical practices. Balsam alerts us to the care with which such inevitable comparisons in the female analyst–female patient dyad need to be understood and interpreted if analysis is to afford optimal integration and freedom for female patients. Balsam's clinical examples also support our notions that the refrain "I don't want to be like my mother" is the conscious negation of the unconscious competitive wish to take mother's place. Or as one young mother reported in her analytic session, "Mirror, mirror on the wall, I've become my mother after all!"

Balsam also demonstrates that girls' body images oscillate; there may indeed be moments when the more familiar comparisons to the male body and genitals seize the foreground, but these can and should be discriminated from enduring attention to the body of the same-sexed parent. The physicality of the mother, says Balsam, "deserves a place in our theory of female development as it relates to psychosexuality, gender role identity, and body image" (p. 420). We strongly agree with her conclusion that "we have not sufficiently developed reactions in developmental progress about aspects of the female body other than the genital" (p. 424).

Babies and Pregnancy Fantasies

Girls can have babies and boys cannot; what does this fact mean in the development of the triangular situations in boys and girls? By the time a little girl is four or so, she usually knows that her body will someday be able to accommodate a baby. This formidable idea, however rudimentary, colors her experience of the triangular situation as she fantasizes, from her little girl's point of view, what it might mean. She thinks that she might be a Mommy, with her Daddy as partner (or with her mother as her partner) as she dreams of being Cinderella or Wonder Woman. She pretends to feed baby dolls or plays out Barbie's romances with Ken. She tries to imagine how she might give birth to a baby: Would she swell up like Mommy? Would her tummy pop like a balloon? Would it hurt? How do babies get there in the first place? Maybe it would be better to forget it and play hide and seek?

Our colleagues who work with children tell us how often these fantasies occur in their little girl patients. The desire to get large with child and give birth is part of the triadic family dynamic and reflects the little girl's identification with her mother and her competition with her as well. Of course, little boys fantasize that they can make babies, too, but it is only little girls who will be able to actualize these wishes when they grow up and who see that they have bodies which will be like their mothers' bodies someday.

During the triangular period, boys and girls try out both parental roles. We have observed the following examples: A little girl sticks out her tummy and says "I'm going to have a baby and marry Daddy." Another little girl glides down the stairs with a baby doll under her skirt and announces, "I'm the Daddy and I have a penis and Mommy and I made a baby!" Psychoanalysts have documented unconscious and symbolic representations of tumescence and de-tumescence can certainly refer to the penis, but we have found that fantasies of growing large and small may also relate to pregnancy and often are missed or misunderstood (in both boys and girls).

Phyllis Greenacre (1977) studied and elucidated the bodily changes in Alice in Wonderland: "*Alice's Adventures in Wonderland* is replete with descriptions of bizarre and unassimilated body feelings, which reproduce—in various body parts as well as in the total body—the phallic form and changes. Alice's body becomes enormously and suddenly elongated or collapses and shrinks sadly. Her *neck* particularly becomes so serpent-like that she is actually mistaken for a serpent hiding in a tree. Her arm and leg, each in turn, seem strange, far away, and hardly part of herself in their grotesquely enlarged form. All of these changes follow eating or drinking" (pp. 217–218). Greenacre does not comment here on the obvious inference that the bodily changes following eating and drinking may equally refer to infantile theories of pregnancy—oral impregnation fantasies.

She does, however, speculate along these lines when she discusses the interest in bodily changes of author Lewis Carroll, whose real name was Charles Lutwidge Dodgson. Dodgson was the oldest boy and third child in a sibship of ten; he saw three new babies arrive before he was five. Greenacre wrote: "Another contributing determinant to Charles Dodgson's concern with body size and changes lay in his repeated observation of his mother's pregnancies, with inevitable notice of her sudden changes from obesity to thinness. Just as the Alice books reflect so much the unassimilated phallic problems as well as the recrudescence of the early primary-process type of thought, so his early drawings are striking in their presentation of the fat-thin contrasts" (p. 218).

Freud reduced the girl's maternal instincts to penis envy, with the baby a displacement for the envied penis, but contemporary psychoanalysts (Parens et al., 1976; Chodorow, 1978; Benjamin, 1988; Tyson and Tyson, 1990; Balsam, 1996) have abandoned that one-sided conceptualization in favor of the complex process of identification. They see the girl's wish to have babies as coming from positive sources—recognition of the potentials of her own body and identification with her mother and her mothering functions. In their observations, for example, Parens and colleagues identify as early as twelve to fourteen months the appearance of an interest in babies in girls, associated with identification with the mother. What does the little girl make of her mother's expanding pregnant body? The child's sometimes excited, sometimes fearful, and often fiercely envious identification has been ignored, by and large, but it is a frequent clinical phenomenon. Rosemary Balsam (2001) demonstrates with extensive clinical illustrations the importance of the image of the pregnant mother's body to the little girl as "the most important icon of grown-up physical femaleness" (p. 1341).

The 2006 film *Pan's Labyrinth*, directed by Guillermo del Toro, depicts a young girl's fear-filled fantasies about sexuality and childbirth. The action takes place during the Spanish Civil War. The heroine, Ofelia, about nine or ten years old, retreats to an inner fantasy world to cope with the terrors of the war and her mother's relationship with a sadistic fascist captain. The mother is ill and pregnant with the captain's baby, so that neither she nor her daughter can escape him. While Ofelia's fantasies mirror the realities of the violence she experiences around her, they also reflect developmental issues typical of all young girls—a sadomasochistic view of the primal scene, with the male seen as the tormentor, and exaggerated ideas of what bearing a baby would do to the body.[4] There is also a clear Persephone motif: In a scene depicting her fantasy she enters the underworld and is enjoined, just as Persephone, not to eat or she will be trapped with a salacious and viciously cannibalistic man and unable to get back to her mother again. Also striking is the ending in which the girl is finally able to escape and steals away with the newborn brother, her Persephonal ("Oedipal") baby.

In the Persephone story there is also a (somewhat puzzling) episode where Demeter takes over another woman's baby. She does this in order to bestow immortality upon the child in a ritual of fire. She throws him into the flames, an act misinterpreted by the mortal mother, Metinera, who snatches him out again. The stealing of another woman's child is a fantasy frequently revealed in the analysis of adult females. It often represents the competitive wish for the baby her father gave her mother. Many of the Baubo figures have a face depicted on the abdomen, which evokes the image of a fetus within the belly. Thus, the joke for Demeter in the Baubo episode may be not only the sexual pleasure suggested by the sight of the genitals, but the reminder of her fertility and the possibility of bearing children.

Bodily Anxieties

Although some bodily anxieties stem from the early dyadic phase, we will focus here on concerns that emerge during the triadic period in the context of the girl's blooming sexuality and competitiveness. As punishment for incestuous wishes, the girl fears bodily damage and loss of her mother. These fears of bodily damage are not identical to the fears of castration that have been posited for the boy in the Oedipal complex. These female fears, which we will describe below, include fears of being penetrated, having her female genitals mutilated or ruined, or losing her reproductive capacities. Later a girl's fears of punishment for her sexual and rivalrous feelings can become transferred to worries about infertility, frigidity, or giving birth to a defective baby.

Early psychoanalysts (Horney, 1924; Klein, 1928; Jones, 1935) painted a dramatic picture of the little girl's fears and fantasies during the triangular phase. Her sexual fantasies about her father and intercourse arouse fears of being damaged by his big penis, as oral sadistic projections are often intermingled with these fantasies. Unresolved conflicts about such fears result in fears of sexual intercourse and childbearing in adulthood or adolescence. Horney describes a case of a woman who suffered from such fears:

> I told you that this patient produced fantasies of rape—fantasies which she regarded as fact—and that ultimately these related to her father. . . . Her castration fantasies took the familiar form of imagining that she was not normally

made in the genital region, and besides this she had a feeling as though she had suffered some injury to the genitals. On both these points she had evolved many ideas, chiefly to the effect that these peculiarities were the result of acts of rape. Indeed, it became plain that her obstinate insistence upon these sensations and ideas in connection with her genital organs was actually designed to prove the reality of these acts of violence, and so, ultimately, the reality of her love-relation with her father. The clearest light is thrown upon the importance of this fantasy and the strength of the repetition-compulsion under which she laboured" (1924, p. 62).

Similarly, Marie Bonaparte (1948), an early psychoanalytic pioneer, described girls' fears of penetration, which she felt may lead to frigidity in adulthood. She described the terror some children experience on the introduction of any instrument into any body orifice, as in medical examinations.

Elizabeth Mayer (1995) proposed a major primary feminine genital anxiety, which she called "female castration anxiety," which she contrasted with male castration anxiety. This involves the feared loss or closing of the genital opening and allied fears of the loss of openness as a trait of the personality.

Doris Bernstein (1993) articulated three specific "female genital anxieties," which she classified as fears of access, diffusivity, and penetration. Access refers to the girl's sense that she does not have ready access to her vagina, which she cannot see easily or manipulate in a sexualized way, with an opening over which she has no control. Diffusivity refers to the nature of female sexual sensations, which may generate a generalized feeling of helplessness. Penetration anxiety is especially prominent during the Oedipal period, according to Bernstein. Girls fear damage to their small bodies from fantasies about the exciting, penetrating, and large paternal penis (pp. 101–142). Expanding on Bernstein's classification, Arlene Richards (1996) emphasized the flexing of the perineal musculature in the development of female sexual awareness and sensation. The contraction of these sphincter muscles in toilet training results in a spreading sexual excitement which is confused with genital sensation. Richards also described her view of the primary fear of castration in women in terms of a loss of pleasure or function of the female genital apparatus. Richards asserted that girls fear that their *capacity for sexual excitement* may be subject to loss as a punishment for forbidden Oedipal wishes.

We think that all of these bodily anxieties specific to the female body are manifested clinically. They are often linked to triadic conflicts and fears of punishment.

Female Sexual Pleasure

We would like to illustrate how joyous Baubo-like sexuality in a woman may appear in psychoanalysis if we can find better ways in which to recognize it.

We return to Mrs. B., whose analysis we discussed in chapter 8. In the course of her analysis, Mrs. B., a teacher in her early fifties, divorced her husband after a near sexless marriage and returned to school to finish a higher degree. She also worked through some severe sexual fears, inhibitions, and negative feelings about her body. After many pain-filled years, she had finally found pleasure in her body and was enjoying sex with a serious new lover. After ordering some new books, *The Joy of Sex,* and a book of woman's fantasies named *The Secret Garden,* she had a dream in which she recognized, in surprise, that an apparent stranger is a man with whom she once had a long-forgotten sexual relationship. Then she finds herself outside, and it is hot and dry. She starts watering the lawn. And suddenly the lawn is covered with coral-shrimp flowers: "The flowers, they were in all different stages of growth. I guess that equals my growth. I like flowers. If I were a princess, I'd always have flowers around. And lots of flowers in gardens." Her associations to the male stranger led indirectly to her father, and the princess to Cinderella finding her prince.

When this material was presented in a study group, several male analysts suggested that the flowers symbolized penises and this woman's bisexual wishes. Indeed, Mrs. BA had suffered a longstanding envy of the dominant males in her life—her bombastic husband, her critical, rigid father and her preferred older brothers. But while penis envy and corresponding castrating fantasies were important aspects of this woman's mental life, this dream appears to represent her joy in her rediscovered feminine pleasures and sexuality, in her beautiful body, as symbolized by the growing flowers with the coral color of female genitalia. Her associations to the "lover from the past" led to details that linked him to her father. Thus, in addition to the meanings of psychic growth, this dream expressed Mrs. BA's regret over her lost years and her unconscious Persephonal wishes to be able to replay her rediscovered sexuality with her father.

Summary

We began this chapter by tracing the meanings of a more obscure portion of the Persephone myth, which in each of its variations introduces the fascinating personage of Baubo. We believe Baubo's actions reflect a pleasure in the female genitals and reproductive capacities, a pleasure that has not been sufficiently appreciated in psychoanalytic theory and clinical work. Without a concept of female pleasure, we have in effect a sexual phase for girls without accounting for sexuality and its powerful drives.

We then attempted to address the girl's body, not solely its lacks, which Freud emphasized, but its capacities. And we emphasized its unequivocal importance to be considered in the triadic picture. We suggest that the female genitalia and imagined capacity to have babies in the future shape her fantasies and fears in uniquely gender-specific ways. We want to clarify that we are not parroting Freud's idea that "anatomy is destiny," but rather, that the female body is part of the staging of this important drama.

Notes

1. See Little Hans; the little boy Hans, when he saw his baby sister naked, had the fantasy that "her widdler" was growing.

2. In Western societies even in the twentieth century clitoredectomies were performed on women and girls who were observed to masturbate excessively.

3. Freud states, "There is yet another surprising effect of penis-envy, or of the discovery of the inferiority of the clitoris, which is undoubtedly the most important of all. In the past I had often formed an impression that in general women tolerate masturbation worse than men" (p. 255).

4. Boys appear to have similar fantasies, but the identifications and the end results may be different.

CHAPTER TEN

~

Adolescence and Beyond

Come, civil night,
Thou sober-suited matron, all in black,
And learn me how to lose a winning match,
Play'd for a pair of stainless maidenhoods:
Hood my unmann'd blood, bating in my cheeks,
With thy black mantle; till strange love, grown bold,
Think true love acted simple modesty.
Come, night; come, Romeo; come, thou day in night;
For thou wilt lie upon the wings of night
Whiter than new snow on a raven's back.
Come, gentle night, come, loving, black-brow'd night,
Give me my Romeo;

(Shakespeare, *Romeo and Juliet*, 3:2.10–21)

Kore/Persephone was a carefree young adolescent, on an outing with other girls her age, when she was seized by Hades. She wandered from her mother's protection, and events are suddenly set in motion. This is a familiar story. Adolescent girls love outings, but they may run into trouble—sometimes big trouble—when they stray too far from the safety of home and mother (Good, 2006). Yet, eventually, they must leave their mothers. In this sense, it can be said that the Persephone-Demeter myth represents an initiation rite (Lincoln, 1991).

Adolescence is noted for major developmental challenges. Adolescents must incorporate sexual maturation—bodily and hormonal—into their body schemas, identities, and lives; they must separate psychologically from their parents; they must consolidate their personal identities and integrate them within the larger social order. And, inevitably, in the context of these very real and urgent physical, psychological, and social changes, triangular issues emerge with a new and heavy emphasis. Triadic issues are a crucial part of the developmental tasks of adolescence. Psychoanalytic interpretations of adolescence stress its "Oedipal" struggles, although in traditional terminology, especially when it comes to females (Blos, 1962, 1979; Loewald, 1979; Laufer and Laufer, 1984; Plaut and Hutchinson, 1986; Schmukler, 1999). For example, Peter Blos (1962) writes: "As far as the resolution of the Oedipus complex is concerned, once more, we must remember that neither in the boy nor in the girl do we encounter resolutions which live up to the ideal models. In both sexes there remain residues of positive and negative Oedipal strivings: that is to say, relics of feminine strivings remain in the boy, and the girl maintains for a long time fantasies of a phallic nature. The analysis of adolescent girls has shown that the resolution of Oedipal conflicts prepares her [sic] for heterosexual love" (p. 108). Today psychoanalysts do not speak of the *resolution* of Oedipal strivings, but rather of an adaptive *integration* of these strivings into the adult personality.

In her study of female adolescence through works of literature, Katherine Dalsimer (1986) begins by asking the same questions we do: "At every phase of adolescence, not only at its ending, but from its beginning, it is necessary to consider how the distinctive nature of the girl's experience may shape developmental processes. For both girl and boy, I have said, adolescence is set in motion by a biological event, the advent of puberty. But this is a different event for the girl than for the boy—and its psychological ramifications different, I believe, in ways that have not yet been fully articulated" (p. 10).

In this chapter, we will try to address contemporary thinking about female development and integrate it with our understanding of the triadic issues important to female adolescents. We will consider the important changes in the female body during adolescence: menarche; the real possibility of bearing children; and the loss of virginity. We will also discuss a triadic component of the preponderantly female syndromes of bulimia and anorexia, and a common and very important clinical/social phenomenon which we have observed in adolescent girls grappling with social interactions, which we call "twos versus threes." We will touch on the way triangular issues occur throughout women's lives, especially at such important junctures as menarche, defloration, marriage, childbirth, career changes, and menopause.

The Persephone myth teaches that the insistent cyclicity of the female reproductive system is ever-present in the representation and experience of the female self. This recognition underlies much of our discussion.

Bodily Changes

Onset of Puberty

The onset of puberty delivers huge bodily changes for the girl—her shape changes, her breasts develop, pubic hair appears. She begins to menstruate, and unseen hormones fuel strong sexual desires that push her in unexpected ways. The feelings, fantasies, and conflicts around her body, which we spelled out in the previous chapter, exist now in a newly intense context: Now the girl really *can* have babies, now her new body *can* compete effectively with her mother's for male attention, including that of the father. Her sexual feelings are suddenly very hard to ignore, and as social pressures push her into sexual exploration, her world expands to include new and scary, yet exciting, personalities and possibilities.

Malkah Notman (2003) remarks on the comparisons an adolescent girl makes with her mother's body, which resemble the comparisons that younger girls make during the triangular phase. She writes: "The changes in the adolescent female body bring the girl closer to the mother's shape, inducing many fantasies and expectations of her own mature female body. The younger girl notices her mother's body with its curves, larger, fuller breasts. The preadolescent girl waits for her breasts to develop, sometimes eagerly, sometimes reluctantly" (p. 580). It is neither adequate nor accurate to locate feelings like these on a "phallic" continuum; comparisons between the "lacking" body of a girl and a male's better endowed one. Rosemary Balsam (1996) also emphasizes that girls compare their bodies with their mothers' along many dimensions, and their comparisons evoke many different meanings and feelings, both positive and negative. These female-to-female comparisons are intricately woven into the girl's triangular conflicts and rivalries but were not considered in traditional accounts of the "female Oedipal complex."

One woman patient put all this into words as she looked back at her adolescence: "I remember trying to outshine my mother. When I was a teenager I remember thinking I was thinner and prettier than my mother. I felt *I* was my father's favorite. I felt I was victorious. I felt guilty and frightened. About my mother, I thought, 'I feel guilty if I look better than you. What if I'm cuter than you?' . . . The inside of my body is secret always. Now even more so. I'll think I might see something wrong. I remember being freaked out about a discharge.

Something yellow. I was worried what my mother would think. I thought it was just happening to me and nobody else. Things were coming out of me. Things I had to keep hidden. The fear that I'd be discovered. That I did things wrong. I was paranoid about my period. Was I bleeding too much? Too little? Are my breasts too big? Too little? This relates to my mother. She would use tampons. I felt, still feel, that's not natural—something stuck in my body. Something invading. I was so afraid of sexual feelings."

Such emerging sexual feelings and conflicted incestuous fantasies often leave adolescent girls afraid to be alone with their fathers, and their fears may of course be reinforced by the corresponding sexual responses in the fathers. In chapter 3, we described fairy tales from many cultures in which girls run from away from widowed fathers who want to "marry" them. Some fathers are too interested in their blossoming teenage daughters and comment on their development in ways that embarrass them. Some fathers defend against sexual interest by retreating from a once loving and close relationship to a more distant one. And some fathers, confronted with a nubile daughter's new attractiveness, may become harsh, constraining, and suspicious of her sexuality and her behavior. All of these responses can impact upon a girl's feelings about her own sexual identity. This patient was able in her analysis to recognize the guilt-ridden sexual wishes underneath all her fears.

Menstruation

Every female patient we have met remembers her first menses—when it happened, where it happened, what she was told about it, what she was not told about it, how she felt, and so on. Girls wait for their periods to come and compare its timing with that of their peers. They remember their mothers' explanations of what menstruation means and how to cope with the bleeding and describe their disappointment if the explanations were inadequate. Menarche is a major moment in the life of a woman and may be greeted with the whole range of human emotions, from apprehension to shame to joy. Doris Bernstein (1993) elaborated bodily anxieties around menstruation: "Wetness necessarily invokes a regressive potential to all the anxieties and conflicts surrounding early bladder and sphincter control" (p. 46). Similarly, Elina Reenkola (2005) writes, "One of women's primary horrors and causes of shame is her menstrual flow unexpectedly leaking into the sight of others. This shame emerges from her inner space which she cannot control, from the permeability of her body's boundaries. . . . Although menstruation is a visible, red message indicating a feminine inner space and fertility, it is nevertheless kept hidden" (p. 107). Menstruation is another bodily secret, as discussed in the last chapter; a source of shame and pride.

The first flow of monthly blood is unmistakable physical evidence of the passage from childhood to sexual maturity. Girls may try to hide or deny the blood and its meanings (which may be associated with toilet functioning as well as sexuality), but a successful adolescent passage demands they ultimately accept it and their sexual maturity. It brings them into their mother's domain. Menstruation is the marker of the female body preparing for motherhood.

And along with fear and conflict, menarche brings with it the promise of excitement and pleasure. That sense of wonder is captured poignantly by the fifteen-year-old Anne Frank in her diary (1995):

> I think that what's happening to me is so wonderful, and I don't just mean the changes taking place on the outside of my body, but also those on the inside. I never discuss myself or any of these things with others, which is why I have to talk about them to myself. Whenever I get my period (and that's been only three times), I have the feeling that in spite of all the pain, discomfort and mess, I'm carrying around a sweet secret. So even though it's a nuisance, in a certain way I'm always looking forward to the time when I'll feel that secret inside me once again" (pp. 158–159).

Bruce Lincoln (1991) describes the complex meanings of the pomegranate in Greek mythology: "Furthermore, the red color evokes associations not only of mortal wounds but also of menstrual blood, the blood of defloration, and the blood of parturition; blood of life as well as of death, sexual blood, women's blood. The prodigious number of seeds within a pomegranate has always made it a symbol of exuberant female fertility, but there are male associations as well" (p. 85). Remember that Persephone eats a pomegranate seed, in spite of the agreement between Zeus and Demeter that she will be released from the underworld if she eats nothing. As in the biblical story of Adam and Eve, the woman brings on her own, and entire mankind's downfall by eating the forbidden fruit, traditionally depicted as a red apple. Thus menstrual blood is universally seen as very dangerous and powerful, used to cure diseases, as a love charm, or as a potent toxic substance. Fears and fantasies about menstrual blood are frequently mixed up in people's minds with the blood of defloration and/or other kinds of wounds.

In previous work we have documented these cross-cultural meanings (Holtzman and Kulish, 1997, pp. 43–63). Menarche is met with great ambivalence by all adolescent girls, whatever culture or era they belong to. It is fearsome; it is exciting; the culture reinforces both aspects of the ambivalence.

The ambivalence is related to the fact that menstruation puts the girl on equal footing with her mother. It concretizes the girl's ability to compete with her mother; it signifies the maturational capacity to have babies like her mother; it means she can be called a sexual adult; thus it adds reality to her Persephonal fantasies. All of the unconscious and frightening wishes to outdo or get rid of mother and win father become more real.

Defloration

Defloration is another milestone in the lives of female adolescents, and like menarche, it is often accompanied by bleeding and pain. The breaking of the hymen (not inevitably, but usually, as part of first intercourse or penetration) is an experience unique to females. Even in the context of today's relative sexual "freedom," even in the most advanced sexual education of little girls, the hymen is not spoken of; it remains a secret part of the body. In Western cultures, this membrane may not even be listed in books on female anatomy or mentioned in routine lectures about sex in school or included in the words of wisdom mothers share with their daughters. In many other parts of the world, however, and in stark contrast, the girl's honor and the honor of her family depend on the intactness of the hymen, which is considered proof of a girl's virginal status at marriage. We have observed clinically that girls in our contemporary society seek the loss of virginity in pursuit of mastery over concerns about crossing this threshold, at times almost a counterphobic action to put the anxiety-provoking event behind them. Similar unconscious conflicts may underlie the new-fashioned bravado and the old-fashioned avoidance of defloration.

Our major clinical finding (Holtzman and Kulish, 1996, 1997) on the subject of defloration was that girls almost invariably experience thoughts of their mothers in some manner as they give up their virginity. A patient in her twenties comes late to her session. She thinks about how angry her mother got whenever she was late. Her first sexual intercourse came to mind, and she recalled feeling that it was an adult activity: "I think I had in mind that I wanted to lose my virginity that night. I bled a little. I thought this was something my mother would not want me to do. She never talked to me about it. I thought, 'Screw her. I am free to do what I want!' I felt excited and grown-up, but scared."

We have heard our patients describe this phenomenon as they recount their sexual experiences and have recognized it also in countless literary accounts of defloration. Our data persuade us that the loss of virginity inevitably brings triangular issues with it: Like Persephone, the fully sexual young woman is entering what she has perceived as her mother's realm. As she does so, however, she faces a dual task—to take on an adult woman's sexual role, competing in fact with her mother for male attention, but also separating from her and leaving her. Fears of losing mother and of separation from her are paramount in the triangular stage for girls, and they are front and center at the time of defloration.

Another patient remembers her freshman year at college: "I was in a strange city. It was dark, dangerous, near a bad neighborhood. I felt isolated by myself. What I remember most was always being so afraid that someone would break in and rape me and then kill me. I'd go to sleep and then wake up with the slightest noise and have an anxiety attack. The fear was about being alone, alone in this weird city, this other place. Vulnerable to something terrible happening. Everybody who loved me wouldn't even know. I suppose that would really mean my mother. I wanted to be independent. It would be violent. I'd be hurt. If I were near to my mother, she could help me. That's silly because even if I lived in the same city, no one would know. No one would know even now. This terrible fear and anxiety comes up."

Here again is the Persephone theme of willingly leaving the safety of mother and childhood and placing oneself "in harm's way." The mother, like Demeter, does not even know what is happening. Note the oscillation in this woman's mind between the wish to be independent and the fear of separating from her mother. The "Persephonal" triangle, although disguised, is visible—mother, daughter, and father. The girl's sexual desire is disavowed and projected and is transformed into a fearful rape fantasy. She finds herself, like Persephone, drawn by a dangerous dark world of sexuality and in danger of losing the comfort and security of her mother.

These themes appear repeatedly in works of fiction. In *Tess of the d'Urbervilles*, the heroine leaves her mother's home as a virgin; she is raped, and returns with her baby. She tells her mother that she would never have left if her mother had helped her to understand what might happen to her. On the eve of her marriage, the novelist Edith Wharton asked her mother what to expect. Her mother coldly referred her to the statues of men that are displayed in art museums (R. W. B. Lewis, 1985, p. 53). Wharton suffered from what we have called "threshold anxiety" accompanied by panic attacks (Wharton, 1933, pp. 16–18)—literally fears of crossing over thresholds—which we interpret as reflecting Wharton's incestuous fantasies and childhood fears of intrusion into her body by the male genital. Wharton's early memories encompass a vivid love between her and her father and the time and interests they shared; their long walks together, her little hand in his big one, and the hours they spent in his vast library. Several of her famous stories and poems include overt references to Persephone and thinly veiled incestuous themes. *Ethan Frome*, for example, a story read by most high school students, tells of the sorrows, conflicts, and hatreds that arise when a younger woman enters the life of a husband and wife and evokes the familiar family triangle (Holtzman and Kulish, 1997).

In his novel *Saturday*, Ian McEwan (2005) provides another excellent illustration of how the mother inhabits a woman's mind when she loses her virginity. The protagonist Henry is reminiscing about the first time he had sex with Rosalind, his wife-to-be, when she was nineteen and a virgin. A neurosurgeon, he met her when she was an emergency patient under his care.

"After their love affair began months later, past midnight, in the cabin of a ferry on a wintry crossing to Bilbao, she teased him about his 'long and brilliant campaign of seduction.' A masterpiece of stealth she also called it" (p. 47). He mused, "There were two women to consider, and to earn the trust of the daughter he would have to know and like everything about the mother [who had died three years earlier when she was sixteen]. . . . This ghost would have to be courted too.

Marianne Grammaticus [the mother] was not so much grieved for as continually addressed. She was a constant restraining presence, watching over her daughter, and watching with her. This was the secret of Rosalind's inwardness and caution" (p. 48). Henry realized that he was in competition with the mother, and that he, like Hades, would have to lure her away.

Anorexia and Bulimia

Themes of fertility and birth are woven throughout the Persephone myth, and so they are through the original triangular phase and its recapitulation in adolescence. As we have said, the forbidden eating of the pomegranate seeds has been interpreted as an early fantasy of oral impregnation. Children often suppose that swallowed seeds, as from a watermelon, will grow in a woman's tummy and eventually produce a baby. Another common childhood fantasy is that a woman may be impregnated by sucking a man's penis and swallowing the semen. We suggest that eating disorders, which occur preponderantly in females, may be related to this early constellation of unconscious conflicted triangular wishes for a baby—perhaps to have a baby with the father as mother did (or to have a baby with the mother, as little girls naively may have those wishes, as well). The distorted bodily perceptions of anorexic or bulimic girls may well hide such unacceptable wishes. For example, girls are so afraid that their bodies will be like their mothers' pregnant bodies that they starve themselves. But behind the fear is the wish to be like mother, or to be mother.

There is a voluminous literature on anorexia and bulimia (Bouchard, 1994; Bruch, 1973; Wilson, 1987) which emphasizes sociological and psychological pressure on the adolescent girl's body image. One major dynamic that has been posited is a girl's need to control her body though intake and expelling of food. The relation of anorexic/bulimic symptom otology to the bodily changes of adolescence has been also been well documented. That is, the anorexic girl wants to stop maturation, the development of her body, and her burgeoning adult sexuality, and often actualizes these wishes through starving herself. Clinicians note the girl's frequent desire to make the body boy-like and to control its urges. This control of food represents an unconscious attempt to control emesis, urination, defecation, and menstruation. Such control may be felt to be necessary because of intense and arousing wishes to engage in sex that would bring loss of control. Moreover, at adolescence the intensity of feeling out of control over a changing body increases the proclivity toward such clinical conditions. Anorexia and bulimia may be considered extreme examples of the phenomenon described by Gilligan of girls silencing their sexuality at adolescence.

From our somewhat limited experience with eating disorders we speculate about pregnancy fantasies not frequently mentioned in the literature about anorexia and bulimia. In bulimics, binging and purging can express a persistent unconscious fantasy of getting pregnant and ridding the self of the baby. For example, one of our patients, a bulimic girl in her late teens, reports a dream in which she is stealing cookies from her mother's purse. Her associations lead to a story of competition with her mother—a recent shopping trip, in which she felt she wanted to be as thin and as beautiful as her mother in order to wear a special sexy dress. She remembers how she would ask her father to buy her chocolate chip cookies when she was little, and how she baked them for him in early adolescence. She had adored her father and was consciously attracted to men who reminded her of him.

Analysis showed that for this patient, eating was an expression of an early theory of pregnancy. Her dream of stealing cookies expresses the wish to take in oral goods that belong to her mother. Indeed, her childhood idea of how babies were made was that "you suck on a penis and you get pregnant." Her thoughts about purses were also connected with her mother and her mother's demands upon her; her mother always wanted her to carry a purse. Thus, the cookies in the mother's "purse" could be interpreted as the father's penis or perhaps as seeds in the mother's vagina or womb. In any case, this young woman wanted the sweet goodies that her mother got from her father. With her binging and purging, she enacts such wishes and dangerous pleasures, and then undoes them. Vomiting, of course, is a side effect of pregnancy, and in her case it was both a way of "aborting" the wished-for pregnancy and her punishment for it. It was an attempt to be as thin and as attractive as she saw her mother and to be the chosen one by her father.

The patient had symptoms of kleptomania as well as her eating disorder. In her case, analysis revealed that the kleptomania reflected the unconscious

wish that she might possess her father's penis. On other occasions, the patient had stolen feminine accoutrements such as lipstick, earrings, lingerie,
and sweaters.

Woman to Woman Competition

With adolescence, a daughter becomes able to compete with her mother on
an equal footing—woman to woman. Her newly matured body and blossoming sexuality are formidable endowments, and one way or another, she knows
it. The following material is derived from the first year of the psychoanalysis
of a woman in her seventies. Mrs. E was married, but never had children. She
remembers the painful conflicts of her adolescence—triadic conflicts. Her
sexual wishes, and her defenses against them, appeared in the form of fears of
penetration and rape fantasies, as described in the last chapter. These common fantasies—we are talking about fantasies, not the terrible realities of abduction, molestation, and rape—can often be understood as unconscious incestuous wishes, in which conflict and guilt turn the active wish to be a
sexual subject into the wish/fear of enforced victimization, where there is no
responsibility for choice. In the transference with the analyst she is reliving
an adolescent's anxious competitive comparison with her mother. In the patient's mind, the analyst/mother is older and prettier than she.

Mrs. E started immediately by scanning the analyst: "Your hair looks
pretty." Expressing feelings of inadequacy, she says, "I don't know how to do
this thing [that is, the analysis] right." Returning to her primary concern, her
body, she recalls how others used to consider her clumsy. Then she reports a
dream that seemed very real: "I was trying to escape 'not nice' men. I was
afraid they might do me bodily harm and I was running up to the roof to escape. In the dream I felt powerless. And there is another scene where I paint
my arms brown."

She associates to the dream: "I *don't* remember father spanking me." This
seemingly non sequitur becomes understandable as the negation of a wish for
sexualized attention from her father. (See our discussion on beating fantasies
in the previous chapter.) And she goes on about what her father did and did
not give her—"sometimes over-generous, and sometimes not forthcoming."
This oscillating image of a good and generous father versus a bad and at-
tacking one reflects the way little girls often think.

Mrs. E continues by listing painful experiences, such as, "dentists, for example. It's painful what they do in your mouth." Her thoughts then veered
to her friend D whose husband was twenty years older and very paternalistic: "Can you imagine, D's daughter accused him of molesting her. Can it be
true? How a man could invade . . . do that to his own daughter, or any child?

Invasion, the threshold is gone over and once you invade it, it's torn. Really the body, the vagina . . . I think of blood, pain, and horror. If I were a man maybe I would have to do such things. The bodily harm. That's different than just a bullet through the heart. It's different if you're a woman." Her imagery conjures up the loss of virginity, the breaking of the hymen, and first intercourse, all in a sadomasochistic context in which both roles are perceived as frightening.

Mrs. E then associates to the "roof" in the dream: "Falling off the roof [the old slang expression for menstruation]. Blood. Pain. Menstruation. I remember something related probably to my first menstruation. I always associated my skulking around with falling on stage in the school play. But perhaps it was really related to starting my period about that time. I didn't know a lot about it. Just had these little hints about it. My mother didn't say anything, and when she discovered blood in the bathroom she left me a Kotex pad and a belt. I do know that it was my father that I would get some sympathy from."

"All I can think about, when I was eleven things happened, like the play and clumsiness. Funny. I can hardly remember, but that is when I began to menstruate. I was embarrassed. I didn't want people to know it happened to me. That's a significant reaction. I don't want people ever to know how I feel. I feel that all the time. It is hard for me to show my true feelings or thoughts, because then I don't say anything or suddenly I blurt them out or do or say something wrong."

When the analyst asked for elaboration of this, the patient answered in another seeming unrelated response, "I don't know if I told you about this dentist. I broke my front tooth, also when I was eleven. He put his hand on my breast. I hated it. I was embarrassed and wouldn't go back. I lost the nerve in the tooth because I refused to go back. My mother finally took me back and the dentist said with tender eyes, sympathetically, 'Did I ever hurt you? Ever do anything to you?' I said no. I thought *I* did something wrong." The patient answers the analyst's question about what she might feel she had done wrong with a mixture of guilt, taking blame for the molestation by the dentist, and fantasies of being punished/castrated—in the sense of breaking a part of the body.

The brown in the dream reminded the patient of feces and recently having a colonoscopy—another bodily intrusion by a male. She sums up all this by musing, "My adolescence was painful and I thought of myself as not attractive and clumsy—not svelte. My hair never looked pretty, like yours."

Now at last the rivalry with the analyst slips out clearly in this recapitulation of the beginning of the session. The analyst's "pretty hair" represents the patient's pretty mother, to whom she had compared herself as a clumsy teenager. The adolescent crisis is now fully delineated, in all its triangular "Persephonal" fullness:

She says, "I thought of my father again yesterday. Was he overprotective of me? When I was about twelve or thirteen, he took me for a ride one hot evening to find the 'coolest spot on a hot day.' He never said anything specific but was overly fearful of something happening. Rape was not a word bandied about." In her description, the evening ride sounds almost like a date, and she projects her wish to be penetrated by her father onto him—he, not she, was the one who was thinking about rape.

"He was so sympathetic to me. When I got my period, and all the other times, he would bring me Kotex from the store. There was a frightening thing that happened when I was little—a girl was sexually attacked and killed while selling Girl Scout cookies. A nice man in the neighborhood was the guilty one—can you imagine that?" Thus she disavows her own erotic imaginings about her father.

In the next session, Mrs. E returned to the subject of the dream and her sense of doing something wrong. She linked her infertility to punishment for wrongdoing, for what happened with the dentist. The dream and its associations showed that the wrongdoing concerned incestuous triadic wishes. This connection is a frequent one in women who fantasize, sometimes even consciously, that masturbation and other forbidden sexual wishes have led to the punishment of infertility. And we can see her horrified confusion between rape and her own unacceptable erotic desires.

Little girls link what they imagine is going on sexually between their parents, between adults, sadomasochistically, to an idea they call "rape"—confusing their imaginings with the real rapes that occur in the world. Girls do not actually want to be raped; they want to be doing what mother and father are doing, which they may out of confusion, anxiety, and guilt, label rape. The "rape fantasies" that are so common in this case of Mrs. E (and many others) are best understood as the conflation of the wish for sexual intercourse and the expectation of punishment implicit in it.

The Psychological Pressures of Adolescence, and the Triangular Phase

Carol Gilligan's influential work (1982, 1991, 2003) elucidates the psychological and social pressures that seem to crush adolescent girls in this culture. Gilligan and her colleagues demonstrate in extensive research the feistiness and confidence of school-age girls, but how, after puberty, they seem to back away from their former selves and lose their voices. Their adolescent crisis of identity takes the shape of uncertainty about their opinions and a fear of voicing them. Adolescent girls fear that being outspoken and overtly competitive means being rejected and judged as unfeminine.

A patriarchal society exerts strong pressures on women to define and to shape themselves to masculine prerogatives. "When women feel excluded from direct participation in society, they see themselves as subject to a consensus or judgment made and enforced by the men on whose protection and support they depend and by whose names they are known" (1982, p. 66). We acknowledge the importance of the social and cultural pressure on adolescent girls, which has been so well elaborated by social researchers, but our focus will be on the inner life.

Deborah Tolman, a colleague of Gilligan, discusses the difficulties of coming of age in a culture in which female sexual desire is silenced, obscured, and denigrated (1991, pp. 55–69). The new inhibitions of adolescence bear down very heavily on sexual pleasure. Gilligan (2003) writes, "Picking up the voice of pleasure in girls at the edge of adolescence, I came to the places where this voice drops off and a tragic story takes over" (p. 17). Gilligan emphasizes that the major developmental crisis for girls is not as much at the age of four or five, in the "Oedipal phase," but at adolescence.

We agree that adolescence is a major time of psychic reorganization, but would stress that there are several critical stages of development, points of crisis that must be mastered if full development is to proceed. A major organizing and structural formation occurs between three and six, in which consolidation of erotic, incestuous, and rivalrous fantasies comes to the fore. A second major time of psychic reorganization is that of puberty and adolescence. Part of its challenge is that it demands reengagement with earlier, perhaps inadequately mastered, developmental tasks, as well as bringing newer compelling challenges.

Triangular issues reemerge clearly at important moments in women's lives, such as marriage, motherhood, career changes, and menopause. They often have a familiar cast to them, and with good treatment and/or support, they can be addressed and reintegrated to allow for better understanding and greater freedom.

Adolescent loves—hetero- or homosexual—are moves away from the parents, but often they are moves cast in the parents' shadows and composed of pieces of identifications with them. Elisabeth Young-Bruehl (2003) has provided perhaps our most detailed demonstration of how our love objects are bisexual composites, formed out of the identifications we make with the primary objects of our childhoods—parents, grandparents, siblings.

The friendships and love relationships formed by adolescents often are long-lasting and deep. "The adolescent's emotional needs and the cognitive capacity to find a place separate from the immediate family change the whole context of his or her life. As the adolescent goes out to meet the world, the people he or she meets, studies with, works with, and makes love with become lifelong friends, comrades, and often mates, never to be forgotten. All of this is experienced with perhaps the deepest intensity and emotion of one's life" (Kulish, 1998, p. 541).

Oscillating Love Objects

In the beginning of adolescence there is a repetition of the oscillation between mother and father, female and male love objects that characterized the earlier Persephonal period. Nowhere is this more beautifully described than in the diary by Anne Frank (1995).

She writes about the changes taking place in her body and recent embarrassment over her mother and father. Then comes the passage about menstruation quoted above. In the same entry, she describes a homoerotic love:

> Unconsciously, I had these feelings even before I came here. Once when I was spending the night at Jacque's, I could no longer restrain my curiosity about her body, which she'd always hidden from me and which I'd never seen. I asked her whether, as proof of our friendship, we could touch each other's breasts. Jacque refused. I also had a terrible desire to kiss her, which I did. Every time I see a female nude, such as the Venus in my art history book, I go into ecstasy. Sometimes I find them so exquisite I have to struggle to hold back my tears. If only I had a girlfriend! (p. 159).

By the entry the very next day, Anne describes a wonderful feeling looking into a boy's eyes, and denies her new heterosexual interest: "You mustn't think I'm in love with Peter, because I'm not. If the van Daans had had a daughter instead of a son, I'd have tried to make friends with her" (p. 160). Thus she immediately reverts to an interest in a girl, but a month later she is clearly fixated on Peter.

In her analysis of this passage and Anne's reported dreams during that time frame, Dalsimer (1986) documents the multilayered nature of this object choice. Anne's associations in her diary around the dreams link Peter to a series of important people in her life—another young man named Peter, maternal and paternal grandmothers, mother, and father. Dalsimer concludes that Peter is a triadic love choice, condensing feelings toward both parents. "But if Anne's feeling for Peter bears 'the unmistakable stamp of Oedipal love,' it also bears the imprint of her earlier love for her mother" (p. 64).

Twos and Threes

Feelings of rivalry and worries about being "left out" are intense among pre-pubescent and adolescent girls and give rise to striking group oscillations between twosomes and threesomes. (We see this phenomenon earlier in childhood as well, but it comes to the fore in adolescence.) Triadic dynamics are clear in this phenomenon: There is always a threesome, and every threesome is always threatening to become a twosome from which one party is excluded. When this happens, the excluded party seeks to restore her access to the twosome by excluding one of them. We have observed that jockeying for position in the context of a threesome is a major preoccupation in female social behavior. This mirrors Persephone's dilemma and the central motif of trying—sometimes more successfully and sometimes less—to balance a three-party system.

It is harder to negotiate issues of loyalty and equality of affection among three parties than between two. When two draw closer to each other, the "third" is wounded in a deep and painful way that re-evokes the feelings of exclusion and humiliation at triangular experiences. Girls are keenly aware both of the desire to assure their safety by excluding the threatening other and the opposing wish of "not wanting to hurt someone's feelings." These scenarios occur often when one girl wants to be closest to the second and leaves the third out.

This behavior is particularly clear and poignant when one girl begins to date and spend time with a boyfriend at the expense of her relationship with a female "best friend." The girl left behind feels painfully alone and excluded. The oscillations may move from broadly speaking homoerotic desires and heterosexual ones, between the so-called "negative Oedipal" desires and "positive Oedipal" desires, reflecting old "Persephonal" conflicts between loyalty to mother and to father. The alienation of the excluded member reminds us of a patient who as a child once saw her parents having sex. At that moment she thought, "I don't recognize what they have turned into. They pay no attention to me. It feels like they are animals!"

Alliances among girlfriends oscillate fluidly. The oscillations are formed by shifting identifications among the threesome—with the secure mother/daughter dyad, with the guiltily betraying girl, with the mother/father dyad, with the rivalrous mother, etc. The excluded one often unconsciously represents the mother, whom the girl guiltily betrays. When there have been earlier problems in the relationship with the mother, they may remain alive in the daughter, emerging in such two-against-three patterns in childhood and adolescence. They may also infiltrate social relations among adult females. While these relational patterns are often seen as manifestations of sibling rivalry, we think that more powerful dynamic is triangular, and that it arises from the so-called "Oedipal"/Persephonal phase. That is, the wish to turn a threesome into a twosome, and the attendant unconscious conflicts, occupies much of a girl's social life.

Since Persephonal issues arise with a vengeance at adolescence, this phenomena emerges with more saliency at this time. Competition with other girls is heightened, as is the need to manage the accompanying fears of rejection. Throughout the lifespan, girls work and rework the dilemma of managing a threesome. The cast of characters may vary, but the task remains the same: to orchestrate two into three or three into two.

We have also noted that girls have a more difficult time than boys in managing "two versus three" in relationships through adolescence and beyond and are more obsessed with the problem than boys. (We speculate that this difference is another example of the heightened importance girls place on relationships and the "Persephonal" conflicts we have been delineating. That is, they face the dilemma of holding onto their mothers as they move away into the world of adult sexuality.)

Reports of these instances are frequent in analyses of females: A young married woman patient is pregnant with her first baby and very excited. She had told her family and one very good friend, swearing them to secrecy, but had not yet told her close circle of girlfriends. Her mother, unable to keep the news a secret, told her manicurist, and the news was out. When the girlfriends learned the news, each was hurt that the patient had not told her first. The pain was especially potent between the woman whom the patient *had* told first and the patient's other "best" friend, part of a threesome. The patient came into her session distraught at having hurt everyone's feelings and spent many hours discussing this seemingly "unimportant" (to her) matter, which brought back memories of similar dilemmas in her early adolescence.

During her next pregnancy, this woman carefully mapped out a strategy for telling her friends in such a way that no one would be hurt. It was very difficult for this young woman to acknowledge the competitiveness involved in all of these concerns over not hurting her girlfriends, and in all of their preoccupations with who learned what when—that is, who was the better friend. Triangular issues directly involving the mother also lurked underneath the turmoil here; in her anger at her mother for leaking the news, the patient recalled how her mother's competition with her often led her to treat her like a little girl, not a grown woman, dismissing her expressed wish as though she had no right to her own secrets.

Ms. T, a single lawyer in her early thirties, reports the following dream. "I'm kissing a guy in a weird way in a corner. I look and where spectators are standing is his wife. And she was talking about how her relationships with people are always a problem." Ms. T's thoughts turn to experiences in early adolescence: "Girls are excluders. They are able to go in twos and not threes. I'm always feeling in the middle. It's just not fair." She complains about what happens when she introduces her friends to each other. She feels the two become friends, displaying no loyalty to her, and she becomes marginalized.

A friend was giving a party to which she was not invited. The reason, she was told, is that one of the intended guests, Ms. P, is her supervisor at work, and would be uncomfortable if Ms. T were there. Ms. T complains bitterly that P is more important and therefore her needs must be catered to. "Like I am dangerous and/or going to hurt her!" Ms. T said.

This association sparks the memory of another part of the dream: "I'm stuck outside a house. I walk around with just a towel on and I try to find the entrance to get back in." The image of a towel had come up many times in Ms. T's analysis. It alluded to an important primal scene experience in which her parents had hurriedly covered themselves with a towel when she walked in upon them. "P is just like my mother, insecure," Ms. T goes on. "I felt that my mother would feel left by me, and jealous maybe if I was prettier, younger, and more successful in school than she was. I was supposed to be loyal to her, just like P expects me to be loyal to her. I felt this loyalty thing when I talking to her about how this other guy in the firm is such a great lawyer and I wanted to work with him. P yelled, 'I'm fed up with hearing about him!' I guess she didn't want to hear me praising a man and feeling that he was so great, better than her maybe. I felt that both mother and P wanted to thwart my development."

"I felt that I couldn't love both my mother and my father; that it could only be one or the other or they would be jealous." The loyalty conflict of the Persephone story could not be put any clearer than in this statement.

Beyond Adolescence: Infertility, Motherhood, the Workplace, and Menopause

Our clinical work with adult women, examples of which we have sprinkled throughout this chapter and this book, has convinced us that triadic conflicts of the Persephonal rather than Oedipal type reverberate throughout women's life spans.

Infertility and Motherhood

We spoke of women, like Mrs. E above, who experience gynecological and infertility problems as punishment for their sexual misdeeds—masturbation, masturbation fantasies, incestuous wishes, perceived sexual misbehavior during adolescence, etc. We have found that when we can help our patients recognize and understand their guilty fantasies about sexuality, they are relieved from a burden that had added to their stress from gynecological problems.

A woman who has been struggling with fertility problems finally becomes pregnant and now is afraid of losing the baby. She tells her analyst: "I am pregnant now and that is a secret, and I feel that the secret is oozing out, coming out. I had a dream about all of this: I go to the bathroom, and see drops of blood. I am so afraid I am going to get my period. I don't want people to know about the pregnancy—I don't want to tell my mother—telling her will make it real. I have always been afraid of bleeding. I remember panicking when I was a little kid and I played a game with a boy in kindergarten. We hit each other over the head. But then he put something like a can in the bag instead of just the soft plastic and my head cracked open. It hurt and it was bloody when I put my hand up there and that was bad. My mother always panicked when she saw blood. I thought I was going to die and my insides were coming out. I thought I was getting brain damaged."

"Blood—I do recall my mother's bloody tampons—why did I have to see that? Mother and father sometimes just walked around nude. But I think it bothered me to see my father and his pubic hair and his penis. He was so popular with the neighborhood women who thought he was so handsome. When mother thought he was having an affair, I was devastated. How could he do that and betray his family and betray me? Who would he love more and why?"

She returns to her fear of finding blood and the disappointment she may feel. "The inside of my body is a secret always. Now even more so. Everything is very secret. I think I'll see that something is wrong with me and I will try to hide it. Private things are wrong—I would realize that people will know that I am not perfect."

She remembers a concern about discharge from adolescence. "I wanted to keep it a secret. I thought it just happened to me, because there was something wrong with me. I was paranoid about my breasts and my period. The perfect woman is what I wanted."

The analyst asked, "What is the perfect woman?"

"The perfect woman would have no discharge, a consistent period, no deviations." She described her disgust and horror at the idea of inserting tampons into her vagina. "An invader. . . . This relates to my mother—she used them . . . I think she had a D and C. Memories of blood. That was all scary."

The analyst interpreted: "You wanted to be the one your father chose— the perfect woman—you thought he picked another woman because your mother bled, etc. You were the younger woman and wondered why he did not pick you. You feel that because you loved your father and felt angry toward your mother, you will be punished by not being able to keep the pregnancy." And with this, the patient calmed down.

But when women finally do become mothers it can become a time of rec-onciliation—both within themselves and in their relationships with their mothers. They can step more happily into their identifications with their mothers. While old conflicts can still haunt a new mother, the conflicted feelings of "I don't want to be like my mother" can be erased by the pride and fulfillment of being a mother. Balsam (2000) writes about this possibility in new mothers who enter treatment. New motherhood is complex, she says, and "it is inevitable that a woman will internally encounter as 'remembered present' the intimate actions and attitudes of her primary caretakers as they have imprinted themselves with her" (p. 482). But, "such observation be-comes only a psychological starting point, as used here, for a discussion of the psychological power of internalization." She stresses the fluidity and not the fixity of these internalizations and "a sense of the possibilities for fresh access at different points in the life cycle at which mother and daughter are rein-venting their internal closeness" (p. 484).

Triadic Conflicts in the Business World
In a series of work-focused psychotherapies and organizational consultations, Laura Huggler (personal communication, 2007) clearly and dramatically documented female triadic dynamics in the workplace. In particular, she has found that newly promoted and/or hired female CEOs often have difficulties with the female COOs who are supposed to report to them.

She has found evidence of the oscillating identifications that are charac-teristic of young and adolescent girls in the relationships among newly pro-moted or hired female CEOs with female executive subordinates. Male CEOs, she finds, have little hesitation in dealing with real or perceived com-petitors within the executive ranks, including disruptive or provocative sub-ordinates. Women involved in such troublesome situations, however, agonize over such situations, finding it a struggle even to speak with the subordinate directly about the problematic behavior, let alone initiate any more drastic action.

New female CEOs perceive, often in a distorted way, the subordinate "other woman" as hypercritical, unpleasant, or unduly withholding and con-trolling. Therapeutic intervention usually leads to an understanding that the CEO is ashamed of, guilty about, and frightened by the intensity of her ag-gression. She would like to get rid of the other executive but finds herself in-hibited by unrealistic fantasies of being criticized by others and unable to find a suitable replacement. By herself (that is, without therapeutic intervention) she is often unable to contain the inconsistent and detrimental behavior in such relationships.

Huggler reported that in her consultations, women CEOs in these situations found themselves thinking frequently of their own mothers and entertaining anxious fantasies about getting rid of the office "mother"—that is, the one who was there first, and who may be preferred by the board of directors. The CEO unconsciously perceives the board of directors as male, even though it may be made up of men and women, and wants to win its love.

This is another unconscious carryover of triadic conflicts into the work situation and an illustration of how they may inhibit even highly competent CEOs who remain uncomfortable with competition. This is an illustration from adult life of the dilemma that distinguishes Persephone's maturation from her Oedipus's. It is the persistent need to maintain the good will of the mother, which is not at issue for boys who are not rivals with their mothers, which makes a girl's mastery of competition a more precarious endeavor than it is for boys.

Menopause

Even in menopause, triadic conflicts may emerge with full and sometimes painful force. Nowhere is this better expressed that in Thomas Mann's disturbing yet brilliant novella, *The Black Swan* (1953), which we see as a cross-generational triadic or Persephonal tale. Rosalie von Tummler, who lives with her grown daughter and teenaged son, is fifty years old and a widow. She is bitterly lamenting the end of her menstrual cycle when she falls in love with her son's handsome and receptive young tutor, Ken. Her daughter is appalled by her mother's obvious sexual interest in the young man, but when Rosalie finds herself bleeding once again, she is convinced that this is a reward for her sexual longings, a "victory." "What a miracle!" she exclaims to her daughter (p. 88). She berates Anna for wishing her to subside obediently into matronhood. But Rosalie's miracle is the harbinger of tragedy. The "blessed" blood flow is not the sign of vigorous new womanhood but of an ovarian cancer that means her death.

Here, in menopause, a love affair—a classic triangle between a man and two women—is contemplated in order to dispel the fears of aging. The forbidden desire and its punishment are written in the language of the female body, in the ebb and flow of its blood.

Reenkola (2005) comments, "The end of menstruation, the phenomena of menopause, may also feel shameful. Women want to conceal the hot flashes, blushing, sweating, even the end of menstruation. Aging and the corresponding physical changes, wrinkles and creases brought by experience, a bending back, are all shameful, the ideal being a young woman's body. . . . On the other hand, shame can also be alleviated during menopause if the end of her fertile period means that the woman regains control of her body and possession of her sexuality" (p. 107). Once again we are reminded of the story of Persephone; in this phase of woman's life cycle of fertility, ownership of sexuality remains a central issue.

Conclusion

In this chapter we have examined how the specifically female concerns of the triangular phase intensify as girls grow into the sexual maturity and psychological separateness of adolescence. We have also sketched the added stress of societal pressures against women's ownership of their own sexuality, which makes the challenges of adolescence more rigorous than they might otherwise be. Competition, envy, and incestuous longings reclaim the psychological foreground in adolescence, and the issues of maturity and autonomy that appear first in the triangular period come to a far more definitive blossoming in adolescence. We emphasize not a recrudescence of the original triangular phase at adolescence but a new chapter in life, with its own powerful triadic dynamics and issues. While our clinical cases focus on inhibitions and anxiety, pubescent girls also feel validated and proud of their bodies and their beauty. The triadic issues that come up in adolescence are easily discernable, and they appear in the analyses of women of every age, both in memories of adolescence and at later turning points of sexuality and maturation. A better and more complete understanding of female development will mean a much fuller picture of adolescence as well, and of the later phases of the female sexual life cycle.

CHAPTER ELEVEN

∽

Triadic Countertransferences and Clinical Misperceptions

With most people disbelief in a thing is founded on a blind belief in some other thing.

(Georg C. Lichtenberg, German physicist and satirist)[1]

In this chapter we will consider how changes in theories about the female triadic situation may affect technical considerations and interpretive attitudes in the treatments of female patients by clinicians of both sexes. We will try to demonstrate how outmoded thinking about the female Oedipus can mire patient and therapist in overlong, stalemated, or even derailed treatments. We will address, too, how shared cultural stereotypes about women and personal countertransferences and blind spots can interfere with the clinical understanding of triangular material in women. Established theory frequently reinforces these countertransferences, making for formidable clinical difficulties.

Everyone—psychoanalysts included—tends to resist recognition of the triangular drama. Ivri Kumin (1985/1986) called the dysphoric feelings evoked by the awareness of erotic transference and countertransferences "erotic horror." According to Kumin, the analyst's task is to accept the patient's sexual desire without either seductiveness or avoidance. In an often overlooked but perhaps prophetic article, Bela Grunberger (1980) spoke of both individual and institutional resistances to the Oedipus complex, what he called that "nodal complex" (p. 607). He pointed out narcissistic elements central to the Oedipal conflict that often are not resolved by analysts in their own analyses, and warned that these lacunae have consequences—not only in our analytic work but also in our theoretical deliberations, some of which aim to obliterate or minimize the Oedipus complex theoretically or to alter psychoanalytic institutions broadly.

With this axiom about the basic and ever-present resistance to the triangular drama in mind, we will outline some typical countertransferences to "Oedipal material" with *female* patients.

Review of the Literature on Countertransferences to Triadic Material with Female Patients

Female Analysts and Female Patients

The psychoanalytic literature includes many discussions of the benefits to women patients at work with woman analysts. One common idea is that this female-to-female interaction can foster positive feminine identifications for female patients who lack such models. Ellen Ruderman (1986), for example, wrote of the "creative and reparative uses of countertransference" in treatments of women by women. She advocated the idea that female analysts continually need to rework and reexamine their own relationships with their mothers with reference to themes of separation and individuation. (This interesting emphasis may reflect the positive value women place on relationships, as suggested in previous chapters.)

However, this celebration of the benefits of the woman/woman dyad may obscure other issues. Female analysts may share some of the same developmental blind spots as their patients and may miss or misinterpret triadic (or paternal) transferences. According to many writers (Bernstein and Warner, 1984; Ruderman, 1986), some female analysts respond defensively to the competition and envy of their female patients and often resist being seen as the rival triadic mother. Instead, they tend to get involved—or lost—in earlier "pre-Oedipal" mother/daughter issues (Mendell, 1993) or to become over-identified with their patients (Bigras, 1990). They may become "too maternal" and overprotective (Moldawsky, 1986). Helen Meyers (1986) warned of another pitfall—collusion in an idealized, and sometimes erotized, "good" mother transference. The bad mother image is split off and displaced on a person outside the therapeutic situation (often, in our experience, the husband or lover). Also, the erotized female-to-female therapeutic situation may mask unrecognized erotic triadic father transference.

The problem of over-identification is mentioned by several writers in differing contexts (Notman, 1984/1985). Frequently, when a woman chooses a woman analyst with the *conscious* idea that this will guarantee her support for her attitudes, sometimes this wish is reinforced by the analyst's over-identification with the patient. Doris Bernstein (1991) warned that it might be easier for a woman analyst to identify with another woman's hostilities toward men than to analyze them. We would add that focusing of resentment on men outside the office also serves the purpose of routing hostility away from the analyst-patient relationship—a hostility that often has triadic origins and remains clearly challenging for many adult women.

The sentiment that women analysts need to mentor their female patients (Kestenbaum, 1984/1985; Eisenbud, 1986) is another that has been widely expressed in the literature. Yet such sentiments and enthusiasm are potentially dangerous, as mentoring may blur therapeutic boundaries, foster the analyst's own agenda and values, or allow unexamined countertransferences to germinate.

In a comprehensive and perceptive article, Bernstein (1991) discussed the dangers in the woman/woman dyad. She highlighted the awakened competitiveness, both pre-Oedipal and Oedipal, in the female analyst toward the patient and the patient's mother. The fantasy is "we are going to do it better." The analyst may foster a powerful regression in the presumable service of growth, but this may also become a resistance. The stance of insisting how bad the original mother was may also hide far more threatening erotic, loving feelings toward their mothers that both analyst and patient fear.

Kirsten Dahl (1989) proposed that the common fantasy of the terrifying "witch mother," commonly understood as a pre-triadic fantasy associated with the daughter's hostile attachment to her mother, is better understood as triadic construct. Dahl points out that the fantasy of the witch mother is multifaceted. It is characterized by projections onto the mother of envious, hostile, and jealous aspects of the daughter's love and experiences of the mother as malignantly destructive of the daughter's sexual freedom, but it also includes efforts to obtain genital pleasure from other sources, a secret excited longing for the mother and her body and a wish to be the mother's erotic partner. This wish oscillates with the fear that the mother would destroy her daughter if she knew that her daughter had an alternative erotic object tie to a man. Dahl's belief is that earlier fantasies may be incorporated into the idea of the "witch mother" but are now reworked in the triadic context. We find these ideas congenial with our own thinking.

Male Analysts and Female Patients
Male analysts who are biased in their expectations of women may foster traditional female sex roles and replicate patriarchal power structures (Broverman et al., 1970; Lerner, 1982; Myers, 1982). They may also unwittingly fos-

ter unhealthy compliance in their female patients. The male analyst may unconsciously encourage this behavior as a boost to his ego (Person, 1983). Male analysts who unknowingly assume a socially sanctioned paternal role may trap their female patients in an "Oedipal" dynamic, or paradoxically, infantilize them. There is overwhelming evidence that male therapists are more vulnerable than women therapists to acting upon strong erotic countertransferences seductively or overtly (Myers, 1982; Meyers, 1986; Bigras, 1990; Kernberg, 1995). Sexual boundary violations occur most frequently between male analysts and female patients (Dahlberg, 1970; Seiden, 1976; Butler and Zelen, 1977).

Social stereotypes and gender roles may silently generate unconscious biases in analysts toward their patients. While such unconscious attitudes may not, strictly speaking, be classified as countertransferences, they nonetheless exert powerful influences in the analytic process which need examination. Teresa Bernardez (1987) has labeled these characteristic reactions "cultural countertransferences."

Cross-gender Countertransferences

Analysts have various degrees of comfort in experiencing the self in the guises of the opposite sex. Cross-gender triadic transferences may be the most difficult to deal with and engender the most pervasive countertransferences or blind spots. (Kulish, 1984, 1986, 1989). These blind spots, which have been discussed by a number of authors (e.g., Chasseguet-Smirgel, 1984; Renik, 1990), affect the analyst's openness to experiencing triadic transferences that cast him or her in the role of the erotically desired, cross-gendered parent.

It has been suggested in the literature that the triadic transference is usually along the lines of the manifest gender of the analyst, while the feelings toward the opposite sex are displaced onto an outside figure (Kulish, 1989). (For example, in the female to female dyad, the patient directs erotic fantasies onto her analyst's husband, and perceives her as a rivalrous mother.) While this may be so, it is also true that an analyst's capacity for bisexual empathy and identification may be strained in these circumstances (Meyers, 1986; Lasky, 1989). For example, a male analyst might be uncomfortable experiencing himself as the "Oedipal" mother, or as a "castrated" being or sexual object that can be penetrated. It is may be easier for the male analyst to focus on the pre-triadic maternal identification, before the mother is defined by her genital. On the other hand, a female analyst may have difficulty experiencing herself as the "Oedipal" father.

In a research project that set out to examine some of these suggestions, Kulish and Mayman (1993) found evidence that therapists encouraged the development of gender-consistent transferences. More specifically, male therapists were more sensitive to competitive Oedipal issues, especially with *male* patients. Female therapists described more transferences pertaining to earlier oral issues, especially with their female patients, and less often recognized triadic "Oedipal" material than did male therapists. We might conclude that women may lean toward avoidance in the countertransference to patient's triadic sexual fantasies but have less difficulty with maternal/infant transferences, which include anal and oral erotogenic components (Lester, 1990; Wyre and Welles, 1989). These findings correspond with our thesis that adherence to older theories about women may steer therapists away from recognition of triadic material in their female patients.

Deafness to the Maternal Erotic Transferences

Harriet Wyre and Judith Welles (1989) have described maternal erotic transferences, which they contend are often incompletely explored in psychoanalytic therapies. These transferences illuminate conflicted early erotic and sensual feelings, Oedipal and pre-Oedipal, of the girl toward her mother. They argued that maternal transferences may be anchored in pre-Oedipal matrices but are erotic in their own right and can reflect "Oedipal, genital erogeneity" (p. 673). Beverly Burch (1997) has drawn attention to the neglect, in psychoanalytic theory and practice, of the mother/daughter side of the family romance and the homoerotic transferences which may reflect it. Joyce McDougall (1986) provides a now well-known example of this fear of the erotic maternal transference. She described her countertransference reaction to a female patient—"deafness" to the homosexual, "negative Oedipal" dimensions of the patient's fantasies. In clinical practice we have seen that the incestuous meanings of a homoerotic love are very fiercely defended against.[2]

Our point is that a strong and accurate theory about female development makes it more likely that such triadic blind spots can be found and empathy achieved.

Clinical Examples

We will present clinical material which demonstrates these sorts of biases, avoidances, repressions, and countertransferences and how they become upheld by theoretical convictions.

A Case of Being Mired in the Dyadic Mother/Daughter Relationship

In this first case, the countertransference of a female analyst to a female patient derailed the treatment for awhile. Mrs. B, a middle-aged teacher whom we discussed in chapter 8, was approaching the end of her analysis. She had sought treatment because of severe anxiety and because social phobias and inhibitions were restricting all areas of her life, especially the sexual. She was the overly protected youngest child of strict, but loving parents. She and her siblings were expected to put up a good front at all times and live up to the highest ideals of conduct. The father was a staunchly conservative army man who kept tight and critical watch on his children, especially his daughter. He was especially vigilant lest she stray sexually. Mrs. B's mother was more permissive but gave the patient mixed messages. She adjured her daughter to be popular with the boys but to stay away from sex. At the same time she bragged about her own past and present sexual capacities.

Mrs. B approached her treatment as she did the rest of her life—like a good and obedient girl, acquiescing to her parents' demands. It took several years of analysis before this characterological defense shifted enough for her underlying rebelliousness and anger to emerge toward the analyst. Working through these conflicts in the transference, Mrs. B was able to free herself gradually from her inhibitions and leave her unhappy and sexless marriage. It seemed to the analyst that through much of the analysis the transference had remained on a "pre-Oedipal" level. The patient's loneliness and her wish to be to taken care of was a frequent theme. She would complain angrily about how she had to be alone on vacations, for example, and that the analyst should somehow make this all better. At the same time, she feared that her angry demandingness would drive the analyst away.

The following sequence of material occurred as she was working through her anxieties about seeking new relationships with men and trying to release her severe inhibitions about sex. She had just begun to see a man who was interested in her. C was separated, but his divorce was not yet final. In the week before this sequence, the patient had talked anxiously about feeling competitive with some of her female coworkers about their standing with their male boss.

She reported that C had told her about a big brouhaha with his wife. According to Mrs. B's report, the wife had acted very angrily and very bizarrely, pulling off her blouse, pushing her breasts into C's face, and demanding, "You see these? Aren't these better than your new girlfriend's?"

The patient said, "I can see that he is still entangled with her and the divorce isn't happening quickly enough. I just stepped back. Withdrew. I could feel myself doing it. Maybe it triggered something to do with my anxieties about anger. As he described the extent of his wife's rage it also made me think of how it was with T (her ex-husband) and my father. What instills such a rage in a woman? I am afraid it's a dead end."

While the patient's words—"a dead end"—referred consciously to her fear that the relationship with C was going nowhere, they may speak as well of *unconscious* fears: the murderousness of her competition with the wife, the end of the relationships between mother and daughter or analyst and patient, or deadened genital.

The analyst observed that there was anger and jealousy about sex in this story—the wife seemed to be reacting to Mrs. B as a rival:

"Hmmm. Now I'm 'the other woman.' That's interesting." But, she said, she couldn't enjoy sex with C after what had happened. The analyst interpreted that she could not allow herself to be the victor in this competition, and Mrs. B was interested in that, too.

At the next session the patient felt better. She had been thinking about the issue of being victorious. That struck her, even though it was a victory by default. "I don't even know her. It's not like I am in a race and she was the opponent."

"But symbolically it's a victory," the analyst said.

Mrs. B began to associate to C's wife's anger—appalled and envious at the same time. She herself had felt that kind of rage but been too scared to express it. "I wish I could have been so outrageous, really. . . ."

"This whole idea of being chosen, being the special one. . . . He must have sensed that I pulled back [for example, suddenly stopped enjoying sex]. I glommed on to details about him that aren't important and criticized him to myself, like he is too old for me. [In reality C was only a few years older than the patient. This dynamically determined exaggeration reflects the triadic Persephonal meaning of the relationship for this woman.] Perhaps that diminished the victory. Oh that's something to ponder. With a victory, part of it feels good, but part of it makes me feel uneasy. It must make me feel uneasy, this idea of victory . . . because I'm blanking out." Silence. She continued, "Victorious over someone. Being chosen. Hmm. Why do I keep going back to my mother?"

She laughed. "That's so Oedipal! [The patient had some acquaintance with psychoanalytic ideas.] I don't know if I experienced her as being victorious. Maybe it's just a fantasy. . . . I remember a time she was with me at the gynecologist's office, when I was having all those problems. She bragged about how good her sex life was, and how she always had orgasms. How could she say that at a time when I was feeling there was something the matter with me sexually, as a woman? I could really hate her for that. But she doesn't have a clue. She would be horrified if she knew what she had said hurt me. . . ."

Here analyst and patient are working through an important dynamic: Mrs. B's conflict about being victorious. In the transference, the patient expresses her experience of the analyst as hurtful in displacement, via the memory of her mother at the gynecologist's office. Moreover, she defensively makes the mother and analyst clueless, "nice," without hostile intent. Nor can she acknowledge her own rage and competitiveness comfortably. The conflict is, as she defensively recognized it herself, "Oedipal."

The analysis seemed to be progressing, and the analyst was pleased. But the patient came in depressed, discouraged, and complaining—the analysis should have produced more results by then, and the analyst was not helping her. She bemoaned her failure to have a good relationship with a man. This was a retreat from the ostensible recognition of the "Oedipal" material of the day before and a return to the seemingly pre-triadic themes that had dominated the analysis persistently until then. Now Mrs. B reported a recurrence of the repetitive dream she sometimes had of being stranded and alone in a cabin in the middle of winter. In the past, the analyst had always responded to this kind of material with pre-triadic interpretations of the patient's needs for better understanding and care from her mother and her anger about feeling these needs were unmet.

This time, however, perhaps because the material of the last week had been so dramatic, the analyst became aware of a pattern that she had not recognized before. These dreams, and the expressions of disappointment that came with them, occurred when the patient was feeling competitive towards a woman, either within the transference/countertransference, or within her life.

The patient's reaction to C's in fact yet wife had unsettled her completely. The competitive response to the wife's behavior had awakened fears of her evoking her mother's wrath and losing her continued support and love. Her rage toward the rival was expressed briefly, and then was quickly followed by recollections of miserable times alone.

Mrs. B had understood the analyst's interpretation of her "victory" as a criticism; this in itself was the patient's simultaneous disavowal of her own competitive feelings and her projection of them onto the "other woman." She had experienced the focus on her own conflict as a criticism and a threat, a competitive put-down by the analyst/mother, and she felt hurt by it. In the patient's mind, the analyst was deliberately and competitively keeping the patient from having a man of her own. The analyst's own competitive triadic strivings were probably at play here as well, in her perhaps overly zealous interventions. In this context, the analytic interaction had become a repetition of the patient's original experience of her triangular strivings.

The analyst realized that she had fallen (repeatedly fallen, she understood now) into the common mistake of taking separation-related *content* (such as the patient's wishes to be nurtured and her anger at being left) as indicative only of pre-triadic separation issues. Yet while the frequently expressed fear of being alone may sometimes correctly be perceived as dyadic, it may be *mis*perceived as well (see chapter 6). In this case, the analyst here had been blind to the underlying competitive and triadic Persephonal issues—the girl's fears of being abandoned by her mother because of her own wishes to be rid of her—which might have sharpened her interpretive focus and relieved the patient of her guilt about her anger at the analyst. Psychoanalytic theory, as well as the analyst's unconscious preference for being in the role of the nurturing and giving mother, rather than the threatening and competitive one, had combined to slow down the treatment for some time. The analyst's interpretation of dyadic separation issues and her avoidance of triadic ones had probably reinforced the patient's belief that competitive feelings were forbidden and to be ignored.

Now, however, as the analysts began to address the patient's triangular and competitive conflicts, the treatment took a decidedly progressive turn. The patient began to acknowledge and own her rivalrous feelings, which freed her to move forward with her new relationship.

Here we see clearly that the analyst needs to be acquainted with and have worked through their own triangular desires, competition, and angers in order to recognize and to tolerate expression of these feelings in their patients.[3]

It is often easier to recognize such countertransferential struggles in someone else. Re-analyses frequently offer glimpses of possible blind spots in previous analytic work. It is not unusual in our experience with re-analyses to discern evidence of triadic countertransferences in the first analyst, which have entangled what appeared otherwise to have been beneficial treatments. The following vignette provides such an example.

A Case of Re-analysis

Ms. R, a talented professional musician, was an only child. She had idealized her father but had never married and was trying to find a suitable mate. She began a second analysis a year after leaving a lengthy first attempt with Dr. E in which she had come to feel infantilized and stuck. The early analytic work had been enjoyable for both parties. The patient had always felt deprived, devalued, and ignored by her mother, who nonetheless took narcissistic credit for Ms. R's accomplishments. Now, however, she experienced her woman analyst as lovingly "re-mothering" her.

Ms. R's second analyst was also a woman, and she soon came to suspect that her predecessor, Dr. E, had reacted to, but not analyzed, the patient's triangular competitive transferences. Very quickly, rich triadic material began to emerge. The patient dreamed and spoke often of triangular scenarios involving two women and a man. She complained about her relationships with women as well as her trouble finding a mate. Several years into her second treatment, she had finally begun to enjoy satisfactory sexual relations and to talk of her wishes to marry and have children in the future. The second analyst had just returned from a week away.

In this session, Ms. R described one of her hours with Dr. E. At that point in the first analysis, she had been dating a new man: a psychiatrist, Dr. Robert. Ms. R had been extolling his virtues to Dr. E since she had met him, speaking of her attraction to him and her admiration for his psychological sensitivity and perceptiveness, implying that Dr. E did not have these characteristics. When she told Dr. E that she had decided to go on a short vacation with him—which meant that she would miss some analytic sessions— she felt that Dr. E was annoyed and jealous. Finally Dr. E blurted out, "I'm tired of hearing about him. You prefer seeing this guy to me!" Ms. R had been told by a friend that Dr. E was divorced and now single, and with hindsight, she could see that she [Ms. R] had tried to make Dr. E jealous by negatively comparing her over and over to Dr. Robert. This was a turnaround of what her mother had done to her, often comparing her to an older male cousin.

Now, the patient mused retrospectively, "I think Dr. E was just like my mother. She was insecure. She expected me to be loyal to her, just like my mother did. I felt that both my mother and Dr. E were jealous of me, wanted to thwart my development, and didn't want me to get ahead and get married."

Then Ms. R reported a dream in which Dr. E appeared—for the first time in years, according to the patient: She had asked her for a referral to a male therapist, and Dr. E had backed away. That is what her mother had done when she displeased her, Ms. R said, and that is what Dr. E. had seemed to do toward the end of the treatment.

"Any other thoughts about backing away?" the analyst asked.

The patient said obediently that it must have to do with the analyst's vacation, but then went back to Dr. E. "My asking her for a referral to a male would for sure have made Dr. E back away. I always felt that I couldn't love both my mother and my father; it could only be one or the other. And my mother was very jealous." The patient had spent a lot of time in her second analysis praising and exalting the male analyst of her current boyfriend, expecting to make her new analyst feel as jealous, frustrated, and guilty as had her former analyst. In the first analysis, the triadic material was never addressed. Patient and analyst seemed to be locked in an attempt at a reparative re-mothering.

But now she went back to the analyst's vacation. "This is *not* a complaint about the inconsistency of our sessions," she began, and went on to talk about familiar triangular themes and conflicts about loyalty. But this time the triangle had shifted and now *she* was the excluded one, the third wheel. She complained about a close girlfriend who was breaking dates with her to go out with a serious new boyfriend. Ms. R described oscillating triangles, alternately in and out of the coupled twosome. She returned to praising her boyfriend's male analyst.

Feeling herself left by girlfriend and analyst, Ms. R retaliates by setting up a triangle in which—she hopes—the analyst will feel like the odd one out, less valued than the male analyst. She is trying to turn the tables and make the analyst feel rejected, as she felt as little girl when her mother chose the father over her. Her issues about being excluded go in tandem with her fears of being left. That is the Persephonal dilemma.

Well, the analyst said, if she wasn't complaining about the missed sessions, perhaps it was because she feared that if she did, the analyst might break off their relationship. But Ms. R had a different view. "No, it's not that you'll break off with me. But you won't be nice anymore. I feel you are confident with yourself. Dr. E was insecure and jealous and envious. She didn't want me to do that well. I sense you want me to soar, to do well. I think Dr. E was more like my mother, and at that point when she got mad, it really came out. My mother was envious of me."

Being alert to competitive issues wrapped up with separation and loyalty concerns helped the second analyst steer clear of the shoals on which Dr. E crashed. Perhaps Dr. E's countertransference contributed to the infantalization, or pre-Oedipalization, that the patient experienced within a prolonged first analysis. In the second analysis this was not a problem; however, we can see that it may contain elements of its own countertransference, that is, competitiveness by the current analyst with the former analyst. This triadic Persephonal competitiveness is a frequent countertransference danger in second analyses or treatments. *In this case, the patient's competitive conflicts took the form of fear of the analyst not being "nice," meaning a withdrawal of affection, nurture, or closeness from her. Attendant upon the primary Persephonal conflict is a secondary one—that to act on competitive wishes risks losing her mother's love and nurturing care.* Also, the patient's healthy strivings toward sexuality and maturity could be fostered only through a sense of a safe and stable relationship with a maternal analytic figure, who could tolerate her hostility and aggression and recognize their manifestations, even when, as in this instance, they were inverted from passive into active. If the analyst were not thinking along Persephonal lines, she might have gone off on a lengthy tangent about the patient's penis envy and overevaluation of men and missed the patient's triadic competitiveness with her. While this vignette concerns a female analyst, this sort of problem can occur with male analysts and their female patients.

A Case of Triadic Shame

A female analyst came for consultation on an analytic case that had evolved into a complicated and intense transference, to which she was having unsettling counter-reactions. The patient was a younger and beautiful woman, married to a wealthy industrialist. After several years of holding herself back, she had now become openly competitive with the analyst and was flaunting her youth, wealth, beauty, and success. Through her social connections, the patient had become active with some colleagues of the analyst in a fund-raising project. She bragged about how friendly she had become with the "big cheese" psychoanalysts, the analyst's analyst among them.

The analyst presented the following clinical material: The patient had been talking about how warm and interested in her the male analysts were. She waxed eloquent in anticipation of an upcoming event that both she and the analyst were likely to attend. The analyst said that she was aware that something was awry, but she didn't know what; uncharacteristically, she had nothing to say to the patient, and she was having a hard time in the consultation as well.

It was apparent to the consultant that the patient had found her analyst's "Achilles heel." She pointed out how competitive the patient was with her analyst, how she had been goading her. The patient, probably not consciously or fully owning up to these feelings, was acting them out. The analyst could then begin to talk, shamefully, about her realization that she felt demoralized, jealous, and that her male colleagues preferred her patient to her.

In this case, triadic competition had evoked childhood feelings of rejection and humiliation in the analyst that stimulated unconscious rage at the patient. The patient was unconsciously experienced as the analyst's rival, whom she perceived as beautiful, more socially adept, and chosen by the father-figure. And, both of these feelings were unacceptable to the analyst who had to back away from them. Consciously the analyst was oblivious to the early triadic shame which had been re-aroused in her by the patient's making her feel diminished and inferior.

The analyst was unable to recognize or own up to her guilt and shame about her competitiveness and could not help the patient own up to hers and to her acting out. The Persephone model alerts us to this common dilemma in woman patients and therapists alike. In this case, it was the *analyst* who fell behind her patient in acknowledging her competitiveness. She was inhibited in allowing such feelings because she was afraid of being rejected—by the patient, her colleagues, and significant figures from her past.

In the Homeric hymn there are hints that Persephone at first tries to hide that she is eating the pomegranate seeds from Demeter; she misrepresents the situation. Can we see here a girl's shame and guilt at having engaged in this symbolic sexual act, which binds her to Hades, and at displeasing her mother in her move toward a life of her own?

A Case of Triadic Competition

The following illustrates resistance in the analyst to an emerging triangular transference in her female patient. A young female psychoanalytic candidate was working in supervision to be more comfortable with an analytic position and less "supportive." The candidate identifies with her patient—a divorced woman with small children—and is very empathic towards her. The patient feels burdened and tends to present herself as martyred by her own high expectations of herself as a working mother. A recurrent theme in the analysis has been the patient's idealizing of her father and devaluing of her mother, whom she describes as inadequate. The candidate characterized the transference as largely maternal and dyadic, centering around issues of control and nurturance. The supervisor, however, was struck by the triangular themes in the patient's unrelenting criticism and contempt toward her mother and her jealousy toward her ex-husband's new younger wife.

As the candidate began to recognize and interpret these dynamics, the patient began to show a softened attitude toward her mother and simultaneously more confidence in herself. A new and surprising refrain emerged as well: The patient was feeling pleased with her progress and thinking about stopping sometime soon.

This was the context in which the candidate reported the following session. The patient was a good mood. She was feeling more positive and trusting toward her boyfriend and might possibly consider remarriage, an idea she had eschewed until then. She elaborated plans for redecorating her house and taking a class to advance her career. Then she returned to the familiar theme of anger at her mother, complaining about how much attention her father gave her. The patient commented enviously that the analyst had a husband to go off with on vacations. (In previous supervisory sessions the possible "Oedipal" or triadic primal scene meanings of this kind of material had been discussed.) Then, displaying her new self-confidence, the patient began to talk about her determination to try for a higher-paying and more responsible position at work. She was as capable and could do as good a job as her female superiors, she said. In fact, she might be able to take over her female supervisor's role and do it better.

The supervisor felt that the material bristled with triangular competitiveness and energy, but the analyst had intervened along her familiar motherly lines, "helping" the patient to be "more realistic" and put fewer demands on herself. In fact, the candidate's intervention contained the words, "you have these *megalomaniac* goals."

The candidate was at first unaware of how demeaning those words were and of the unconscious need to put the upstart down that they conveyed. Together, however, supervisor and candidate were able to recognize a countertransference reaction to the competitive, triadic, Persephonal challenge in the transference. The candidate had been unable to acknowledge and tolerate *within herself* the unconscious competitive rivalry that she felt toward the patient. This is an instance in which the maternal transference was defensively experienced by the analyst as a dyadic nurturing one. We also suspect that the talk of a premature termination of a training case contributed to the candidate's countertransference, perhaps stirring up unconscious conflicts about separation and loss in the context of triangular dynamics.

Here once again the analyst was stuck attending to early "pre-Oedipal" dynamics and tended to miss triangular competitiveness in herself and her patient. She was not sufficiently alert to the subtle ways the patient expressed her hostility and to her own hostility in response. A greater appreciation of Persephonal issues would have helped her to clarify the clinical interaction.

Triadic Homoerotic Countertransference

A psychoanalytic candidate had been analyzing a young woman artist for several years. When the patient was three or four, her father ran off with another woman, established a new family, and had more children. His departure left the patient's mother depressed and needing to go to work to support her young children. Understandably, fears of being left, unappreciated, and unlovable haunted the patient and appeared as recurring themes in the analysis. The patient often was late and tried to keep herself from becoming too dependent or attached to the analyst. The candidate had worked well with the patient to interpret the patient's fears in the transference and link them to her feelings about her absent father and often disappointing mother. In the fourth year of analysis, the patient began to be able to approach her yearnings for the analyst. She resented that she seemed to mean less to the analyst than the analyst did to her. The patient poignantly voiced the idea of wanting to be special to *someone*.

The patient asked the analyst if she would come to a major showing of her art that was planned in the near future. The analyst was working well with the patient in trying to understand the many meanings this request carried, but the demands increased nonetheless. Finally the patient demanded, "Why don't you come?" The analyst blurted out, "But I can't anyway. It is my husband's birthday!" She was both surprised and dismayed by this outburst. In trying to understand what prompted it, the candidate admitted that she must have been threatened by the patient's erotic yearnings—probably homoerotic, which made her throw her husband in the patient's face. Up until then, the candidate had speculated that the patient's repressed sexual yearnings in the transference were aimed at the betraying father. But this episode suggested another possibility: that the patient was at that time yearning for her mother. Indeed, after the enactment, the patient, clearly rebuffed, moved away from her direct demands and expressed yearnings for the analyst and spoke about never feeling she would matter to anyone. She had memories of her mother always being too busy working and involved in her own feelings of rejection by the father to pay enough attention to her daughter's needs. She spoke of how judgmental the mother was about sexuality. Unfortunately, the analyst's remark reinforced the patient's fear of her (homo)erotic feelings. This incident illustrated, this time from the analyst's side, how a girl fears that expressing her triadic sexual feelings might drive her mother away.

These clinical examples seem to support the findings in the literature that female therapists/analysts have a special difficulty with being the competitive sexual subject (and object) in the triangular situation. The anxiety around being the humiliated loser and/or the triumphant winner can paralyze the analytic situation. This constellation re-evokes the triangular conflicts in which winning means loss of the mother or her love. And losing means re-experiencing the painful feelings of being left out and not chosen.

Cases of Males' Triadic Paternalism

Over the years in supervision and consultation with male therapists we have observed certain repeated countertranferences to triadic material with female patients similar to those reported in the literature. It is not that that they do not recognize the triadic material, but rather they become pulled in by it and respond inappropriately to it. (We are not referring here to sexual boundary violations in which overt sexual behavior occurs and which have been written about extensively.[4]) Instead, meaning well, they become paternalist and at the same time subtly seductive. In the midst of a "hot" triadic transference, they find themselves giving advice, support, or hugs. They may retreat into genetic interpretations, explaining away the erotic transferences. They seem to be acting on the fantasy that they are being reparative, "good fathers." Like in the cases above, they retreat into a "pre-Oedipalization," supported by theory.

A young male supervisee brought in material about a woman patient who, in spite of what seemed like her solid marriage, was expressing fantasies of divorcing her husband and voicing very strong fears of doing so alone. He understood this material as indicative of early problems of separation and felt he had to be more "supportive" and empathic toward her. What he was missing was the patient's emerging sexual interest in the therapist, which surfaced as fantasies of leaving her husband. The supervisor surmised that the therapist was unconsciously latching onto the idea of infantile "separation" to distance himself from discomforting triadic material.

Another way male analysts and psychotherapists distance themselves from triadic material is to make arbitrary self-disclosures that leave the patient vulnerable to a disquieting sense of inequality between them. This kind of behavior actually sustains the sexualized triadic transference and maintains a paternalistic imbalance of power, which the woman needs to work out in the first place. In one instance a woman patient expressed her vivid sexual fantasies about the therapist repeatedly in e-mails, all the while the material in the sessions remained rather mundane. The analyst never said anything about the e-mails and let the sexuality remain safely floating in cyberspace. In such modern ways, sexualized triangular transference can remain submerged and unanalyzed.

Conclusion and Summary

In this chapter we have presented clinical material to demonstrate that adherence to outdated or erroneous theoretical propositions, combined with commonly found countertransferences in psychotherapists or psychoanalysts, can contribute to misunderstanding triadic Persephonal issues in their treatments of female patients. We have delineated the contextual clinical clues, here and in previous chapters, which should direct our attention to the triangular issues in female development.

We have argued that allegiance to older and erroneous theory about female development perpetuates individual blind spots and encourages the infantilization, pre-Oedipalization, and cultural stereotyping of females. This limits the effectiveness of their analyses. We have presented some clinical examples that demonstrate ways in which triangular themes and conflicts can be missed, especially if backed up by currently accepted theories about female development. In the first, the dyadic separation material blinded the analyst to important triadic competitiveness in the patient. In the second, a re-analysis revealed triadic dynamics that a first analysis had missed and that now threatened a second. In another case, unrecognized countertransference feelings of shame associated with triangular conflicts threatened to paralyze the analyst's effectiveness. In yet another case, the analyst's unconscious triadically based hostility and competition with the patient slipped out and could have, if unchecked, damaged the progress of an ongoing good treatment. Here, too, attention to early dyadic dynamics and the need to be a "good mother" analyst reinforced her countertransference. In a final case, we saw how the analyst's countertransference anxiety about the patient's homoerotic feelings reinforced the patient's fears of maternal rejection. An increased awareness of the homoerotic aspects of the triadic Persephonal situation would have helped the analyst to understand her patient and herself better and to avoid such enactments.

We do not wish to dismiss dyadic or narcissistic dynamics in women, but only to say that the story does not stop there. Triadic material can be embedded or intertwined with themes of separation, masochism, or seemingly dyadic mother/daughter conflicts. Furthermore, dyadic material can be a regressive defense from triadic material alive in transference.

In describing the transformations of drive by the ego, Arlow (1963) clearly shows the variety and mutations that certain elements take on throughout development. What appears as early, "pre-Oedipal" material may carry triangular meanings that can easily be misread: "Finally there are those oral drive manifestations which are used to express wishes characteristic of the Oedipus phase. For example, a young boy during the Oedipal period gorged himself on marble cake. He explained his behavior by saying 'I'm eating a lot of marble cake. I'm going to become Captain Marvel.' He was acting out the classical cannibalistic fantasy of incorporating the father, his phallus, and his magical prowess. Such a fantasy may lead in later life to various oral symptoms, e.g., globus hystericus, anorexia, etc. The level of regression in such symptoms would not be to the 'oral phase.' It would be a typical regression to an oral fantasy which *originated* [our italics] during the phallic (Oedipal) phase" (p. 17).

Current theories and training often contribute to these ellipses. For many reasons, the Oedipus complex is going out of style and Persephone is misunderstood. The current emphasis in psychoanalysis is not on sexuality but rather on attachment, interaction, and enactment. Our hope is that practitioners and students in the mental health fields might become more responsive and attentive to triadic and Persephonal dynamics and the sometimes difficult countertransferences and transferences that accompany them. A heightened sensitivity to Persephonal triangular conflicts in our patients and in ourselves requires self-vigilance.

If we do not have in mind that the girl's Persephone phase is different from the boy's Oedipal phase, then we run the risk of misperceiving and misinterpreting women patients. Thinking "Oedipal" may tunnel the therapist's vision, blocking out important aspects of a female patient's experience. Without a firm commitment to changes in our theories of female development, and a belief in infantile sexuality, every generation of analysts may repeat these omissions and misunderstandings.

Notes

1. en.proverbia.net/citasautor.asp?autor=14405, accessed April 7, 2007. http://en .proverbia.net/citasautor.asp?autor=14405

2. One way this disguised desire for the mother may be played out is in the way that some homosexual women have identified with the object of mother's desire— most often father or brother.

3. An example of countertransference was an amusing repeated typographic error. Meaning to write the analyst's "own" competitiveness, and after supposedly correct- ing the error, we found time and time again we typed "won" competitiveness.

4. In these instances the underlying dynamics in the female patients are often not triadic. The male therapist or analyst may miss the transference in which he is an am- bivalently needed maternal object, or he may miss the patient's rage, or he may fool himself into thinking he can save the day through love.

CHAPTER TWELVE

~

Summary and Conclusion

"Knowledge throughout women's mythmaking is achieved through personal, intuitive and subjective means. It is never to be derived from prior authority and is always to be tested within the self. This is not to say that the poems, or the truths they represent are merely private. . . . The effectiveness of these poems rests on their power to release meanings that were latent but imprisoned all along in the stories we thought we knew." (Ostriker, p. 235)

(*The Homeric Hymn to Demeter*, lines 490–495, Foley, p. 26)

We began our study of the so-called "female Oedipus complex" with the question of what to name it. While everyone understands the old term, it is part of the problem we were tackling. We believe that the Oedipus complex as elaborated by Freud has given us vital insights into the human psyche—especially the male psyche. But we wanted a satisfactory understanding of the triangular issues in women that we have encountered repeatedly over many years of clinical psychoanalytic practice. When theory has been applied to females, however, theoretical and practical problems have occurred. And the Oedipal story does not work as a touchstone against which to measure and understand females, either theoretically or practically. So we settled for the terms "female triadic phase" or "female triangular situation," which we have used throughout the book.

Yet there are good reasons that myths become paradigms of human experience, and we believe that the study of myth has much to offer psychoanalysts. Myths express shared cultural beliefs, in dramatic and vivid narratives that

183

people understand and remember. With this in mind, we hoped to find an alternative myth that expressed the paradigm of the triangular situation for females as the myth of Oedipus encapsulates the triangular situation for males. We found that many myths have something to tell us about the psychology of women. Yet none capture the female *triangular* situation as elegantly, as comprehensively, and as compellingly as the Persephone-Demeter story. This ancient tale has attracted and inspired poets, artists, philosophers, psychoanalysts, and the general populace across many cultures over thousands of years. It is a story about a young woman's separation from her mother and eventual reunion with her; about her first negotiations of adult sexuality with a father figure; and about how loving and close relationships with *both* mother and father can be balanced. It is a triangular tale of incest and intense emotions. In addition, it captures the cyclical nature of woman's experience—the ebbings and flowings of fertility and childbearing.

Concepts and Language

We propose that the complex of feelings that stem from the triangular situation in women be named the *Persephone complex*. Changing concepts often requires a change in language. The words we use for our concepts, and the names we chose to describe them, establish the context in which we understand them. Language shapes perception and expectation; it organizes our thinking. When we thinking about "Oedipus," we think about "castration" and "penis envy," not about pregnancy or vagina; when we talk about the "phallic-Oedipal" phase in little girls, we distract ourselves from—and thereby foreclose on—the girl's crucial developmental need to identify with her mother.

The Female Triangular Situation
Despite much critical reevaluation of Freud's theories about female development, the idea of a "female Oedipal" phase has not received enough attention. We have attempted in this book to integrate contemporary psychoanalytic thinking about female development into a cohesive picture of this important period and its attendant structures and conflicts.

What do these new perspectives tell us about the female triangular situation? First, that a girl's entry into the Persephonal/triadic stage is not motivated by penis envy or by hostility toward her mother. Rather, a complex set of interacting forces—biological, cognitive, relational, social, sexual, and ideational—the compelling fantasies of the primal scene, for example—contribute to the maturation of a dyadic relationship into a triadic one. Separation from the mother is a crucial issue for girls at this stage and an inescapable aspect of their triangular conflicts. Girls do not *change* love objects, shifting their attention from mother to father, as psychoanalytic thinking assumed for many years; rather they *add* an erotic object, the father, to create a triangular relationship. We have found no evidence of the so-called "negative Oedipal phase," a period of homosexual object choice which has long been assumed to precede the normative heterosexual phase. Instead, a girl's attention and her sexual interest oscillate between both parents, forming patterns that, like a boy's conflicted triangular patterns, may be repeated throughout development. Typical of this phase are issues of balancing loyalty; girls can feel caught by their urges toward mother and father.

The typical family pattern, in which the mother is the primary caregiver, poses a major dilemma for girls compared to boys at this time. With the onset of the triangular stage, children typically become more competitive with the parent of the same sex. A boy's feelings of murderous rivalry are not directed at his mother, the parent on whom he usually depends for his day-to-day well-being—such as being fed or nurtured. But a girl's competitive feelings are aimed at her mother. Out of the fear of alienating their mothers and losing their love and care, many girls back away from their competitive and sexual feelings, hiding them both from their mothers and from themselves. A typical result of this solution is an abdication of the sense of agency over sexual and aggressive urges. This is for us *the* central implication of the Persephone story: The young girl is the "victim" of the father figure Hades, who has abducted her and seemingly forced her into sex.

Aggression and Sexuality

Girls therefore have psychological reasons to handle aggression and competition very differently from the way boys do. Society sharpens the differences by encouraging boys to be aggressive and girls not to be. Girls typically express aggression subtly and indirectly, trying always not to hurt others' feelings and to keep relationships intact. They need to find ways to keep their mother and have their father and lose neither. Persephone demonstrates this dynamic graphically in the compromise solution of the alternating seasons spent with each parent.

Freud insisted that the female superego is weaker than the male one and that girls have a more difficult time than boys in resolving their triangular conflicts. These conclusions followed from his theory that fear of castration motivates the formation of the superego and the resolution of the so-called Oedipal phase; since girls lack penises, they lack this motivation and its end result. We view the situation differently. Contemporary thinking suggests that the superego is formed, in both boys and girls, out of gradual internalizations and identifications with both parental objects. This process begins long before the triangular phase but is consolidated in the context of the intense drama and strong emotions of this period. Like boys, girls suffer from their triadically based feelings of guilt, which may be very powerful. Exquisitely aware of the relationships around them, they feel excluded from the parental duo and hence humiliated and inadequate in the position they find themselves.

Primary Femininity

As originally conceived, the so-called female Oedipal period was defined by supposed deficiencies in the female: It was motivated by the lack of a penis, envious wishes for one, and in general dominated by the vision that the girls (and their mothers) do not have what males do. But contemporary ideas of primary femininity—the early sense of femaleness—now allow us to address the female triadic period in less biased terms and to take into account the realities of the *female* body and its mental representations.

While earlier psychoanalytic theory has emphasized the shame and lack that girls feel, the Baubo episode in the Persephone tale illustrates the reality of sexual pleasure and the delight that women may feel in their bodies and their genitals. Girls do not *only* feel ashamed of their bodies, and it is not *only* boys who display pride, passion, pleasure, and a desire to exhibit, particularly in the triadic phase. Girls' identifications with their mothers, their bodies, and their potential to have babies shape their experience in the triangular phase in uniquely feminine ways. They imagine having babies as their mothers do, being beautiful and alluring, being admired and carried off to rule as powerful queens in their own realms. Pleasureful masturbation with the accompanying triadic masturbatory fantasies is characteristic of this period. The female body and the configuration of the entire female genital allow for multiple modes of masturbation in secret or sometimes unrecognized forms.

Triangular Relational Patterns

With the onset of *puberty and adolescence* come major hormonal pressures, menstruation, and finally the reality of being able to have babies. With these changes triadic fantasies and conflicts reemerge, intensified.

One early example of this arises at puberty or just before, and it is the phenomenon that we have called *twos versus threes*. Often interpreted as sibling rivalry, it is derivative of the experience of the triadic primal scene and reflects girls' difficulties in dealing with threesomes. These worries about how to manage their relationships with other females can occupy the social lives of girls throughout their lives.

Whereas previous comparisons often left them feeling inferior or small, adolescent girls can now actually compete with their mothers, and they begin to take their first steps into the world of adult sexuality. The experience of defloration is the watershed of this rite of passage, in which the virgin Kore became Persephone, queen of the underworld. Triadic conflicts may reappear at other important milestones as well: marriage, motherhood (or infertility), career changes, and menopause.

Over the years a daughter will identify herself variously with her images of an authoritarian mother, a sexual mother, a newly sexual girl, and a betraying and seducing daughter. As these identifications oscillate and shift, the image of her own mother remains a powerful inner voice, a force to be reckoned with. A three-year-old cherishes her desire for and identification with her mother as a secret within herself. She will add other loves, other identifications. Yet however seductive Hades' charms, Persephone and Demeter remain forever linked—separating, searching for each other, reuniting, and separating again.

Theory and Practice

We have found that the "Oedipal" understanding of female development has not always been helpful in clinical work with women. Especially when theory reinforces countertransference tendencies and stereotypical blind spots, treatments of women go awry. A clearer theory of women's triangular issues and Persephonal conflicts should be readily applicable to the clinical situation. It discourages the unwitting infantilization of female patients or the well-documented tendency to leaving their sexual and competitive sides unanalyzed and underground. Throughout this book we have used clinical material—our own or from our supervisory and teaching experiences—to demonstrate how these ideas can be applied.

The Persephone story encapsulates for the girl, as the Oedipus tale does for the boy, a central core of unconscious triadic incestuous fantasies, gratifications, conflicts, and typical solutions. Oedipus wins his mother and defeats his father; Persephone manages to keep both parents, although not at the same time. Oedipus tolerates his guilt by maintaining, "I didn't know I did it"; Persephone tolerates hers by insisting, "Hades made me do it."

But these stories do not set forth ideals of actual functioning. Killing your father, marrying your mother, and having children by her is not the ideal developmental line for young men. Nor is abdication of agency, or alternation of loyalties, the best resolution of triadic problems for girls. Both of these stories are incomplete. They delineate the dilemmas that we must all navigate—the "Oedipal" conflicts that enmesh men, the "Persephonal" ones that entrap women. It is the function of the myths to establish the universal dramas. It is our job, each of us, to work out our own individual solutions, and that is where psychoanalysis comes in.

Our purpose is not, therefore, to sell the Persephone story at all costs or to force it onto clinical data. What *is* important to us is to understand female development and triadic conflicts better. We hope that this paradigm will help clinicians to open their eyes and ears to newer and better understandings of the triadic material of their female patients. The better we understand these universal stories, the stronger the authorship our patients can develop about their own unique stories. The myths take us only so far. Every woman needs a story of her own.

Bibliography

Abelin, E. (1971). The role of the father in the separation-individuation process. In J. McDevitt and C. Settlage (Eds.), *Separation-Individuation* (pp. 229–252). New York: International Universities Press.

Abraham, K. (1909). Dreams and myths: A study in folk-psychology. *Clinical Papers and Essays on Psychoanalysis*. New York: Basic Books, 1955.

———. (1922). Manifestations of the female castration complex. *International Journal of Psychoanalysis, 3*, 1–29.

———. (1924). A short study of the development of the libido, viewed in the light of mental disorders. In *Selected Papers of Karl Abraham* (pp. 418–501). New York: Brunner/Mazel.

Agha-Jaffar, T. (1952). *Demeter and Persephone: Lessons from a Myth*. Jefferson, N.C.: McFarland.

Appignanesi, L., & Forrester, J. (1992). *Freud's Women*. New York: Basic Books.

Applegarth, A. (1976). Some observations on work inhibitions in women. *Journal of the American Psychoanalytic Association, 24*, 251–269.

———. (1985). Some reflections on superego development in women. Unpublished paper presented to the Michigan Psychoanalytic Society, Dearborn, Michigan, November 2.

Arlow, J. A. (1961). Ego psychology and mythology. *Journal of the American Psychoanalytic Association, 9*, 371–393.

———. (1963). Conflict, regression and symptom formation. *International Journal of Psychoanalysis, 44*, 12–22.

———. (1969). Fantasy, memory, and reality testing. *Psychoanalytic Quarterly, 38*, 28–51.

———. (1980). Object concept and object choice. *Psychoanalytic Quarterly, 49*, 109–133.

Arthur, M. (1994). Politics and pomegranates: An interpretation of the Homeric Hymn to Demeter. In H. Foley (Ed.), *The Homeric Hymn to Demeter* (pp. 214–242). Princeton, N.J.: Princeton University Press.

Ashliman, D. L. (1997). Incest in Indo-European folktales. Electronic Texts. www.pitt.edu/~/incest.html (accessed August 2, 2005).

Bachofen, J. J. (1967). *Myth, Religion, and Mother Right*. (R. Manheim, Trans.) New York: Bollingen Foundation.

Bakhtin, M. M. (1981). *The Dialogic Imagination*. Austin, Tex.: University of Texas Press.

Balsam, R. H. (1996). The pregnant mother and the body image of the daughter. *Journal of the American Psychoanalytic Association, 44*, 401–427.

———. (2000). The mother within the mother. *Psychoanalytic Quarterly, 69*, 465–492.

———. (2001). Integrating male and female elements in a woman's gender identity. *Journal of the American Psychoanalytic Association, 49*, 1335–1360.

———. (2003). The sound of silence. Unpublished paper presented to panel on the language of female development, at the American Psychoanalytic Association, Boston, June 21.

———. (2007) Toward less fixed internal transformations of gender. Commentary on: femininity and obsessive-compulsive masculinity: sex differences in melancholy gender by Meg Jay, Ph.D. *Studies in Gender and Sexuality, 8*, 137–147.

Barnard, M. (1958). *Sappho*. Berkeley: University of California Press.

Bassin, D. (1982). Woman's images of inner space: Data towards expanded interpretive categories. *International Review of Psycho-Analysis, 9*, 191–203.

Benjamin, J. (1988). *The Bonds of Love*. New York: Pantheon Books.

Bergmann, M. S. (1992). *In the Shadow of Moloch*. New York: Columbia University Press.

Bergmann, M. V. (1982). The female Oedipus complex. In D. Mendell (Ed.), *Early Female Development* (pp. 175–202). New York: S. P. Medical and Scientific Books.

Bernardez, T. (1987). Gender based countertransference of female therapists in the psychotherapy of women. In H. Braude (Ed.), *Women, Power and Therapy* (pp. 25–39). New York: Haworth Press.

Bernadez-Bonesatti, T. (1978). Women and anger: Conflicts with aggression in contemporary women. *Journal of American Women Analysts, 33*, 215–219.

Bernay, T. (1986). Reconciling nurturance and aggression: A new feminine identity. In T. Bernay and D. Cantor (Ed.), *The Psychology of Today's Woman: New Psychoanalytic Visions* (pp. 51–80). Hillsdale, N.J.: Analytic Press.

Bernstein, A. E., & Warner, G. M. (1984). *Women Treating Women*. New York: International Universities Press.

Bernstein, D. (1990). Female genital anxieties, conflicts, and typical mastery modes. *International Journal of Psychoanalysis, 71*, 151–165.

———. (1991). Gender specific dangers in the female-female dyad in treatment. *Psychoanalytic Review, 78*, 37–48.

———. (1993). *Female Identity Conflict in Clinical Practice*. Northvale, N.J.: Jason Aronson.

Bettelheim, B. (1975). *The Uses of Enchantment*. New York: Random House.

Bigras, J. (1990). Psychoanalysis as incestuous repetition: Some technical considerations. In H. Levine (Ed.), *Analysis and Childhood Sexual Abuse* (pp. 175–196). Hillsdale, N.J.: Analytic Press.

Blos, P. (1962). *On Adolescence*. New York: Free Press.

———. (1979). *The Adolescent Passage*. New York: International Universities Press.

Blum, H. P. (1976). Masochism, the ego ideal and the psychology of women. *Journal of the American Psychoanalytic Association, 24*, 157–193.

Bonaparte, M. (1935). Passivity, masochism and femininity. *International Journal of Psychoanalysis, 16*, 325–333.

———. (1948). De l'angoisse devant la sexualite [Fear of sexuality]. *Revue Francaise de Psychanalyse, 4*, 475–480.

———. (1953). *Female Sexuality*. New York: International Universities Press.

Borges, J. L. (1972). *The Gold of the Tigers*. New York: E. P. Dutton.

Bouchard, M. A. (1994), trans., Abstract of eating disorders and femininity: Some reflections on adult cases that presented an eating disorder during adolescence by Janine Chasseguet-Smirgel. (*Canadian Journal of Psychoanalysis/Revue Canadienne de Psychanalyse* 1, no. 1, 1993, pp. 101–122.) *Psychoanalytic Quarterly, 63*, 821–822.

Brenner, C. (1982). *The Mind in Conflict*. New York: International Universities Press.

Brickman, H. R. (1993). Between the devil and the deep blue sea: The dyad and the triad in psychoanalytic thought. *International Journal of Psychoanalysis, 74*, 905–915.

Britton, R. (1989). The missing link: Parental sexuality in the Oedipus complex. In J. Steiner (Ed.), *The Oedipus Complex Today* (pp. 83–101). London: Karnac Books.

Britton, R., Feldman, M., & O'Shaughnessy, E. (1989). *The Oedipus Complex Today*. London: Karnac Books.

Broverman, I., Broverman, D., Clarkson, F., Rosenkrantz, P., & Vogel, S. (1970). Sex-role stereotypes and clinical judgements of mental health. *Journal of Consulting and Clinical Psychology, 32*, 1–7.

Brown, L. J. (2002). The early Oedipal situation: Developmental, theoretical, and clinical implications. *Psychoanalytic Quarterly, 71*, 273–300.

Bruch, H. (1973). *Eating Disorders*. New York: Basic Books.

Bryan, D. (1930). Bisexuality. *International Journal of Psychoanalysis, 11*, 150–166.

Bulfinch, T. (1979). *Bulfinch's Mythology*. New York: Crown Publishers.

Burch, B. (1997). *Other Women*. New York: Columbia University Press.

Butler, J. (1995). Melancholy gender-refused identification. *Psychoanalytic Dialogues, 5*, 165–180.

Butler, S. E., & Zelen, S. (1977). Sexual intimacies between psychotherapists and their patients. *Psychotherapy: Treatment, Research and Practice, 14*, 143–145.

Byatt, A. S. (2004). Happy ever after. *The Guardian*, Saturday, January 3, 2004.

Campbell, J. (1959). *Masks of God*. New York: Viking Press.

Carlson, K. (1997). *Life's Daughter/Death's Bride*. Boston: Shambhala.

Cavell, M. (1998). Triangulation, one's own mind and objectivity. *International Journal of Psychoanalysis, 79*, 449–467.

Chasseguet-Smirgel, J. (1970). Feminine guilt and the Oedipus complex. In J. Chasseguet-Smirgel (Ed.), *Female Sexuality: New Psychoanalytic Views* (pp. 94–134). Ann Arbor: University of Michigan Press.

———. (1976). Freud and female sexuality: The consideration of some blind spots in the exploration of the 'Dark Continent.' *International Journal of Psychoanalysis, 57*, 275–286.

———. (1984). The femininity of the analyst in professional practice. *International Journal of Psychoanalysis, 65*, 169–178.

Chehrazi, S. (1986). Female psychology: A review. *Journal of the American Psychoanalytic Association, 34*, 141–162.

Chodorow, N. J. (1978). *The Reproduction of Mothering: Psychoanalysis and the Sociology of Gender*. Berkeley: University of California Press.

———. (1994a). Family structure and feminine personality. In H. Foley (Ed.), *The Homeric Hymn to Demeter* (pp. 243–265). Princeton, N.J.: Princeton University Press.

———. (1994b). *Femininities, Masculinities, Sexualities*. Lexington: University Press of Kentucky.

Chomsky, N. (2002). *On Nature and Language*. Cambridge: Cambridge University Press.

Chomsky, N., & Halle, M. (1968). *The Sound Pattern of English*. New York: Harper and Row.

Cixous, H. (1998). *Stigmata: Escaping Texts*. London: Routledge.

Clower, V. I. (1975). Significance of masturbation in female sexual development and function. In M. Marcus and J. Francis (Eds.), *Masturbation: From Infancy to Senescence* (pp. 107–144). New York: International Universities Press.

Cupitt, D. (1982). *The World to Come*. London: SCM Press.

Dahl, E. K. (1989). Daughters and mothers: Oedipal aspects of the witch-mother. *Psychoanalytic Study of the Child, 44*, 267–280.

Dahlberg, C. C. (1970). Sexual contact between patient and therapist. *Contemporary Psychoanalysis, 6*, 107–124.

Dalsimer, K. (1986). *Female Adolescence*. New Haven, Conn.: Yale University Press.

Daly, C. D. (1943). The role of menstruation in human phylogenesis and ontogenesis. *International Journal of Psychoanalysis, 24*, 151–173.

Dervin, D. (1998). The Electra complex. *Gender and Psychoanalysis, 3*, 451–470.

Deutsch, H. (1925). The psychology of women in relation to the function of reproduction. *International Journal of Psychoanalysis, 6*, 405–418.

———. (1944). *Psychology of Women* (Vol. 1). New York: Grune and Stratten.

———. (1982). George Sand: A woman's destiny. *International Review of Psychoanalysis, 9*, 447–459.

Diamond, M. J. (1995). Someone to watch over me: The father as the original protector of the mother-infant dyad. *Psychoanalysis & Psychotherapy, 12*, 89–102.

————. (2006). Masculinity unraveled. *Journal of the American Psychoanalytic Association*, 54, 1099–1130.

Donovan, J. (1989). *After the Fall: The Demeter-Persephone Myth in Wharton, Cather, and Glasgow*. University Park: Pennsylvania State University Press.

Donovan, M. W. (2005). Demeter and Persephone revisited; ambivalence and separation in the mother-daughter relationship. In E. Toronto, G. Ainslee, M. W. Donovan, M. Kelly, D. Kreffer, and N. McWilliams (Eds.), *Psychoanalytic Reflections on a Gender-Free Case: Into the Void*. New York: Routledge.

Dooley, L. (1938). The genesis of psychological sex differences. *Psychiatry*, 1, 181–195.

Downey, T. W. (2000). The unfolding anatomy of aggression in one girl. Paper presented at the winter meetings of the American Psychoanalytic Association, New York, December.

Downing, C. (1989). *Myths and Mysteries of Same-Sex Love*. New York: Crossroad.

Eckert, P., & McConnell-Ginet, S. (2003). *Language and Gender*. Cambridge: Cambridge University Press.

Eco, U. (1984). *Semiotics and the Philosophy of Language*. Bloomington: Indiana University Press.

Edgecumbe, R., & Burgner, M. (1975). The phallic-narcissistic phase: A differentiation between Pre-Oedipal and Oedipal aspects of phallic development. *Psychoanalytic Study of the Child*, 30, 161–180.

Edgecumbe, R., Lunberg, S., Markowitz, R., & Salo, F. (1976). Some comments on the concept of the negative Oedipal phase in girls. *Psychoanalytic Study of the Child*, 31, 35–61.

Eisenbud, R. (1986). Lesbian choice: Transferences to theory. In J. Alpert (Ed.), *Psychoanalysis and Women: Contemporary Reappraisals* (pp. 215–233). Hillsdale, N.J.: Analytic Press.

Eliade, M. (1963). *Myth and Reality*. (W. R. Trask, Trans.). New York: Harper and Row.

Elise, D. (1997). Primary femininity, bisexuality, and the female ego ideal: A re-examination of female developmental theory. *Psychoanalytic Quarterly*, 66, 489–517.

————. (1998). Gender repertoire: Body, mind, and bisexuality. *Psychoanalytic Dialogues*, 8, 353–371.

————. (2007). Excitements and entwinements; women, sex, and gender. Unpublished paper presented at the Michigan Psychoanalytic Society, Novi, March 17.

————. (In press). The black man and the mermaid. *Psychoanalytic Dialogues*.

Emerson, R. W. (1982). *Emerson in His Journals* (J. Porte, Ed.), Cambridge, Mass.: Harvard University Press.

Estes, C. P. (1992). *Women Who Run with the Wolves*. New York: Ballantine Books.

Fabricius, D. (2004). Guilt, shame, disobedience: Social regulatory mechanisms and the "inner normative system." *Psychoanalytic Inquiry*, 24, 309–327.

Fairfield, S. (1994). The Kore complex: The myths and some unconscious fantasies. *International Journal of Psychoanalysis*, 75, 243–263.

Fast, I. (1979). Developments in gender identity: Gender differentiation in girls. *International Journal of Psychoanalysis*, 60, 443–445.

Fenichel, O. (1931a). The pregenital antecedents of the Oedipus complex. *International Journal of Psychoanalysis*, 12, 141–166.

———. (1931b). Specific forms of the Oedipal complex. *International Journal of Psychoanalysis*, 12, 412–430.

Ferber, L. (1975). Beating fantasies. In M. Marcus and J. Francis (Eds.), *Masturbation: From Infancy to Senescence* (pp. 205–222). New York: International Universities Press.

Fischer, R. S. (2002). Lesbianism: Some developmental and psychodynamic considerations. *Psychoanalytic Inquiry*, 22, 278–295.

Foley, H. P. (Ed.). (1994). *The Homeric Hymn to Demeter*. Princeton, N.J.: Princeton University Press.

Frank, A. (1995). *The Diary of a Young Girl*. New York: Bantam Books.

Frazer, J. G. (1922). *The Golden Bough: A Study in Magic and Religion*. New York: MacMillan.

Frenkel, R. S. (1996). A reconsideration of object choice in women: Phallus or fallacy. *Journal of the American Psychoanalytic Association*, 44, 133–156.

Freud, A. (1936). The ego and the mechanisms of defence. In *The Writings of Anna Freud* (Vol. 2, pp. 3–191). New York: International Universities Press.

———. (1965). Normality and pathology in childhood: Assessments of development. In *The Writings of Anna Freud* (Vol. 6). New York: International Universities Press.

Freud, S. (1900). The interpretation of dreams. *Standard Edition*, 4, 241–276.

———. (1905). Three essays on sexuality. *Standard Edition*, 7, 130–243.

———. (1908). On the sexual theories of children. *Standard Edition*, 9, 205–226.

———. (1910). A special type of object choice. *Standard Edition*, 11, 163–275.

———. (1915). A case of female paranoia running counter to psychoanalytic theory of the disease. *Standard Edition*, 14, 261–272.

———. (1916a). A mythological parallel to a visual obsession. *Standard Edition*, 14, 337–338.

———. (1916b). Some character types met with in psychoanalytic work. *Standard Edition*, 14, 309–333.

———. (1916–1917). Introductory lectures on psycho-analysis. *Standard Edition*, 16, 1–240.

———. (1919). A child is being beaten: A contribution to the study of the origin of sexual perversions. *Standard Edition*, 17, 175–204.

———. (1921). Group psychology and the analysis of the ego. *Standard Edition*, 18, 65–144.

———. (1923a). The ego and the id and other works. *Standard Edition*, 19, 67–106.

———. (1923b). The infantile genital organization. *Standard Edition*, 19, 140–145.

———. (1924). The dissolution of the Oedipus complex. *Standard Edition*, 19, 171–180.

———. (1925). Some psychical consequences of the anatomical distinctions between the sexes. *Standard Edition*, 19, 241–258.

——. (1926a). Inhibitions, symptoms, and anxiety. *Standard Edition, 20,* 75–174.

——. (1926b). The question of lay analysis. *Standard Edition, 20,* 177–258.

——. (1931). Female sexuality. *Standard Edition, 21,* 221–243.

——. (1933). "On Femininity." The new introductory lectures on psychoanalysis. *Standard Edition, 22,* 112–135.

——. (1937). Analysis terminable and interminable. *Standard Edition, 23,* 209–253.

——. (1940). An outline of psycho-analysis. *Standard Edition, 22,* 141–207.

Friday, N. (1978). *My Mother Myself.* New York: Delacorte Press.

Friedman, R. C., & Downey, J. I. (1995). Biology and the Oedipus complex. *Psychoanalytic Quarterly, 64,* 234–264.

Gabbard, G. O., & Wilkinson, S. M. (1996). Nominal gender and gender fluidity in the psychoanalytic situation. *Gender and Psychoanalysis, 1,* 463–481.

Gagne, L. B. (2002). The use of darkness. *Christianity and Literature, 51,* 275–277.

Galenson, E., & Roiphe, H. (1971). The impact of early sexual discovery on mood, defensive organization, and symbolization. *Psychoanalytic Study of the Child, 26,* 195–216.

——. (1982). The pre-Oedipal relationship of a father, mother, and daughter. In S. Cath, A. Gurwitt, and J. Ross (Eds.), *Father and Child: Developmental and Clinical Perspectives* (pp. 151–162). Boston: Little, Brown.

Gill, H. S. (1991). Internalization of the absent father. *International Journal of Psychoanalysis, 72,* 243–252.

Gilligan, C. (1982). *In a Different Voice.* Cambridge, Mass.: Harvard University Press.

——. (1991). Women's psychological development: Implications for psychotherapy. In C. Gilligan, A. G. Rogers, and D. T. Tolman (Eds.), *Women, Girls, and Psychotherapy: Reframing Resistance* ed. (pp. 5–31). Binghamton, N.Y.: Haworth Press.

——. (2003). *Birth of Pleasure: A New Map of Love.* New York: Vintage.

Gilman, R. D. (1982). Pre-Oedipal and early Oedipal components of the superego. *Psychoanalytic Study of the Child, 37,* 273–281.

——. (1990). The Oedipal organization of shame—the analysis of a phobia. *Psychoanalytic Study of the Child, 45,* 357–375.

Gingold, H. (2007). Hermione Gingold. Wikipedia. en.wikipedia.org/wiki/Hermione _Gingold (accessed January 8, 2007).

Gluck, L. (1975). *The House on Marshland.* New York: Ecco Press.

Goldberger, M. (1999). Obsolete terminology constricts imaginative thinking. *Psychoanalytic Quarterly, 68,* 462–466.

Good, M. I. (2006). Seduction, abduction, and the disposition to trauma: The work of Karl Abraham and the myth of Persephone. Unpublished paper presented to the American Psychoanalytic Association, June 2006, Washington, D.C.

Graves, R. (1960). *The Greek Myths.* (Vol. 1). New York: Penguin Books.

Gray, P. (2000). On the receiving end. Facilitating the analysis of conflicted drive derivatives of aggression. *Journal of the American Psychoanalytic Association, 48,* 219–236.

Gray, S. H. (1996). Superego aspects of intellectual achievement. *Journal Academy of Psychoanalysis, 24,* 16–27.

Greenacre, P. (1952). *Trauma, Growth, and Personality.* London: Hogarth Press, 1970.

———. (1977). *Swift and Carroll: A Psychoanalytic Study of Two Lives.* New York: International Universities Press.

Greenberg, J. R. (2006). What Daimon made you do this? Thoughts on desire in the consulting room. Unpublished paper presented to the Michigan Psychoanalytic Society, Plymouth, April 1.

Grimm, J. L. C. & W. C. (1972). *The Complete Grimm's Fairy Tales.* New York: Pantheon Books.

Grossman, W. I. (1995). Psychological vicissitudes of theory in clinical work. *International Journal of Psychoanalysis, 76,* 885–889.

Grossman, W. I., & Stewart, W. A. (1976). Penis envy: From childhood wish to developmental metaphor. *Journal of the American Psychoanalytic Association, 24,* 193–213.

Grotstein, J. S. (2004). Notes on the superego. *Psychoanalytic Inquiry, 24,* 257–270.

Grunberger, B. (1980). The Oedipal conflicts of the analyst. *Psychoanalytic Quarterly, 49,* 606–630.

Guzder, J., & Krishna, M. (1991). Sita-Shakti: Cultural paradigms for Indian women. *Transcultural Psychiatric Research Review, 28,* 257–301.

Halberstadt-Freud, H. C. (1998). Electra versus Oedipus: Femininity reconsidered. *International Journal of Psychoanalysis, 79,* 41–56.

Hamon, M.-C. (2000). *Why Do Women Love Men and Not Their Mothers?* New York: Other Press.

Hansell, J. H. (2000). Mourning and melancholia in superego development and resistance to change. *Journal of Clinical Psychoanalysis, 9,* 255–277.

Harris, A. (2005). *Gender as Soft Assembly.* Hillsdale, N.J.: Analytic Press.

Herman, N. (1989). *Too Long a Child: The Mother-Daughter Dyad.* London: Free Association Press.

Herzog, J. M. (2000). Female aggression and its relationship to the family, the culture and the individual. Paper presented at the winter meetings of the American Psychoanalytic Association, New York, December.

Hirsch, M. (1989). *The Mother/Daughter Plot: Narrative, Psychoanalysis, Feminism.* Bloomington: Indiana University Press.

Hoffman, L. (1996). Freud and feminine subjectivity. *Journal of the American Psychoanalytic Association, 44,* 23–44.

———. (1999). Passions in girls and women. *Journal of the American Psychoanalytic Association, 47,* 1145–1168.

Holtzman, D., & Kulish, N. (1996). Nevermore: The hymen and the loss of virginity. *Journal of the American Psychoanalytic Association, 44*(S), 303–332.

———. (1997). *Nevermore: The Hymen and the Loss of Virginity.* Northvale, N.J.: Jason Aronson.

———. (2000). The feminization of the female Oedipal complex, part 1: A reconsideration of the significance of separation issues. *Journal of the American Psychoanalytic Association, 48,* 1413–1437.

———. (2003). The feminization of the female Oedipal complex, part 2: A reconsideration of the significance of aggression. *Journal of the American Psychoanalytic Association*, 51, 1127–1151.

Horney, K. (1924). On the genesis of the castration complex in women. *International Journal of Psychoanalysis*, 5, 50–65.

———. (1926). The flight from womanhood. *International Journal of Psychoanalysis*, 12, 360–374.

———. (1928). The problem of the monogamous ideal. *International Journal of Psychoanalysis*, 9, 318–331.

———. (1932). The dread of women. *International Journal of Psychoanalysis*, 13, 348–360.

———. (1933). The denial of the vagina. *International Journal of Psychoanalysis*, 14, 57–70.

Hyde, J. S. (2005). Notes on Dr. Abraham's article on the female castration complex. *International Journal of Psychoanalysis*, 3, 327–328.

Irigaray, L. (1985). *This Sex Which Is Not One*. Ithaca, N.Y.: Cornell University Press.

———. (1991). *Marine Lover of Friedrich Nietzsche*. (J. C. Gill, Trans.). New York: Columbia University Press.

———. (1994). *Thinking the Difference*. New York: Routledge.

Jacobson, E. (1965). *The Self and the Object World*. London: Hogarth Press.

Jakobson, R., & M. Halle. (1956). *Fundamentals of Language*. The Hague: Mouton.

Jones, E. (1922). Notes on Dr. Abraham's article on the female castration complex. *International Journal of Psychoanalysis*, 3, 327–328.

———. (1933). The phallic phase. *International Journal of Psychoanalysis*, 14, 1–13.

———. (1935). Early female sexuality. *International Journal of Psychoanalysis*, 16, 263–273.

Jung, C. G. (1915). *The Theory of Psychoanalysis*. New York: Journal of Nervous and Mental Disease Publishing Company.

———. (1934). The archetypes of the collective unconscious. In *The Collected Works of C. G. Jung* (Vol. 7, pp. 90–113). New York: Bollinger Foundation, published 1953.

———. (1967). The psychological aspects of the Kore myth. In C. G. Jung and K. Kerenyi (Eds.), *Essays on a Science of Mythology, The Myth of the Divine Child* (pp. 156–177). Princeton, N.J.: Princeton University Press.

Kalinich, L. J. (1993). On the sense of absence: A perspective on womanly issues. *Psychoanalytic Quarterly*, 62, 206–228.

Kaplan, L. J. (1991). *Female Perversions*. New York: Doubleday.

Kaschak, E. (1992). *Engendered Lives: A New Psychology of Women's Experience*. New York: Basic Books.

Keiser, S. (1953). A manifest Oedipus complex in an adolescent girl. *Psychoanalytic Study of the Child*, 8, 99–107.

Keller, E. F. (1985). *Reflections on Gender and Science*. New Haven, Conn.: Yale University Press.

Kernberg, O. F. (1995). *Love Relations*. New Haven, Conn.: Yale University Press.

Kestenbaum, C. J. (1983). Fathers and daughters: The father's contribution to feminine identification in girls as depicted in fairy tales and myths. *American Journal of Psychoanalysis, 43*, 119–127.

———. (1984/1985). The public and the private woman. *Bulletin, the Association for Psychoanalytic Medicine, 24*, 1–19. G. J. Stein and E. Auchincloss, reporters.

Kestenberg, J. S. (1968). Outside and inside, male and female. *Journal of the American Psychoanalytic Association, 16*, 457–520.

Kirkpatrick, M. (2003). The nature and nurture of gender. *Psychoanalytic Inquiry, 23*, 558–571.

Kleeman, J. A. (1945). The Oedipus complex in the light of early anxieties. Reprinted in R. Britton, M. Feldman, & E. O'Shaughnessy. *The Oedipus Complex Today* (pp. 11–82). London: Karnac Books (1989).

———. (1975). Genital self-stimulation in infant and toddler girls. In M. Marcus and J. Francis (Eds.), *Masturbation: From Infancy to Senescence* (pp. 107–144). New York: International Universities Press.

———. (1976). Freud's views on early female sexuality in the light of direct child observation. *Journal of the American Psychoanalytic Association, 24*, (suppl.) 2–29.

Klein, M. (1928). Early Stages of the Oedipus Complex. In *Love, Guilt and Reparation and Other Works: The Writings of Melanie Klein, V 1.* (pp. 186–198) London: Hogarth Press, 1975.

———. (1945). The Oedipus complex in the light of early anxieties. Reprinted in Britton, R., Feldman, M., and O'Shaughnessy, E. (1989). *The Oedipus Complex Today*. London: Karnac Books, pp. 11–82.

Kohlberg, L. (1973). *Collected Papers on Moral Development and Moral Education*. Moral Education Research Foundation, Harvard University: Cambridge, Mass.

Kohut, H. (1971). *The Analysis of the Self*. New York: International Universities Press.

Kossman, N. (2001). *Gods and Mortals: Modern Poems on Classical Myths*. Oxford: Oxford University Press.

Krausz, R. (1994). The invisible woman. *International Journal of Psychoanalysis, 75*, 59–72.

Kris, E. (1956). The recovery of childhood memories in psychoanalysis. *Psychoanalytic Study of the Child, 11*, 54–88.

Kulish, N. (1984). The effect of the sex of the analyst on transference: A review of the literature. *Bulletin of the Menninger Clinic, 48*, 95–110.

———. (1986). Gender and transference: The screen of the phallic mother. *International Review of Psychoanalysis, 13*, 393–404.

———. (1989). Gender and transference: Conversations with female analysts. *Psychoanalytic Psychology, 6*, 59–71.

———. (1991). The mental representation of the clitoris. *Psychoanalytic Inquiry, 11*, 511–536.

———. (1998). First loves and prime adventures: Adolescent expressions in adult analyses. *Psychoanalytic Quarterly, 67*, 539–565.

———. (2000). Primary femininity: Clinical advances and theoretical ambiguities. *Journal of the American Psychoanalytic Association*, 48, 1355–1379.

———. (2002). Female sexuality: The pleasure of secrets and the secret of pleasure. *Psychoanalytic Study of the Child*, 57, 151–176.

Kulish, N., & D. Holtzman. (1998). Persephone, the loss of virginity and the female Oedipal complex. *International Journal of Psychoanalysis*, 79, 57–71.

———. (2002). Baubo: Rediscovering women's pleasures. In A. M. Alizade (Ed.), *The Embodied Female* (pp. 109–119). London: Karnac.

Kulish, N., & Mayman, M. (1993). Gender-linked determinants of transference and countertransference in psychoanalytic psychotherapy. *Psychoanalytic Inquiry*, 2, 286–305.

Kumin, I. (1985/1986). Erotic horror: Desire and resistance in the psycho-analytic situation. *International Journal of Psychoanalytic Psychotherapy*, 11, 3–20.

Lacan, J. (1968). *Speech and Language in Psychoanalysis*. Baltimore, Md.: John Hopkins University Press.

Lacoff, R. (1972). Language in context. *Language*, 48, 907–924.

Lampl de Groot, J. (1927). The evolution of the Oedipus complex in women. *International Journal of Psychoanalysis*, 9, 332–345.

Lansky, M. R. (2004). Conscience and the project of a psychoanalytic science of human nature: Clarification of the usefulness of the superego concept. *Psychoanalytic Inquiry*, 24, 151–174.

Lasky, R. (1989). Some determinants of the male analyst's capacity to identify with female patients. *International Journal of Psychoanalysis*, 70, 405–418.

Laufer, M., & Laufer, M. E. (1984). *Adolescence and Developmental Breakdown*. New Haven, Conn.: Yale University Press.

Lax, R. F. (2003). The daughter's seduction by her father is her enticement into the Oedipal phase. *Journal of the American Psychoanalytic Association*, 51, 1305–1309.

Lerner, G. (1986). *The Creation of Patriarchy*. Oxford: Oxford University Press.

Lerner, H. E. (1976). Parental mislabeling of female genitals as a determinant of penis envy and learning inhibitions in women. *Journal of the American Psychoanalytic Association*, 24, 269–283.

———. (1980) Internal prohibitions against female anger. *American Journal of Psychoanalysis*, 40, 137–148.

———. (1982). Special issues for women in psychotherapy. In M. T. Notman and C. C. Nadelson (Eds.), *The Woman Patient* (Vol. 3). *Aggression, Adaptations and Psychotherapy* (pp. 273–286). New York: Plenum.

Lester, E. (1976). On the psychosexual development of the female child. *Journal of the American Academy of Psychoanalysis*, 4, 515–527.

———. (1990). Gender and identity issues in the analytic process. *International Journal of Psychoanalysis*, 71, 435–444.

———. (1993). Boundaries and gender: Their interplay in the analytic situation. *Psychoanalytic Inquiry*, 2, 153–172.

Lewis, H. B. (1971). *Shame and Guilt in Neurosis*. New York: International Universities Press.

Lewis, R. W. B. (1985). *Edith Wharton*. New York: Fromm.

Lichtenberg, J. (2004). Commentary on 'the superego'—A vital or supplanted concept? *Psychoanalytic Inquiry, 24*, 328–339.

Lincoln, B. (1991). *Emerging from the Chrysalis*. New York: Oxford University Press.

Litowitz, B. E. (2002). Sexuality and textuality. *Journal of the American Psychoanalytic Association, 50*, 171–198.

———. (2003). A case study in the relationship of theory to language, unpublished presentation at the meetings of the American Psychoanalytic Association in Boston, June 21.

Loewald, H. W. (1962). The superego and the ego-ideal. *International Journal of Psychoanalysis, 43*, 264–268.

———. (1979). The waning of the Oedipus complex. *Journal of the American Psychoanalytic Association, 27*, 751–775.

Long, K. M. (2005). The changing language of female development. *Journal of the American Psychoanalytic Association, 53*, 1161–1174.

Lubell, W. M. (1994). *The Metamorphosis of Baubo*. Nashville, Tenn.: Vanderbilt University Press.

Lykke, N. (1993). Questing daughters: Little Red Riding Hood, Antigone and the Oedipus complex. In J. van Mens-Verhul (Ed.), *Daughtering and Mothering* (pp. 5–25). Routledge: London.

Maccoby, E., & Jacklin, C. (1974). *The Psychology of Sex Differences*. Stanford, Calif.: Stanford University Press.

MacCormack, C., & Strathern, M. (1980). *Nature, Culture, and Gender*. Cambridge, Cambridge University Press.

Mahon, E. J. (1991).The "dissolution" of the Oedipus complex: A neglected cognitive factor. *Psychoanalytic Quarterly 60*, 628–634.

Malinowski, B. (1992). *Malinowski and the Work of Myth* (I. Strenski, Ed.). Princeton, N.J.: Princeton University Press.

Mann, T. (1953). *The Black Swan*. Berkeley-Los Angeles: University of California Press.

Marcus, I. M., & Francis, J. J. (1975). *Masturbation: From Infancy to Senescence*. New York: International Universities Press.

Masters, W., & Johnson, V. (1966). *Human Sexual Response*. London: J. and A. Churchill.

Matthis, I. (1981). On shame, women and social conventions. *Scandinavian Psychoanalytic Review, 4*, 45–58.

May, R. (1980). *Sex and Fantasy*. New York: Norton.

Mayer, E. L. (1995). The phallic castration complex and primary femininity: Paired developmental lines toward female gender identity. *Journal of the American Psychaoanalytic Association, 43*, 17–38.

McClelland, D. C. (1975). *Power: The Inner Experience*. New York: Irvington Publishers.

McDougall, J. (1986). Eve's reflection: On the homosexual components of female sexuality. In H. C. Meyers (Ed.), *Between Analyst and Patient: New Dimensions in Countertransference and Transference* (pp. 213–228). Hillsdale, N.J.: Analytic Press.

McEwan, I. (2005). *Saturday*. New York: Anchor Books.

Melville, A. D. (1986). *Ovid's Metamorphoses*. Oxford: Oxford University Press.

Mendell, D. (1993). Supervising female therapists: A comparison of dynamics while treating male and female patients. *Psychoanalytic Inquiry, 13*, 270–285.

Meyers, H. (1986). Analytic work by and with women: The complexity and the challenge. In H. C. Meyers (Ed.), *Between Analyst and Patient: New Dimensions in Countertransference and Transference* (pp. 159–176). Hillsdale, N.J.: Analytic Press.

Michels, R. (1986). Oedipus and insight. *Psychoanalytic Quarterly, 55*, 599–617.

Moldawsky, S. (1986). When men are therapists to women: Beyond the Oedipal pale. In T. Bernay and D. Cantor (Eds.), *The Psychology of Today's Woman* (pp. 291–303). Hillsdale, N.J.: Analytic Press.

Moulton, R. (1970). A survey and reevaluation of penis envy. *Contemporary Psychoanalysis, 7*, 84–104.

Myers, M. F. (1982). The professional woman as patient: A review and an appeal. *Canadian Journal of Psychiatry, 27*, 236–240.

Nadelson, C. C., Notman, M., Miller, J. B., & Zilbach, J. (1982). Aggression in women: Conceptual issues and clinical implications. In M. T. Notman and C. C. Nadelson (Eds.), *The Woman Patient* (pp. 17–28). New York: Plenum Press.

Nagera, H. (1975). *Female Sexuality and the Oedipus Complex*. New York: Jason Aronson.

Nersessian, E. (1998). A cat as fetish: A contribution to the theory of fetishism. *International Journal of Psychoanalysis, 7*, 713–725.

Neumann, E. (1955). *The Great Mother: An Analysis of the Archetype*. Bollingen Foundation, New York. Princeton, N.J.: Princeton University Press.

Notman, M. T. (2003). The female body and its meanings. *Psychoanalytic Inquiry, 23*, 572–591.

Notman, N. (1984/1985). The public and the private woman. *Bulletin, the Association for Psychoanalytic Medicine, 24*, 1–19, G. J. Stein & E. Auchincloss, reporters.

Novick, J., & K. K. Novick. (1972). Beating fantasies in children. *International Journal of Psychoanalysis, 53*, 237–242.

———. (2004). The superego and the two-system model. *Psychoanalytic Inquiry, 24*, 232–256.

Ogden, T. (1987). The transitional Oedipal relationship in female development. *International Journal of Psychoanalysis, 68*, 485–498.

O'Leary, J., & Wright, F. (1986). Shame and gender issues in pathological narcissism. *Psychoanalytic Psychology, 3*, 327–339.

Olender, M. (1990). Aspects of Baubo. In D. M. Halperin, J. J. Winkler, & F. I. Zeitlin (Eds.), *Before Sexuality* (pp. 83–118). Princeton, N.J.: Princeton University Press.

Orgel, D. (2003). *My Mother's Daughter*. Brookfield, Conn.: Roaring Brook Press.

Orwell, G. (1949). *Nineteen Eighty-Four*. New York: Penguin, 2003.

Ostriker, A. S. (1986). *Stealing the Language: The Emergence of Women's Poetry in America.* Boston: Beacon Press.

Palmer, A. J. (1988). Heidi's metaphoric appeal to latency. *The Psychoanalytic Study of the Child, 43,* 387–398.

Parada, C. (1997). *Greek Mythology Link.* homepage.mac.com/cparada/psyche.html (accessed January 26, 2006).

Parens, H. (1980). An exploration of the relations of instinctual drives and the symbiosis/separation-individuation process. *Journal of the American Psychoanalytic Association, 28,* 89–113.

———. (1990). On the girl's psychosexual development: Reconsiderations suggested from direct observation. *Journal of the American Psychoanalytic Association, 38,* 743–772.

Parens, H., Pollock, L., Stern, J., & Kramer, S. (1976). On the girl's entry into the Oedipus complex. *Journal of the American Psychoanalytic Association, 24,* 79–107.

Parsons, M. (2000) Sexuality and perversion a hundred years on: Discovering what Freud discovered. *International Journal of Psychoanalysis, 81,* 37–51.

Perrault, C. (1697). Cinderella, or the little glass slipper. In A. Dundes (Ed.), *Cinderella, a Folklore Casebook* (pp. 14–21). New York: Garland, 1982.

Person, E. S. (1982). Women working: Fears of failure deviance and success. *Journal of the American Academy of Psychoanalysis, 10,* 67–84.

———. (1983). Women in therapy: Therapist gender as a variable. *International Review of Psychoanalysis, 10,* 193–204.

———. (1985). The erotic transference in women and in men: Differences and consequences. *Journal of the American Academy of Psychoanalysis, 13,* 159–180.

———. (1988). *Dreams of Love and Fateful Encounters: The Power of Romantic Passion.* New York: Penguin.

———. (2000). Issues of power and aggression in women. Paper presented at the winter meetings of the American Psychoanalytic Association, New York, December 2000.

Piers, G., & Singer, M. B. (1953). *Shame and Guilt.* New York: Norton, 1971.

Plaut, E. A., & Hutchinson, F. L. (1986). The role of puberty in female psychosexual development. *International Review of Psychoanalysis, 13,* 417–432.

Powell, S. (1993). Electra: The dark side of the moon. *Journal of Analytical Psychology, 38,* 155–174.

Ramas, M. (1985). Freud's Dora, Dora's hysteria. In C. Bernheimer and C. Kahane (Eds.), *In Dora's Case* (pp. 149–180). New York: Columbia University Press.

Rank, O. (1914). *The Myth of the Birth of the Hero.* (F. Robbins and E. J. Smith, Trans.). New York: Journal of Nervous and Mental Disease Publishing Company.

Reenkola, E. M. (2002). *The Veiled Female Core.* New York: Other Press.

———. (2005). Female shame as an unconscious inner conflict. *The Scandinavian Psychoanalytic Review, 28:*101–109.

Reinach, S. (1912). *Cultes, mythes et religions.* (Vol. 4). Paris.

Renik, O. (1990). Analysis of a woman's homosexual strivings by a male analyst. *Psychoanalytic Quarterly, 59,* 41–53.

Rich, A. (1976). *Of Woman Born: Motherhood as Experience and Institution.* New York: Norton.

Richards, A. K. (1992). The influence of sphincter control and genital sensation on body image and gender identity in women. *Psychoanalytic Quarterly, 61,* 331–351.

———. (1996). Primary femininity and female genital anxiety. *Journal of the American Psychoanalytic Association* 44(S):261–281.

Riordan, M. (1987). *The Hunting of the Quark: A True Story of Modern Physics.* New York: Simon & Schuster/Touchstone.

Ritvo, S. (1989). Mothers, daughters, and eating disorders. In H. Blum, Y. Kramer, A. K. Richards, & A. D. Richards (Eds.), *Fantasy, Myth, and Reality: Essays in Honor of Jacob A. Arlow* (pp. 371–380). Madison, Conn.: International Universities Press.

Rizzuto, A.-M. (1991). Shame in psychoanalysis: The function of unconscious fantasies. *International Journal of Psychoanalysis, 72,* 297–312.

Robbins, M. (1996). Nature, nurture, and core gender identity. *Journal of the American Psychoanalytic Association, 44*(S), 93–117.

Roheim, G. (1950). *Psychoanalysis and Anthropology.* New York: International Universities Press.

Ruderman, E. (1986). Creative and reparative uses of countertransference by women psychotherapists treating women patients: A clinical research study. In T. Bernay and D. Cantor (Eds.), *The Psychology of Today's Woman* (pp. 339–363). Hillsdale, N.J.: Analytic Press.

Rutter, V. B. (2000). *Embracing Persephone.* New York: Kodansha International.

Ryle, G. (2003). *The Concept of Mind.* Chicago: University of Chicago Press.

Sachs, L. J. (1962). A case of castration anxiety beginning at eighteen months. *Journal of the American Psychoanalytic Association, 10,* 329–337.

Salome, L. A. (1915). Anal et sexual. Translated by J. Chambon as A perusal of "Anal et sexual." *Revista de Psicoanalis, 37* (1973), 179–190.

Schafer, R. (1960). The loving and beloved superego in Freud's structural theory. *Psychoanalytic Study of the Child, 15,* 163–188.

———. (1974). Problems in Freud's psychology of women. *Journal of the Psychoanalytic Association, 22,* 459–485.

Schmukler, A. G. (1999). Detours in adolescent development: Implications for technique. *Psychoanalytic Study of the Child, 54,* 47–67.

Scott, J. (2005). *Electra after Freud.* Ithaca, N.Y.: Cornell University Press.

Seelig, B. J. (2002). The rape of Medusa in the temple of Athena. *International Journal of Psychoanalysis, 83,* 895–911.

Segal, H. (1974). *An Introduction to the Work of Melanie Klein.* New York: Basic Books.

———. (1989). Introduction to Britton, R., Feldman, M., & O'Shaughnessy, E., *The Oedipus Complex Today* (pp. 1–10). London: Karnac Books.

Seiden, A. M. (1976). Overview: Research on the psychology of women II; Women in families, work and psychotherapy. *American Journal of Psychiatry, 133*, 1111–1123.

Sexton, A. (1971). *Transformations*. New York: Houghton Mifflin.

Shakespeare, W. *The Winter's Tale* In *Shakespeare*. Edited by Hardin Craig (1958). Palo Alto: Scott Foresman and Company.

Shainess, N. (1982). Antigone, the neglected daughter of Oedipus: Freud's gender concepts in theory. *Journal of the American Academy of Psychoanalysis, 10*, 443–455.

Shaw, R. (1995). Female genital anxieties: An integration of new and old ideas. *Journal of Clinical Psychoanalysis, 4*, 315–329.

Sherfey, M. J. (1966). The evolution and nature of female sexuality in relation to psychoanalytic theory. *Journal of the American Psychoanalytic Association, 14*, 28–128.

Silverman, M. A. (1982). The latency period. In D. Mendell (Ed.), *Early Female Development: Current Psychoanalytic Views* (pp. 203–226). New York: SP Medical and Scientific Books.

Simmons, R. (2002). *Odd Girl Out: The Hidden Culture of Aggression in Girls*. New York: Harcourt.

Sjoo, M., & Mor, B. (1975). *The Great Cosmic Mother*. New York: Harper and Row.

Sophocles. *Oedipus Rex*. (R. C. Jebb, Trans., M. Hadas, Ed.). New York: Bantam Books, 1967.

Spitz, E. H. (1992). Mothers and daughters: Ancient and modern myths. *Analytic Reflections, 2*, 32–48.

Spitz, R. A. (1958). On the genesis of superego components. *Psychoanalytic Study of the Child, 13*, 375–404.

St. Andrews, B. A. (2000). Persephone. *Literary Review, 43*, 494–498.

Steiner, G. (1984). *Antigones*. Oxford: Clarendon Press.

Stewart, G. B. (1979). Mother, daughter, and the birth of the female artist. *Women's Studies, 6*, 127–145.

Stiver, I. P. (1991). Beyond the Oedipus complex: Mothers and daughters. In J. V. Jordon, A. G. Kaplan, J. B. Miller, I. P. Stiver, & J. L. Surrey (Eds.), *Women's Growth in Connection* (pp. 97–121). New York: Gilford Press.

Stoller, R. (1972). The "bedrock" of masculinity and femininity: Bisexuality. In J. B. Miller (Ed.), *Psychoanalysis and Women*. New York: Penguin, 1973.

———. (1976). Primary femininity. *Journal of the American Psychoanalytic Association, 24*, 59–78.

Strong, L. (2005). The myth of Persephone: Greek goddess of the underworld. www.mythicarts.com/writing/Persephone.htm.

Talbot, M. (2002). Girls just want to be mean. *New York Times*, February 24, p. 24.

Tolman, D. L. (1991) Adolescent girls, women and sexuality; discerning dilemmas of desire. In C. Gilligan, A. G. Rogers, and D. T. Tolman (Eds.), *Women, Girls, and Psychotherapy: Reframing Resistance* (pp. 55–69). Binghamton, N.Y.: Haworth Press.

Torok, M. (1970). The significance of penis envy in women. In J. Chasseguet-Smirgel (Ed.), *Female Sexuality* (pp. 135–170). London: Karnace, 1985.

Tylor, E. B. (1871). *Primitive Culture: Researches into the Development of Mythology, Philosophy, Religion, Language, Art and Custom.* London: J. Murray.

Tyson, P. (1989). Infantile sexuality, gender identity, and obstacles to Oedipal progression. *Journal of the American Psychoanalytic Association, 37,* 1051–1069.

———. (1996). Female psychology: An introduction. *Journal of the American Psychoanalytic Association, 44,* 11–20.

———. (1997). Love and hate and growing up female. Paper presented to the Miami Psychoanalytic Society, Miami, Florida, November 9.

Tyson, R. L. (1991). The emergence of Oedipal centrality: Comments on Michael Feldman's paper "Common ground: The centrality of the Oedipus complex." *International Journal of Psychoanalysis, 72,* 39–44.

Tyson, P., & Tyson, R. L. (1990). *Psychoanalytic Theories of Development: An Integration.* New Haven, Conn.: Yale University Press.

Walker, B. G. (1983). *The Woman's Encyclopedia of Myths and Secrets.* San Francisco: Harper Row.

Warner, M. (1994). *From the Beast to the Blond.* New York: Farrar, Straus and Giroux.

Weinstein, V. (1996). *Persephone's Underworld Journey: Reclaiming a Resurrection Narrative for Women.* 3 October 2007. www.geocities.com/kerrdelune/crone2.html.

Wharton, E. (1933). *A Backward Glance.* New York: Charles Scribner's Sons, 1964.

Whorf, B. L. (1940). Science and linguistics. *Technology Review, 42,* 229–231, 247–248.

Wilkinson, S. (1993). The female genital dress-rehearsal: A prospective process at the Oedipal threshold. *International Journal of Psychoanalysis, 74,* 313–330.

Wilkinson, T. (1996). *Persephone Returns.* Berkeley, Calif.: Page Mill Press.

Wilson, C. P. (1987). *The Fear of Being Fat: The Treatment of Anorexia Nervosa and Bulimia.* Northvale, N.J.: Jason Aronson.

Wurmser, L. (2004). Superego revisited—Relevant or irrelevant? *Psychoanalytic Inquiry, 24,* 183–205.

Wyre, H. K., & Welles, J. K. (1989). The maternal erotic transference. *International Journal of Psychoanalysis, 70,* 673–684.

Young-Bruehl, E. (2003). Are human beings by nature bisexual? In *Where Do We Fall When We Fall in Love* (pp. 179–212). New York: Other Press.

Young-Eisendrath, P., & Wiedenman, F. (1987). *Female Authority.* New York: Guilford.

Zipes, J. (1994). *Fairy Tale as Myth and Myth as Fairy Tale.* Lexington: University Press of Kentucky.

Zuntz, G. (1971). *Persephone: Three Essays on Religion and Thought in Magna Graecia.* Oxford: Oxford University Press.

Index

abduction fantasies, 118

Abelin, Ernst, 74

abortion, 126n2

abortion fantasies, eating disorders and, 151

Abraham, Karl, 12

access, 142

Adam, 65

adolescence: aggression in girls, 92; anorexia and bulimia, 150–52; defloration, 148–50; developmental changes and, 143–44; female superego and, 114; menstruation, 146–48; psychological pressures of, 154–59; puberty, 145–46; triadic issues and, 144; triangular relational patterns and, 157–59, 186–87; woman-to-woman competition, 152–54

Adonis, 33

adoption, 126n2

adult sexuality: object addition and, 76; separation from the mother and, 76; triadic separation and, 126n1. *See also* female sexuality; sexuality

Aegisthus, 24

Aeschylus, 24, 25, 40

Agamemnon, 24

aggression: in adolescent females, 114; as biologically determined, 88; female superego and, 107; gender-related patterns, 86; homoerotic impulses in the triangular phase and, 101; Parens' study of, 62–63; phallic, 62; "relational," 91; sexuality and, 185–86; in tales about males, 86. *See also* female aggression

aggressive play, boys and, 101

Agha-Jaffar, T., 65

"aischrologia," 128

Akragas (Sicily), 41

Alice's Adventures in Wonderland (Carroll), 137–39

amputation, 84n3

anal phase, 107–8

"Analysis Terminable and Interminable" (Freud), 55

analysts, countertransferences and, 166–69

"ana suramai," 128

207

~

About the Authors

Nancy Kulish is a psychoanalytic practitioner, teacher, and writer. She is an associate professor in the Department of Psychiatry, School of Medicine at Wayne State University and an adjunct professor of psychology at the University of Detroit. Dr. Kulish has written and lectured extensively on female sexuality and development, gender, and the therapeutic endeavor. She has received many awards for her writings and contributions to the training of students in mental health and for her support and mentoring of young women in their careers. Named the National Psychoanalytic Woman's Scholar by the American Psychoanalytic Association in 2006, she is in private practice in Birmingham, Michigan, as a psychoanalyst and psychotherapist.

Deanna Holtzman is a training and supervising analyst and past president of the Michigan Psychoanalytic Institute. Dr. Holtzman is an associate professor in the Department of Psychiatry, School of Medicine at Wayne State University and an adjunct professor of psychology at the University of Detroit. She is well-known for her work on female psychology and sexuality and has many publications, including *Nevermore: The Hymen and the Loss of Virginity* (1996), co-authored with Dr. Kulish. She has published articles in the *Journal of the American Psychoanalytic Association*, the *International Journal of Psychoanalysis*, the Film Forum's "Projections," and was a contributor to *Female Psychology: An Annotated Psychoanalytic Bibliography* and *The Freud Encyclopedia*. The president of the Sigmund Freud Archives, she is in private practice in Bloomfield Hills, Michigan.